Whitman's Drama of Consensus

WHITMAN'S DRAMA OF CONSENSUS

Kerry C. Larson

The University of Chicago Press

Chicago and London

The University of Chicago Press, Chicago 60637
The University of Chicago Press, Ltd., London

97 96 95 94 93 92 91 90 89 88   5 4 3 2 1

Library of Congress Cataloging-in-Publication Data

Larson, Kerry C.
   Whitman's drama of consensus / Kerry C. Larson.

      p.   cm.
   Bibliography: p.
   Includes index.
   ISBN 0-226-46907-7 : $32.00.   ISBN 0-226-46908-5 (pbk.) : $15.95
   1. Whitman, Walt, 1819–1892—Political and social views.
2. Social contract in literature.   3. Consensus (Social sciences) in
literature.   4. Democracy in literature.   I. Title.
PS3242.S58L37   1988
811'.3—dc19   88-14294
                                                                   CIP

Portions of Part 2 originally appeared as "Voices
in the Grass: Whitman and the Conception of
'Free Growth,'" *Centennial Review* 26 (1982):
199–225, and are reprinted by permission of the
Michigan State University Press.

KERRY C. LARSON is assistant professor of
English at the University of Michigan, Ann
Arbor.

To Lisa

Contents

Abbreviations

CORR   Walt Whitman, *The Correspondence,* ed. Edwin H. Miller, 5 vols. (New York: New York University Press, 1961)

CRE   Walt Whitman, *Leaves of Grass: Comprehensive Reader's Edition,* ed. Harold W. Blodgett and Sculley Bradley (New York: New York University Press, 1965)

DB   Walt Whitman, *Daybooks and Notebooks,* ed. William White, 3 vols. (New York: New York University Press, 1977)

N & F   "Notes and Fragments," *The Complete Writings of Walt Whitman,* ed. Oscar Lovell Triggs (New York: G. P. Putnam's Sons, 1902), vol. 9.

PW   Walt Whitman, *Prose Works 1892,* ed. Floyd Stovall, 2 vols. (New York: New York University Press, 1963)

UPP   *The Uncollected Poetry and Prose of Walt Whitman,* ed. Emory Holloway, 2 vols. (Garden City, N.Y.: Doubleday, Page and Co., 1921)

W   *The Complete Works of Ralph Waldo Emerson,* ed. E. W. Emerson, 12 vols. (Boston: Houghton Mifflin, 1903)

WWC   Horace Traubel, *With Walt Whitman in Camden,* 5 vols. Vols. 1–3 (New York: Rowman and Littlefield, 1961). Vol. 4, ed. Sculley Bradley (Philadelphia: University of Pennsylvania Press, 1953). Vol. 5, ed. Gertrude Traubel (Carbondale: Southern Illinois University Press, 1964).

WWW   *Walt Whitman's Workshop: A Collection of Unpublished Manuscripts*, ed. C. J. Furness (Cambridge, Mass.: Harvard University Press, 1928)

Acknowledgments

Laurence Holland first persuaded me that something really was going on amid all that flag-waving and "promulging." More than that, he also encouraged my first attempts at serious reflection on Whitman's poetry. Sharon Cameron and John Irwin agreed to take on a virtual stranger in need of guidance through the apprenticeship of dissertation writing. Although the present study is entirely different in form and in content from that previous undertaking, whatever rigor and intelligence that can be discerned in these pages is indebted to their exacting standards and generous counsel.

James McIntosh looked over an early version of the first three chapters and asked some tough questions that forced me to rethink my initial assumptions. Jonathan Auerbach and John Kucich also read portions of the manuscript and offered valuable suggestions. Robert Weisbuch's enthusiasm for the project when it was little more than an idea, to say nothing of his continued support and inexhaustible good humor, sustained me over the long haul.

My wife shared fully in the setbacks, joys, frustrations, and labor that went into seeing this book through to completion. It is to her that I owe my greatest debt, one that I look forward to repaying in the years to come.

Introduction

"By great bards only can series of peoples and States be fused into the compact organism of one nation." So declared Walt Whitman in 1860, one year before his cherished "one nation" was plunged into fratricidal war. The kind of juxtaposition suggested in my phrasing, with glorious prophecy set beside dismal fact, may be taken to reflect the spirit of inquiry that has dominated most treatments of Whitman's democratic idealism—an idealism commonly thought to be at best a subsidiary concern marginal to his true achievement as a poet and at worst a product of megalomaniacal fantasies hopelessly out of touch with the social and political complexities of his day. Ever since Santayana, at the turn of the century, branded Whitman the failed crusader for a lost populist cause, the trend in the now extensive body of critical literature devoted to *Leaves of Grass* has indeed been to affirm an increasingly rigid antithesis between "the poet of the self and the self's swaying motion" as it journeys "downward into the abysses of darkness and guilt and pain and isolation" and "the bard of democratic society" who squandered his genius in pursuit of "other forms, other endeavors less appropriate to his talent."[1] The same contrast often guides assessments of the poet's career at large, with his younger, more visceral excursions into the vicissitudes of identity frequently drawn against the platitudes of the "Good Gray Poet," whose later productions trail off into prophetic dogmatism of the most lamentable kind. But whatever the form this dichotomy assumes, it is apt to result in a way of approaching *Leaves of Grass* not far from that once endorsed by T. S. Eliot: "When Whitman speaks of the lilacs or of the mocking-bird, his theories and beliefs drop away like a needless pretext."[2]

More recent efforts to define the ambitions and originality of *Leaves of Grass* are beginning to challenge such judgments, helping us see that for Whitman at least certain "theories and beliefs" are not only inextricably bound up with his poetic vision but instrumental to understanding the dynamics of this verse in its own right.[3] Indeed, one regrettable legacy of the artificial division between "poet of the self" and "bard of democracy" has been to overlook or ignore the radical singularity of Whitman's conception of art, one which extends beyond a simple endorsement of leading democratic creeds and convictions. Neither a faithful transcription of the social world they salute and celebrate nor a visionary attempt to take flight from its conditions, Whitman's songs at their most typical eschew the mirror and the lamp, both the familiar preference for art as a just representation of nature and a Romantic aesthetic of transcendence and transformation. While it is of course true that they incorporate elements from each tradition, as anyone can attest who has admired Whitman's extraordinarily vivid renditions of the American landscape and its inhabitants or who has attended to the vastations of the bard afoot with his vision, the central motive for his poetic requires a different vocabulary to describe its workings. Stated simply, that motive involves the evolution of a consensual framework which the poem does not recommend so much as embody in "one broad, primary, universal, common platform" (*PW* 2:380). By "permitting all and rejecting none," the proper business of the poem is not to sustain a drama, develop a cast of characters, mount an argument, explore a soul, plead a cause, or render a judgment; more fundamentally, its ideal aim is to gather together without artificially dichotomizing a host of "opposite equals" in what amounts to a convocation and tallying of their diverse energies. The voice which issues from this forum of exchange—a forum which is the poem itself—does not in any final or precise sense resemble the third-person voice such as we encounter in omniscient narration, nor can it be likened to the first person voice of autobiographical intimacy such as we discover among the examples of the "egotistical sublime"; rather, it is best approached along the lines of what Donald Pease astutely terms a national "second person" whose characteristic manner suggests an "interlocutive" or "intersubjective" voice. "In place of a fixed identity," Pease observes, Whitman "created what might be called an 'intersubject,' a subjectivity reducible to neither self nor other and not even equivalent to intersubjectivity, but rather a consciousness of the never-ending collocution between self and other." Because he claims a status beyond that of another man of the crowd (though he can play this role as well), the poet presents himself to us not simply as "a separate person but a personification of the 'common place' between persons and things."[4] This emphasis helps explain why many of the moments of highest vision in his *Leaves* tend to be those in which the speaker discovers himself to be worded by an other, as in the exultant ending of "Out of the Cradle Endlessly Rocking" ("the sea whisper'd me") or in the haunted reception of the hermit thrush's "carol of death" at the heart of "When Lilacs Last in the Dooryard Bloom'd" ("And the charm of the carol rapt me"). The peculiar authority of the poet's voice in such cases is not only to "bind us throbbing in one voice," as Hart Crane understood, but to be bound in turn as in confirmation of that proffered "tally, and . . . pact, new bound of living brotherhood."

Through these means Whitman effectively subordinates a mimetic or transcendentalist model of art to a contractual one, the integrity of which is continually affirmed and reaffirmed through the give and take between self and other that identifies the poem's central reason for being. As he began to evolve this notion of verse as exemplifying a transactive process over the years prior to the first appearance of *Leaves of Grass* in 1855, Whitman came to perceive the lineaments of an expression as "gigantic and generous" as the continent it would set down in print. Hence his emphatic objection to a famous statement by Keats that "a Poet is the most unpoetical of anything in existence; because he has no Identity—he is continually in for—and filling some other Body." Running across this quotation sometime in 1848 or 1849, Whitman promptly retorted: "The great poet absorbs the identity of others, and exp[eriences] of others, and they are definite in him or from him; but he p[erceives] them all through the powerful press of himself . . . his own masterly identity."[5] Where Keats assumes the conversion of poet into representative man to entail a necessary annihilation of selfhood that rules out any possibility of exchange, Whitman is quick to insist, even at this early date, on an opposing perspective. His great poet remains the cynosure, but in a fashion which no more implies the forfeiture of other selves (for "they are definite in him or from him") than the loss of his own. It is useful to stress the dynamic implications suggested in Whitman's determination to preserve both sides of this exchange, for rather than merely urging or advocating the union of the many and the one, the "new American expression" undertakes to act out this conjunction of interests as it is distilled through the "powerful press" of the poet's "masterly identity." From his perspective the achieving of consensus can no longer be considered an external theme to think about but an evolving drama integral to the poem's design. Or, put differently, what poetry conventionally isolates as a subject for contemplation—

> . . . there is a dark
> Inscrutable workmanship that reconciles
> Discordant elements, makes them cling together
> In one society . . .[6]

—identifies precisely the mystery Whitman's "great bard" aims to inhabit. In effect, a defining feature of his singularity consists in conceiving poems to be vehicles—or better yet, the occasion—for social cohesion:

> A young man comes to me bearing a message from his
> > brother,
> How shall the young man know the whether and when of
> > his brother?
> Tell him to send me the signs.
>
> And I stand before the young man face to face, and
> > take his right hand in my left hand and his left hand
> > in my right hand,
> And I answer for his brother and for men, and I answer
> > for him that answers for all, and send these signs.
> > ("Song of the Answerer," *CRE*, p. 166)

In response to the reality of social disconnection ("How shall the young man know the whether and when of his brother?"), the Answerer reveals his calling as the connective link for the public discourse, one who does not bear a message for his interlocutors but stands forth as the expressive site and medium for its conveyance. The desired outcome is, in Allen Grossman's felicitous phrase, a "curing [of] the human colloquy"[7] which draws aside conventional methods of social regulation (the pulpit, the court, the Congress) by placing in their stead the living immediacy of a "face-to-face" encounter—the therapy with which the bard fuses a people and their diverse lands and backgrounds into the "compact organism of one nation." It is within the context of this role that we can best measure the seriousness of Whitman's larger aspirations when he declares that "the ambitious thought of my song is to help the forming of a great aggregate Nation . . . to help put the United States hand in hand, in one unbroken circle in a chant" (*PW* 2:726, 463).

To these ambitions Whitman brought an immense and urgent hopefulness, one that was sustained by little more than a truly remarkable faith in the efficacy of literature to bring about a spontaneous religion of the affections as well as an abiding reverence for the common sanctity of any and every thing, be it the beetle on the dunghill or the president in the White House. But if we rightly associate this inclusive reach of generosity—not least of the gifts *Leaves of Grass* has to offer—with its author's loafing and laughing temperament, the factors contributing to his devotion to "a great aggregate Nation" clearly go beyond a matter of personal disposition. To speak of a cure presupposes an illness, one not too difficult to locate in light of the juxtaposition that opens these pages. The constitutional crisis over the issue of slavery, revived with the introduction of the Wilmot Proviso in 1846, accelerated by the passage of the Fugitive Slave Law in 1850, and sealed with the Kansas-Nebraska Act in 1854 and Dred Scott in 1857, developed over a period more or less coterminous with the evolution of Whitman's Answerer. From his editorial post in Brooklyn during the late 1840s, Whitman witnessed much the same portents at first hand in the splintering of the Democratic party, divided like much of the nation over the controversy concerning the extension of slavery into those territories appropriated with the settlement of the Mexican War. As with many of his fellow Free Soilers, he judged slavery to be an anathema primarily because it threatened opportunities for northern (white) laborers; and when it became clear, with the 1848 election, that certain factions of his party ("Doughfaces") willing at all costs to placate the slave power merely prolonged this threat by continuing to elect a procession of mediocrities to the White House, Whitman angrily broke ranks and withdrew from all active participation in the political scene. Instead, some eight years later, in a pamphlet ostensibly written to support John Fremont's bid for the presidency but reaching well beyond this occasion, we find Whitman autobiographically campaigning for a "Redeemer President" whose policy "is not to be exclusive but inclusive" and whose justice would restore the disenfranchised voice of his beloved "workingmen, mechanics, farmers, and all laboring persons" (*WWW,* p. 109).

I introduce these concerns not so much to chart the impact of the impending crisis on Whitman's poetry but to note the widely held view that his shift in allegiance from political to extrapolitical means of realizing his dream of consensus was instrumental in his discovery of a vocation. Because it provides revealing insight into the nature of this shift and, more important for our purposes, equally revealing ambiguities, the pamphlet mentioned above is worth dwelling upon a little further. Never printed in Whitman's lifetime, "The Eighteenth Presidency!" was composed in 1856, though judging from the sound and the fury of its polemic, often taken to uncharacteristically splenetic extremes ("The President eats dirt and excrement for his daily meals, likes it, and tries to force it on the States"), it served as the cathartic release for frustrations of long standing. This jeremiad, described by Gay Wilson Allen as "one of the most eloquent" of Whitman's prose writings, "yet also pathetic in its naivete,"[8] is chiefly remembered today for its endorsement of a "Redeemer President" and its argument for the dissolution of the political party system on the grounds that "America has outgrown parties; henceforth it is too large and they too small" (*WWW*, p. 104). Both appeals are of course closely related, for the unspoken line of reasoning that guides the essay turns on the belief that "if the people would be sufficiently aroused or uplifted," then "all or most of the traditional agencies of authority could be cast aside, to make way for *man himself* in his natural perfection, free for the first time in history from the burden of privileged classes, oppressive governments, and outworn creeds."[9] This is the summary offered by George Fredrickson, whose influential account of northern intellectuals and the crisis of the Union, *The Inner Civil War*, begins by ranking Whitman at the vanguard of those "prophets of perfection" (Emerson, Moncure Conway, William Lloyd Garrison, Theodore Parker, and Wendell Phillips are the others) whose radicalism assumed the form of "a nonpolitical, noninstitutional theory of mass democracy [that affirmed] the anarchist's faith that formal government can be replaced by the spontaneous action of the people."[10] To the extent that these currents of "anti-institutionalism" permeate *Leaves of Grass,* it may be that Eliot was not entirely wrong after all: once the inscrutable workmanship of the Answerer works its will upon us we rise to the realization that "creeds, conventions, fall away and become of no account before this simple idea," that "all statements, churches, sermons melt away like vapors" (*PW* 2:394, 399), for under the "powerful press" of his expansive rhetoric the small-minded realm of political "theories and beliefs" does indeed vanish like "a needless pretext." As the poetic president, his would be a discourse exempt from the competing checks and balances or centralized mechanisms of control which maintain the "sacred compacts" of the Founding Fathers. Although Whitman venerated these men and their visionary design ("I believe its architects were some mighty prophets and gods," he says in "The Eighteenth Presidency!"), it became more than apparent in the years preceding the outbreak of war that the Constitution had woefully failed to secure that "fervid and tremendous IDEA, melting everything close with resistless heat, and solving all lesser and definite distinctions in vast, indefinite, spiritual, emotional power" (*PW* 2:368). Only through the "indissoluble compacts" of the poet and his quasi-mystical vision of democracy could the "fear of conflicting and irreconcilable interiors, and lack of a common skeleton, knitting all close" (*PW* 2:368) be assuaged. For these reasons Whitman would have every cause to agree with William Carlos Williams's proposition that "poetry is a rival government always in opposition to its cruder replicas."[11]

Oddly enough, however, it is rather startling to discover that "The Eighteenth Presidency!" does not in point of fact cast aside any "traditional agencies of authority." On the contrary, much of its rhetorical ferocity is owing to its author's hopelessly divided stand on the subject of these agencies, a division responsible for an impasse in loyalties so pronounced that it seems an enraged rehearsal of similarly balked loyalties gripping many of his countrymen. While denouncing slavery as an intolerable infringement on the rights of white labor and plainly at odds with the intentions of the Founders, Whitman is at the same time constrained to acknowledge the precedence of states' rights in this debate. The only thing worse than the continued spread of the peculiar institution, in other words, would be to override the prerogatives of those individual states where it is already sanctioned— sanctioned not merely by law but by the supreme law of the land, "the organic compacts of America," a fundamental tenet of which asserts that "a State is a perfect mistress of itself." Accordingly, those same "organic compacts" which reveal slavery to be a perversion of the framers' intent also defend, in strict observance of their laws, slavery's existence—an apparent anomaly that Whitman reluctantly confronts in urging adherence to the full "letter and spirit" of the law: "Must the run-away slaves be delivered back? They must. Many things may have the go by but good faith shall never have the go by" (*WWW*, p. 108). In the conflict between ethical obligation and maintenance of the social contract, the latter ("good faith") must take priority. Indeed, "not even the plea of its unrighteousness" can justify disobedience of the contract since a critical provision in that document (article four, section two) stipulates, in Whitman's exact paraphrase, "that any person held to service or labor in one State under its laws, and escaping into another State, shall not be absolved from service by any law of that other State, but shall be delivered up to the person to whom such service or labor is due" (*WWW*, p. 108).[12] While Whitman's scruples regarding state sovereignty no doubt reflect the legacy of Jacksonian principles inherited from his father and deepened during his newspaper days, we should not overlook the larger implication that, as Newton Arvin puts it, "there [is] is a great fund of conservatism in this radical and unexpected practical conformities in this non-conformist."[13] So it is that the visionary kosmos who urges the dissolution of political parties reveals his counterpart in the strict constructionist who declares "there is no remedy" for the present crisis other than those which "the State itself" is prepared to support. Even as the pamphlet ends with an impassioned, insurrectionary plea to "circulate and reprint this Voice of mine for the workingmen's sake," the essential thrust of his polemic counsels prudence: "we must wait, no matter how long" (*WWW*, pp. 111–12, 107).

The point here is not to catch Whitman in a contradiction, even if he prided himself on containing multitudes of them. Still less is it to draw a line of demarcation between the conservatism of his politics and the radicalism of his verse, an antithesis likely to be no less artificial than the one we began with. Rather, what I wish to bring out here is some sense of how both impulses, often compressed in one and the same gesture, result in a conservative radicalism within Whitman's outlook that is evident not only in a topical piece like "The Eighteenth Presidency!" but throughout his texts, poetry and prose alike. It is, for example, more than a local contradiction that the author of *Calamus* could speak on behalf of "the institution of the dear love of comrades" or that the author of *Democratic Vistas* could contend that what "really balances and conserves the social and political world is not so much legislation, police, treaties, and dread of punishment, as the latent eternal institutional sense . . . indeed, this perennial regulation, control, and oversight, by self-suppliance, is *sine qua non* to democracy" (*PW* 2:421), for his avowed "anti-institutionalism" chronically lends itself to invocations of norms and controls commonly associated with these same institutions. Thus, calling for the dismantling of political parties in 1856 did not deter him from christening the newly emerged poet in the 1855 Preface as "the president of regulation"; in the same breath that he proclaims elsewhere "we want no *reforms*, no *institutions*, no *parties*—We want a living *principle* as nature has" (Whitman's emphasis), we also find him asserting that this must be a principle "under which *nothing* can go wrong [and which] *must* be vital throughout the United States" (my emphasis; *WWW*, p. 45). In witnessing how the language of voluntarism here edges irresistibly toward a language of compulsion, we can further note that instead of evincing "an anarchist's faith that formal government can be replaced by the spontaneous action of the people," it would be more precise to say that this is a faith which Whitman is deeply committed to "promulging" even as he is driven by motives no less profound to doubt its reality. He is bent upon persuading himself of this faith no less than ourselves. Much as it would at times like to do so, his verse does not ultimately sponsor a static opposition between legislated union and spontaneous accord but tends to fuse both options into an ongoing dynamic of vacillation which generates the extraordinary clash between aspiration and skepticism that is at the heart of his search for a "living principle" of solidarity.

Not long ago Edwin Fussell took note, as indeed the poet himself often did, of "how Whitman's United States, one and many, singular and plural, were mysteriously constituted into the 'Union' by a written document that in a dark hour proved as tenuous as his own."[14] I want to endorse and expand upon this reminder by adding that the analogy between "the organic compacts of the States" and "a compact, the-whole-surrounding *National Poem*"[15] holds true not only in the sense of a shared historical plight but in prominent ambiguities and improprieties endemic to the act of constitution-making itself. Among these there would have to be included the task of affirming a form of unanimity sufficient to honor the requirements of the many and the one without sacrificing either term; the intrinsically worrisome quest to locate some unquestioned principle of legitimacy or self-evident truth capable of validating that unanimity; the issue of indeterminate language and its problematic bearing on the framers' intent; the equally problematic distinction between constitution as accomplished document (guarantor of established, immutable principles) and constitution as revolutionary act (the instrument for overthrowing the same principles). While Whitman's Answerer—the living embodiment and medium of indisputable Union—comes before us primarily to lay such quandaries to rest, his own urgent work of "curing the human colloquy" can often result in compacts no less susceptible to these afflictions. The strain besetting his creation of "the-whole-surrounding *National Poem*" is no less formal than it is actual; that is to say, his best and most compelling texts seek to remedy by transcending the burdens and deficiencies of their "cruder replicas" only to find themselves often drawn toward a repetition of these same dilemmas. To reflect upon such ironies is not to deny the integrity or consequence of Whitman's democratic idealism; indeed, it is principally through the exploration of these tensions that I hope to make the full authenticity of that vision emerge. It should be possible, in this respect, to appraise the significance of poetry's "indissoluble compacts" without lionizing Whitman as an implacable foe of flawed policies and corrupt institutions or dismissing these concerns as the flimsy pretext for neurotic inhibitions and conflicts.

Because my primary concern involves the risks and rewards of constitution-making as they are acted out in the texts of *Leaves of Grass*, the chapters that follow offer an inside narrative of this drama. They do not, I should add, pretend to offer a thoroughgoing reconstruction of Whitman's life and times. I am less concerned to ascertain specific historical determinants which may have shaped Whitman's vision than to investigate the aspirations and labor that went into sustaining it. Of course, I shall have occasion to return to the crisis of the House Divided when it is especially pertinent, particularly in Part 3, where the poems composed in the period directly before and during the Civil War are discussed. But what chiefly guides my interest are the vicissitudes of a literary experiment, in the sense Whitman desired his readers to appreciate when he remarked "I consider *Leaves of Grass* and its theory experimental as, in deepest sense, I consider our American republic itself to be, with its theory" (*PW* 2:713).

I would like to conclude with two notes on my procedure. To the degree that I have emphasized that Whitman's drama of consensus does indeed unfold as a drama, where the process of securing consent is worked through rather than taken for granted, I have structured my study to reflect this fact. In view of the foregoing comments describing Whitman's aesthetic as above all concerned to evoke a transactive process between the self and the multitude of persons, places, and things that course through it, the intensely apostrophic character of his writing—its manifest delight in acts of summoning, commanding, exhorting, cajoling, and other forms of address—is not surprising. Apostrophe Jonathan Culler has found to be unique among the figures of speech "in that it makes its point by troping not on the meaning of a word but on the circuit or situation of communication itself."[16] There is little mystery as to why this trope should be so heavily favored by texts which, as a rule, do not seek to master a meaning so much as to bring to pass the "common ground" in which a meaningful exchange may take place. As I have hinted, there are innumerable objects of address in *Leaves of Grass;* for the sake of convenience I have narrowed the field to a selection of prominent categories. Part 1 accordingly isolates for analysis Whitman's invocations to the reader, his "you, whoever you are"; Part 2 focuses upon those to his speech, his "uttering tongues" and "leaves of grass"; Part 3 examines the twin concerns of the body and death as the poet approached the cataclysm of fratricidal war. Without rehearsing the individual sections at length I would simply emphasize that in each case it is indeed "the circuit or situation of communication itself" which is most at stake in the readings I advance, not least because the peculiar blend of motives making up Whitman's conservative radicalism compel him to take the rules of exchange between himself and his interlocutors to be his subject and not his sanction, an ongoing issue to be scrutinized rather than something to be safely assumed.

Lastly, a word on my choice of texts. As is well known, Whitman issued a number of editions of *Leaves of Grass* over the course of his career before declaring his preference for the ninth and final installment, the so-called Deathbed edition of 1892. Increasingly, however, scholars have come to dispute the poet's judgment in the belief that the later revisions often sacrifice much of the vitality and imaginative daring of the original texts.[17] I have no wish to challenge this view, though my own sense is that Whitman mended as much as he marred: while most would agree that the deletion of certain key passages in a poem like "The Sleepers" considerably weakens its cumulative power, not many are likely to regret the loss of "out of the rocked cradle" as the first line to one of Whitman's most admired poems. More to the point, there has been a tendency among partisans of the earlier volumes to make their case by profiling the radical experimentation of the younger bard against the more cautious retrenchments of advancing age. Yet as I hope to make clear, these stances can be more profitably understood when viewed as interlocking drives present throughout Whitman's writings rather than discrete impulses divided by a chronological fault line. Consequently, even though the original composition of almost all the lyrics here examined falls between 1855 and 1865, I have chosen the final edition as my primary text in order to emphasize the basic continuity of Whitman's ambitions and the tensions that accompany them. Of course, in those instances where restoration of deleted material is especially revealing or helpful in clarifying issues in a given poem, I have made the appropriate reference.

PART 1

A MORE
PERFECT UNION
Whitman's
"Hymns of You"

*W*hat is poetry? When does poetry cease to be poetic and become something else? In keeping with the spirit of Dr. Johnson's sage advice that it is much easier to say what poetry is not before saying what it is, John Stuart Mill ventures this famous distinction in his brief essay, "What is Poetry?"

> A question will sometimes arise, whether some particular author is a poet, and those who maintain the negative commonly allow that though not a poet, he is a highly eloquent writer. . . . Poetry and eloquence are both alike the expression or utterance of feeling. But if we may be excused the antithesis, we should say that eloquence is *heard*, poetry is *over*heard.

Attempts to rescue poetry from the sullied hands of rhetoric have a long and venerable history, though Mill adds a new twist to the argument. What separates these two discourses has less to do with the subject matter they signify than with the kind of listener they create. In one the audience is openly acknowledged, in the other it is not. "Eloquence is feeling pouring itself out to other minds, courting their sympathy or endeavouring to influence their beliefs, or move them to passion," while "poetry is feeling confessing itself to itself, in moments of solitude." Mill is of course willing to concede that poetry may have eloquent effects, but this is only, so to speak, an accident of composition. He does not need to belabor this point since he writes merely to uphold those silently held conventions that commonly inform one's reading experience. In Mill's essay, those conventions are guided by what has been called, with wise vagueness, the fictional contract, where the common bond between speaker and listener is said to consist in the act of both parties pretending away any such alliance. Tying his definition

3

of poetry to this paradox, Mill accordingly urges that the best way for the poet to honor his contract with the reader is to deny that it exists. Once poetry admits awareness of an audience, once it recognizes itself to be the product of a *shared* agreement, it is no longer poetry but slides into the so-called "lesser" genres of oratory, eloquence, or pamphleteering.[1]

Such opinions are by no means peculiar, and variations on Mill's fabled antithesis between the heard and the overheard come readily to mind. One thinks, for example, of Kant's inquiry into an aesthetic guided by a "purpose without purposiveness," of Yeats's distinction between those quarrels involving ourselves and those involving others, of Eliot's discriminations among "the first" and "the second" voices of poetry, or of Northrop Frye's *mot* that "criticism speaks and all the arts are dumb."[2] Common to each reference is the familiar belief that art in general and lyric poetry in particular is a supremely disinterested activity that holds no palpable designs over us. As such, it lays claim to a condition of "pure persuasion," a term first subjected to serious critical reflection by Kenneth Burke in *A Rhetoric of Motives*. While quick to remind us that "pure persuasion in the absolute sense exists no where," Burke is concerned to demonstrate how "some element of standoffishness, or perhaps better, *self-interference*" is vital to the formation of this "meta-rhetoric."[3] Through the willed intervention of certain obstacles to persuasion or "the interposing of distance" between speaker and recipient, the courtship of appeal may continue endlessly while remaining free of the imputation of ulterior motives or the pursuit of local advantages. Correspond-ingly, in Mill's fictive contract we see how the goal of persuasion is accomplished once it is forsworn, with the desired result that the supposed banishment of the reader from the poet's consciousness here serves in fact to extend a tacit invitation to that reader. Access is predicated upon exclusion, much as Diderot's actor, performing as if the curtain never rose, thrills a packed house. Rather than treating this state of affairs as the hypocritical arrangement that it doubtless is (my speech will rigorously assume your nonexistence so as to make my claim on your attention the more compelling), it is perhaps more fruitful to suggest that Mill's soliloquizing bard and eavesdropping listener idealize a form of communication which takes the conditions for assent to be preestablished—something to

be inferred rather than contested. It would indeed be idle to look
for a *drama* of consensus in such a speech, since that is what Mill's
distinctions are designed to moot. And so far as literary criticism,
along with other modes of reading, takes such conditions for
granted, it may be said, emending Frye, that criticism speaks just
insofar as all the arts are believed to be dumb, that our
interpretation of the texts we address is facilitated by the assurance
that they do not overtly address us. Enjoying the privileged
intimacy of a voyeur, the interpreter, beheld bv no one, beholds all.

Whitman does not wish to be read this way. While Mill's poet
says, in effect, "what I assume, you shall assume," this is a saying
that must remain unspoken. Whitman speaks it out. Taking as its
point of departure what Mill finds so offensive, his verse insists on
"keeping [its] eyes on the listener":

Listener up there! Here you . . . what have you to
        confide to me?
Look in my face while I snuff the sidle of the evening,
Talk honestly, for no one else hears you, and I stay only
        a minute longer.[4]

Simultaneously taken aback and charmed by such outbursts, we
recognize the characteristic accents of a poet who presents himself
not simply as a man speaking *to* men but as one bent on fostering
the illusion of speaking *at* them. Beyond overthrowing the metrical
contract, much of the revolutionary impact of *Leaves of Grass* entails
breaking the mediations conventional to the fictional contract by
devising a mode of address able to traverse the gap between
intimate seductiveness and a generic inclusiveness. We find
ourselves inscribed as readers everywhere in his pages, not only
through directives, imperatives, and other forms of apostrophe but
through the immodest aspirations of a bard who constantly
reminds us that "whether I shall make the POEM OF THE NEW
WORLD, transcending all others,—depends, rich persons, upon
you, whoever you are." Needless to say, Whitman's ubiquitous
"you, whoever you are" hardly represents the internalized audience
of coy mistresses and truant lovers, though something of each role
plays into Whitman's courtship of his reader. Like John Ashbery,
the poet whose experiments with the second person most closely
resemble those of his predecessor, Whitman "prefer[s] 'you' in the

plural,"[5] the you of the "democratic average," the figure "who alone can compact these States."

My interest in these poems does not stop short, however, with the observation that they represent a radical innovation. Strictly speaking, it is in fact doubtful whether they can be considered innovations at all, since a readership as diffuse as Whitman's "you, whoever you are" necessarily looms before us as a fictional construct that is no less shadowy than Mill's banished listener. Quite plainly, though, important differences do stand out between Whitman and the tradition Mill speaks for, most notably the difference between a poetry that takes the grounds for assent to be preestablished or built into its structure of assumptions and a poetry that externalizes the achievement of assent as an active and indeed central feature of its drama. By placing his auditors at the center stage of his verse, Whitman hopes to bring forward and actualize the movement from isolated individuality ("the simple, separate person") to affirmed unanimity ("the word Democratic, the word En-Masse") captured within the "common ground" of the poem itself. So doing, he hopes as well not only to override the mediations between "I" and "you" endorsed by Mill but, more ambitiously, to reconstitute the rules of communicative exchange that govern the social world at large. The next three chapters chronicle the rewards and risks of such an undertaking. Although Whitman's habit of keeping his eyes upon the listener reflects his commitment to the naturalized bonds of "indissoluble compacts," it will also be necessary to see how this habit implies a basic wariness and ambivalence toward all forms of contractual exchange, forms the poet proposes to abolish even as he clings to them. Thus, while the pages that follow retain the concept of the fictional contract, cumbersome and imprecise as it may be, they do so principally because Whitman by no means transcends the dialectic of exclusion and invitation set forth in Mill's essay. Rather, he magnifies both sides of this dialectic, pitching them to new and volatile extremes. His self-styled "hymns of you" permit, in this respect, the tracing of a crisis of readership or, more accurately, a crisis in the attempt to mediate among the diverse wills of this readership in the quest to be all things to all people.

1

Contacts and Contracts

THERE IS NO FORMALLY recognized title for the kind of poem I wish
to discuss in this chapter, even though it comprehends a major portion of *Leaves of Grass*. Its type is best represented by those poems
Whitman grouped under the heading "Chants Democratic" in 1860
and which appear in subsequent editions as miscellaneous "Songs"
between the *Calamus* and "Birds of Passage" sections. A partial listing
of this collection would include "Song of the Rolling Earth," "Song
of the Answerer," "Song of the Open Road," "Song of Occupations," and, unquestionably the finest poem in the sequence,
"Crossing Brooklyn Ferry." These are, however, only more extended
forays into what I shall be calling, for want of a better term, Whitman's second-person poetry.[1] Apostrophes to the reader at large (as
distinct from, say, those to the "curling grass" or "Me Myself") recur
frequently throughout "Song of Myself," and Whitman distributed a
handful of invocations entitled "To You" throughout his *Leaves*.
Whitman's interest in his auditors represents a lifelong concern,
though the appearance of the second-person pronoun diminishes
steadily in editions after 1860.[2]

Most treatments of Whitman's second-person poetry begin and
end with its most unnerving characteristic: its didacticism. Neither
the lyrical confessions of a soul in solitude nor a careful rendering of a
dramatic event, these verses tend to be expostulatory in emphasis,
often to the point where the line between poetry and propaganda
becomes distressingly thin. "The words of the true poems," Whitman
chants in a typical moment, "give you more than poems, / They give
you to form for yourself poems, religions, war, peace, behavior, histories, essays, daily life, and everything else . . ." ("Song of the
Answerer," *CRE*, p. 170). Anyone who knows Whitman knows that
such utterances carry a familiar ring: they are prescriptions for action,
not descriptions; manifestos rather than dramatizations. Unlike

Wordsworth, the American Bard evidently had no qualms about in-
curring the suspicion "of having been principally influenced by the
selfish and foolish hope of *reasoning* [the reader] into an approbation
of these particular poems."³ Mill would no doubt want to observe
that Whitman had forsaken the writer's desk for the lectern, a verdict
many of his most prominent commentators grudgingly accept when
they classify a poem like "Song of the Answerer" as "programmatic"
or as "platform verse." It is hardly surprising, moreover, to find that
there has been far more speculation on the various motives (artistic,
political, and otherwise) behind Whitman's "direct address" than on
its consequences within the poetry itself. We are routinely referred to
the bard's democratic aesthetic, his resolve to shock his audience out
of complacency, his determination that reading should resemble an
arduous "gymnast's struggle," his faith that his poetry will stimulate
"poets to come." More recent scholarship has reminded us of Whitman's early oratorical pretensions and has viewed his lifelong fascination with eloquence as exercising a decisive impact on his verse.⁴

Still, it is one thing to reflect back on the possible sources of
Whitman's "hymns of you" and another to describe the status of that
"you" as it emerges in *Leaves of Grass*. "Crossing Brooklyn Ferry"
offers an admirable point of departure for such a description, both
because it is less polemically charged than the other "songs" I have
mentioned and because it challenges certain well-worn assumptions
about this kind of verse. We need not read far into "Crossing
Brooklyn Ferry," for example, to realize that even so modest a term as
"direct address" may begin to look rather misleading. When Whitman
writes fairly early in the poem "closer yet I approach you," he identifies his reader as a referent capable of being designated in his discourse
in the same breath that he implies the necessity of continued solicitation. The addressee is hardly an implied reader, but neither is he an
utterly accessible presence. The distinction is worth dwelling on because it suggests, curiously enough, that the relationship between
author and reader is not something Whitman works *from* but works
toward. Precisely what most poetry takes for granted Whitman takes
as his explicit subject. Reading further on,

> Closer yet I approach you,
> What thought you have of me now, I had as much as
>   you—I laid my stores in advance,
> I consider'd long and seriously of you before you were
>   born,

we discover a poem which does not silently presuppose the existence of a listener prior to its composition. Instead the act of writing the poem has become virtually coextensive with the act of reaching that listener. It is not at all fanciful to say in this respect that "Crossing Brooklyn Ferry" records nothing less than an anticipation of its own reading. Figuring its reader as putative subject rather than mere recipient, the poem chronicles a sustained attempt to localize that audience, to persuade itself that "It avails not, time nor place—distance avails not" (*CRE,* p. 160). The logic of its vision dictates that the conventional contract between reader and author be not simply recast but formally dissolved ("the simple, compact, well-joined scheme, myself disintegrated, every one disintegrated") in order to reimagine those "ties" to "the others that are to follow me, the ties between me and them." That bond is shown to subsist through the first half of the poem through a range of analogies; from the miscellaneous attractions of the landscape, matters of personal identity, to evil impulses, all of which are significant to the poet primarily to the extent that they afford a shared plane of experiences: "just as you are refreshed by the gladness of the river and the bright flow, I was refreshed, / Just as you stood and leaned on the rail . . . / I stood, / . . . I too was struck from the float forever held in solution . . . I too knitted the old knot of contrariety." Notably, Whitman's stance throughout these sections reverses Mill's dictum regarding the heard and overheard, for now it is the poet, not the beholder, who poses as eavesdropper, urging us to "consider, you who peruse me, whether I may not in unknown ways be looking upon you," for "Who knows, for all the distance, but I am as good as looking at you now, for all you cannot see me?" (*CRE,* p. 163, 164).

As Whitman moves from the external features of the scene at dusk to the "dark patches" of the soul's "hot wishes," everything in the poem aspires to the intimacy of contact, a movement brought to consummation in section eight, as the poet speculates, "what is more subtle than this which ties me to the man or woman that looks in my face? / Which fuses me into you now, and pours my meaning into you?" Following upon the gesture of disintegration that opens the poem, these interrogations bespeak a more triumphant act of integration which allows the poet, his authority redoubled, now to command the landscape he had heretofore only described: "Flow on river! flow with the flood tide . . . Suspend here and everywhere, eternal float of solution! . . . Be firm, rail over the river, to support those who lean idly, yet haste with the hasting current" (*CRE,* p. 164). Correspondingly, the pronomial interplay between "I" and "you" finally merges into "we" in this final section as poet and audience "receive with free sense at last" those "dumb, beautiful ministers": "We use you not, and do not cast you aside—we plant you permanently within us, / We fathom you not" (*CRE,* p. 165). As so often in Whitman's poetry, closure makes itself felt here by projecting a sense of having reached an agreement or a final ratification. As "we fathom you not" suggests, the precise terms of that understanding are perhaps of less consequence than the process of assimilation itself. The depth of such inclusions, moreover, may be the more fully appreciated once we consider as well what the poem excludes. The use of irony, narrative frames, sustained conceits, the introduction of personae—those conventional mediations which induce us to speak of the poem as an objectified perception or the poet as an impersonal force are all refused, since Whitman is quite single-minded in his determination to erase all boundaries, to overcome all distance, to create, in effect, a space in which reader and poem are one. It is a further measure of the remarkable novelty of this project, as bracing today as it no doubt was in 1856, that Whitman's lines do not so much defy those familiar conventions as remain oblivious to them. The primitive force of their solicitations, which invoke rather than assume a beholder, calls to mind William Dean Howells's fine insight that Whitman's verse represents "not poetry but the materials of poetry."[5] For the text of "Crossing Brooklyn Ferry" manifests itself to us not as a cunningly deployed pattern of significances, a shrewdly arranged narrative, not even, in reality, as a "field of action"; it is, before all these, a gesture, summons, or petition. Its immediate ambition is not to insinuate a paraphrasable "theme" or elaborate an archetypal "mythology"; it wants to imagine itself antecedent to such formulations. As we are made to recognize from the first line— "flood tide below me! I see you face to face!"—to the last— "we plant you permanently within us"— the goal is not so much communication as communion.

A more prosaic way of putting this would be to say that the sheer desire for communication has become synonymous with the content of communication. From this standpoint it would seem appropriate for us to abandon talk of *contracts* altogether and speak instead of a poetry of *contact.* This is in fact what Denis Donoghue urges us to do when he identifies "contact" as Whitman's "central term"; "the last grace of [Whitman's] encounter [with his readers] will be a touching, a contact, not a 'seeing.'" His verse craves a "life of continuous intimacy," a "laying on of hands" whose touch can allay the terrible doubt of appearances and whose reach testifies to a longing for a deepened union with others.[6] Perpetually in transit, here but also there, in the past as well as our future, the presence of the Answerer does not occupy this or that side of a dialogue of interests but spans and fuses all interests in order to receive and be received by "free sense at last." Contractual alliances are, by contrast, conventionally thought to be what Kenneth Burke has termed "agonistic instruments." Insofar as the pledge to honor an obligation suggests the possibility that the parties concerned (like a sovereign and his people) might behave otherwise, bonds adjudicated by contract "involve an enemy, implicitly or explicitly."[7] The aim of the poem is to break free of these "agonistic" entanglements; suspending listener and speaker in its "eternal float of solution," it holds no end in view other than the acknowledgment of unconditioned acceptance. Thus, when Santayana takes to task the "barbaric" sensibility of a poet who suffers "the innumerable commonplace moments of life . . . to speak like others" and whose imagination surrenders to "a passive sensorium for the registering of impressions" with "no element of construction . . . and therefore no element of penetration," he is describing Whitman's deepest source of appeal, one that thrives on the promise of indiscriminate receptivity.[8]

Even so, it remains questionable whether our makeshift division between contacts and contracts can withstand much scrutiny. Few would deny that "Crossing Brooklyn Ferry" is a work of compelling and incandescent originality, in every way worthy of Thoreau's high esteem when he first knew it as the "Sun-Down Poem," yet a fuller appreciation of Whitman's quest for consensus requires attention not only to the possible fragility of this distinction, but to how far the poet himself is willing to uphold it. In returning to the poem's most pivotal lines, where the poet alludes to that which "ties me to the man or woman that looks in my face, / Which fuses me into you now and pours my meaning into you now," we may note a peculiar effect. The passage does not so much convey a meaning as tell us that a meaning has been conveyed. However we choose to define the sense of "fusion" here, it is clear that it shares nothing with Eliot's famous celebration of "the fusion of thought and feeling" in the decidedly associated sensibility of John Donne. In drawing the reader into the poem with the fervor of an erotic embrace, Whitman decisively shifts attention away from the content of his "meaning" per se, as if to imply

that any attempt to extrapolate its significance must appear inconsequential in light of the poem's absorptive energy. Lest the force of this
implication be lost on his auditors, Whitman brings home the lesson
of his "preaching" all the more irresistibly by refusing to state it:

> We understand, then, do we not?
> What I promised without mentioning it, have you not
>   accepted?
> What the study could not teach—what the preaching
>   could not accomplish, is accomplished, is it not?
>
> (*CRE,* p. 164)

Questions like these do not expect answers, only assent; to respond
otherwise would not only be a confession of misplaced emphasis but,
one supposes, an act of disqualification. Either we understand or we
do not. (On this score earlier editions are still more emphatic, the last
of the questions above being "What the push of reading could not
start is started by me personally, is it not?") Soft-spoken as they are,
Whitman's coaxing interrogations bear witness to a certain preemptive impulse, here concerned to demonstrate that understanding
is to be achieved despite and not as the result of the "push of reading."
And, so far as this is true, a curious discrepancy emerges. The poem
seems written under the constraint of a double imperative: it desires
to affirm an unparalleled intimacy with its auditor that suggests him
to be absolutely intrinsic to the poem's development at the same time
it is moved to stipulate that those ties which bind listener to author are
absolutely extrinsic to interpretive reflection. What Whitman would
impress upon us is not a method of reading but its irrelevance.

   In a certain sense, there is nothing especially new about this assertion, however newfangled it may sound in reference to Whitman.
There is, after all, a sizable amount of commentary on Whitman which
has held (and continues to hold) that the best way to approach his
verse is to appreciate it. In such cases the stance of the critic is familiar:
less analyst than celebrant, his pretense is to throw off all pretense at
interpretation and delight instead in the verbal fireworks of the text.
Whitman's boast "I am not a bit tamed, / I too am untranslatable,"
becomes his article of faith. The most influential example in this genre
is Randall Jarrell's 1953 essay "Some Lines from Whitman," which
springs from the conviction that "to show Whitman for what he is one
does not need to praise or explain or argue, one simply needs to
quote." Valuable as it unquestionably was in winning for Whitman a

small shred of academic respectability at a time (the heyday of the New Criticism) when the poet badly needed it, Jarrell's homage remains a striking fulfillment of Whitman's prophecy that the bard may indeed weave all things into himself. Animated by an infectious enthusiasm, Jarrell's comments repeatedly exult in their very inarticulateness, as exclamations like "one hardly knows what to point at," "it is like magic," or "something has been done to us without our knowing how it was done" punctuate his observations. Mounting a full-scale interpretation of Whitman, by contrast, is apt to seem somewhat "ridiculous," for it is enough that "the critic points at his qualities in despair and wonder, all method failing, and simply calls them by their names."⁹ The overriding impression, in short, is that this poetry calls for and calls forth a kind of stunned amazement, that it repels explanation in favor of wonder, that it subsumes interpretation in favor of enchantment. This should sound familiar, for it succinctly describes the blissful paralysis of response that grips the "you" of "Crossing Brooklyn Ferry." As such, "Some Lines from Whitman" is itself not so much a response to Whitman as it is absorbed by him. When Jarrell remarks in passing that a line from "Song of Myself" is "evil beyond rejection [and] wonderful beyond any acceptance," we become aware to what extent criticism may come to exist, so to speak, despite itself. Stricken to silence, it too succumbs to the speechlessness of yet another "beautiful dumb minister."¹⁰

These are harsh words, and in fairness it should be added that if Jarrell's analysis falls prey to an especially drastic dissociation of sensibility, it does so with more assurance than his subject. Indeed, this issue would not be worth belaboring were it not for the pains taken by Whitman himself. For what can be emphasized in regard to "Crossing Brooklyn Ferry" is that it is not simply content to imply the dissociation that Jarrell's commentary—"all method failing"—so readily yields to; it virtually prescribes that dissociation. Evidently it is not enough that we intuit what the study could not teach or what the preaching could not accomplish; Whitman tells us that we have as good as done so. It as if the poem, in desiring to make its world safe for the free play of implication, were reluctant to leave too much open to the vagaries of inference. To be sure, when the poet urges us to consider what "the push of reading could not start," there is a sense in which he is merely echoing the Romantic axiom that great art reduces us to awe or silence, like the "thoughts all too deep for words" that seize Coleridge upon hearing Wordsworth first read *The Prelude*. But the crucial difference for Whitman is that any such spirit of ineffable union is no longer trusted to appear as the *product* of our reading but has been inscribed within the text as something to be confronted rather than inferred. And, when pressed to extremes, this orientation can produce startling results. It is one thing to be stirred by the intuition that a writer arouses unanswerable questions, another to find him declaiming "I arouse unanswerable questions" (*CRE*, p. 237). Imagine Keats beginning "Ode On A Grecian Urn" with the announcement "I tease you out of thought" and some sense of the pressures peculiar to Whitman's second-person verse can be gained. This is not to upbraid Whitman for aiming at profundity and doing a poor job of it; artistic ineptitude is beside the point. The paradoxical thrust of these injunctions is of course that they *are* injunctions, that even as they seek to transcend conventional sources of social integration (the lessons in the schools, the preaching in the pulpit) their "push" for intersubjective confirmation of the bonds between self and other may inhibit or perhaps even compromise the promised deliverance of redeemed understanding. While the impulse to leave the contract with his listener open-ended—"leaving you to prove and define it, expecting the main things from you"—must be respected, this competes against the drive to render such expectations inescapably explicit. That the ties which outstrip mere textual understanding should also be set down and ratified within the text suggests not only that Whitman has not entirely left behind the "agonistic instruments" his discourse was to subsume but that he may in fact be loath to do so.

As the harbinger of social attachment, the "equable man" of *Leaves of Grass* is not concerned to restore or reconstruct the legacy of the ·Founding Fathers and their "indissoluble compacts," however much he may have cherished them. As he explains in *Calamus*, "I am neither for nor against institutions." To utter "the password primeval" and to "give the sign of Democracy" is instead to seek out the conditions for a "constitution beneath the Constitution,"[11] an ur-contract characterized by relations that are "calm, subtle, untransmissible by print" (*CRE*, p. 220). That Whitman is repeatedly given to reporting in print on that "which print cannot touch" nevertheless remains a troublesome point of concern and more than one commentator has wondered how it is that "the reader's independence [should be declared] in sentences so obviously meant to tell him what to think."[12] Perhaps, though, outright coercion is not the central issue here; the poet eager to let us know that he has teased us out of thought is not

telling us what to think so much as traveling a thin line between a
desired suspension from traditionally esteemed centers of authority
and the establishment of authority for his own vision. To affirm what
is "promis'd without mentioning it" bespeaks the dream of union
undefiled by prior obligations; to make mention of what must remain
unmentionable speaks to the fear that such consensus may be chimerical, ignored, or, worse yet, perverted. We see at work a similar clash of
motives informing many of these apostrophes, as in the following
lines from "A Song for Occupations":

> I bring what you much need yet always have,
> Not money, amours, dress, eating, erudition, but as
> > good,
> I send no agent or medium, offer no representative of
> > value, but offer the value itself.
>
> There is something that comes home to one now and
> > perpetually
> It is not what is printed, preach'd, discussed, it
> > eludes discussion and print,
> It is not to be put in a book, it is not in this book,
> It is for you, whoever you are . . .
>
> You may read in many languages, yet read nothing about
> > it,
> You may read the President's message and read nothing
> > about it there,
> Nothing in the reports from the State Department or
> > Treasury department, or in the daily papers or weekly
> > papers,
> Or in the census or revenue returns, prices current,
> > or any accounts of stock.
> > > > > > > > > (*CRE*, p. 213)

Restoring the grounds of tacit assent, the "constitution beneath the
Constitution," requires endorsement of self-evident truths whose
power of reconciliation can be made to emerge *only* as an inference,
just as "the new American expression" is "to be indirect and not
direct"—"the words of my book nothing, the drift is everything"
(*CRE*, p. 12). Political reports on the state of the union are consequently mere epiphenomena of this abiding "value" and so derive
from but cannot encompass the "something" which "eludes discus-

sion and print." This the bard can do, coming forward to "offer the
value itself." And yet, like the promise made without being mentioned, this assertion too partly draws toward and partly guards
against the alliance it seeks: the ties that bind must not and yet must be
set down on the page; the value itself must not and yet must be
affirmed. Whitman's stance, in effect, is both prophetic and protec-
tive; he is deeply sensitive to the urgent call for solidarity ("what you
much need") precisely because he is so critically aware of what there is
to threaten it, not only in the world at large but in its very process of
articulation. A delicate balance must be maintained that neither over-
states nor understates the rules of exchange between "I" and "you,"
where either extreme would impair the promise of "free sense."

Here again it is helpful to return to Mill's essay as a point in
contrast. To declare, as Mill does, that "all poetry is of the nature of
soliloquy" is to prescribe, as M. H. Abrams has noted, that "the poet's
audience [be] reduced to a single member, consisting of the poet
himself."[13] Mill, that is, recommends a degree of self-absorption on
the part of the poet so complete that his auditor is held at a safe
distance, thereby insuring his role as interpreter. The poet who declares "I pour my meaning into you" would seem intent on inverting
this formula: he envisions a poetry which absorbs its reader so completely into the text that the beholder virtually *becomes* its meaning,
thereby negating (that is, rendering superfluous) his role as interpreter. As Allen Grossman writes, "divergence of interpretive inference is
one of the obstacles to unanimity which . . . Whitman undertakes to
abolish."[14] Overcoming this divergence can prove, however, to be
very much an an obstacle in its own right, and for this reason those
discrepancies or contradictions in logic so prominent in *Leaves of Grass*
and so often ascribed to muddled thinking or slapdash exuberance
may be more profitably viewed as symptoms of a contractual impasse.
Lines of poetry that tell us to read between the lines, like appeals to a
realm beyond discursive understanding set forth in a bluntly discursive fashion ("I arouse unanswerable questions"), make apparent the
thoroughly volatile character of Whitman's undertaking, where persuasive overtures hoping to consolidate a common interest are
simultaneously advanced and retracted. It would indeed appear in
such cases as though the quality of "self-interference" Burke isolates as
a vital principle of "pure persuasion" had undergone a decisive shift in
emphasis, for we no longer confront a rhetoric that takes the objects
of address to be forever out of reach and so makes the game of

courtship a perpetual activity, like the figures of "wild pursuit" frozen on Keats's urn or the self-enclosed distraction of Mill's solitary bard. In Whitman, self-interference does not describe an enabling stratagem to be worked upon but the behavior of the text itself, most notably in those moments when the virtue of an ungraspable, sacrosanct indeterminacy (the "free sense" of "indirection," the "something" eluding "discussion and print") is urged upon us with a vehemence that invests this ideal with a paradoxically overdetermined character.

In Part 2 of this study we shall have occasion to explore this paradox at greater length, particularly with reference to Whitman's organicism; for the time being we should note that the stalemate that implicitly stands behind it is scarcely peculiar to *Leaves of Grass* but persists in any attempt to affirm what social theorists of the seventeenth and eighteenth centuries were pleased to call the "original compact." Central to the passages we have been discussing and indeed central to Whitman's entire vocation is the belief that constituted power not only can but must be distinguished from the power of constitution-making itself. When this distinction breaks down or is in danger of being forgotten (as the author of *Leaves of Grass* plainly feared that it was), it becomes necessary to uphold its integrity with reminders like "The President is there in the White House for you, it is not you who are there for him" ("A Song for Occupations," *CRE,* p. 215). In a deeper sense, adherence to this needed separation of powers can be felt in the stance of a poet less concerned to shape or direct the general will of the second person than to release it, to "bring what you much need, but always have." As such, his way of thinking remains entirely consonant with the spirit of Thomas Paine's popular stipulation that "a constitution is not the act of a government but of a people constituting a government."[15] Two kinds of convenants, thought to be mutually exclusive, are being invoked here: one a "social compact" ratified between a people and their ruler that ideally sanctions legitimate government, the other a more "original compact" between the people themselves that presumably results in the creation of society. Yet not much reflection is needed to sense the cross-purposes at work in Paine's appeal to that "constitution behind the Constitution," for if his definition is to retain credibility, if it is indeed the case that a "constitution is a thing *antecedent* to a government, and a government is only the creature of a constitution,"[16] then it follows that Paine is imagining—somehow, somewhere—a community whose members join together in sincere and unanimous consent, standing as if for the first time in history in free and original relation. His argument is beset by a vicious circularity: anxious to lay bare the fictional status of all governments empowered by constitution (invented, not discovered), Paine makes it difficult for us to see why his tacit appeal to an "original compact" should escape a similar designation, committing us as it does to a conceivably endless quest for a mythical "state of Nature" where power is disencumbered of all prior constraints. (Needless to add, for Paine this "state of Nature" had just transpired: "we are brought at once to the point of seeing government begin," he writes in the aftermath of the American Revolution, "as if we were at the beginning of time.")[17]

Complications of this kind, while perhaps more easily overlooked in the heat of a polemical tract like *The Rights of Man,* call attention to themselves in Whitman with singular tenacity. In light of the emphasis accorded to *antecedence* in Paine's argument, we can begin to understand why the outstanding concern for the author of "Crossing Brooklyn Ferry" should not be what the push of reading may or may not accomplish but our acknowledgment that "it is accomplish'd by me personally, is it not?" The poet's words must come *before* us; the summons to "consider, you who peruse me, whether I may not in unknown ways be looking upon you" underscores the intimate anonymity of a voice that solicits our response while remaining one step ahead of it. While anticipating our reply may be one way of keeping the give and take of conversation in motion, it also testifies to the insistently *proleptic* drive behind these solicitations. Questions like "Have you practis'd so long to read? Have you felt so proud to get at the meaning of poems?" (*CRE,* p. 34), apart from their delight in ambushing refined sensibilities, seek to establish the preexistent authority of a discourse that underlies all others: "stop this night and day with me and you shall possess the origin of all poems." Like Paine's utopian community, this would be a speech that freely delegates power without being answerable to it. Yet for all the seductive ease Whitman brings to this stance, a strong element of uncertainty remains; in a manner that we have noted elsewhere, the poet who says "I charge you never to expound me" vehemently clings to the very terms of categorical understanding that he is otherwise intent upon banishing. This proleptic urge to come before our own expounding—an urge which must be stated and not simply inferred—often lends to

Leaves of Grass a special pitch of desperation, as in the voice of an "I" which serves notice that "none shall escape me and none shall wish to escape me"; which is "tenacious, acquisitive, tireless, and cannot be shaken away"; whose words "itch at your ears til you understand them"; and which "teach[es] straying from me" in the same breath that it asks "yet who can stray from me?" How to secure the "common ground" of our assent without thereby ceding his authority over that ground would appear to be the common theme of such moments, which bring to mind the original sense of prolepsis as a warding off or deflection of criticism.[18] As such, they also suggest that this is a ground that the "common referee" or "president of regulation"— Whitman's terms for the poet in the 1855 Preface—is not only to stake out and make available but also to preserve and defend.

Much is lost, then, should we assume that the central impetus for these encounters entails a longed-for communion between "I" and "you" unmediated by "discussion and print." It would be more fitting to say that Whitman simultaneously disclaims and depends on these mediations, that the "agonistic instruments" his words are designed to subsume must be qualified against their unwillingness to forsake them. This is not to imply that Whitman's aesthetic of reception is an aesthetic of deception; rather, it is to suggest that the division be-tween constituted authority and the authority of constitution-making, while essential to the "unfinished business" of the poet, is nevertheless an imperative that cannot fully sustain his belief. Thus, when Quentin Anderson wonders how Whitman could in good faith proclaim the authority of his own vision without violating that of his reader we may with equal justice turn the question around by asking how the authority of the reader may be vouchsafed without usurping that of the speaker.[19] Both sides of the question struggle for promi-nence in "Whoever You Are Now Holding Me in Hand," with neither winning out. The poem, first published in 1860 as the third selection in the *Calamus* sequence, usefully summarizes many of the tensions we have been tracing.[20] Calling upon he "who would sign himself a candidate for my affection," Whitman begins by giving us stern warning that "the way is suspicious, the result uncertain, per-haps destructive, / You would have to give up all else, I alone would expect to be your sole and exclusive standard . . ." This caveat lector softens somewhat as the poem soon turns to the recommendation that "thrusting me beneath your clothing, / Where I may feel the throbs of your heart or rest upon your hips; / Carry me when you go forth over land or sea." Yet to this plea for contact Whitman is moved once more to add the necessary rejoinder:

> But these leaves conning you con at peril,
> For these leaves and me you will not understand,
> They will elude you at first and still more afterward,
> I will certainly elude you,
> Even while you should think you had unquestionably
>   caught me, behold!
> Already you see I have escaped you.
>
> (*CRE,* p. 116)

Admonitions such as these no doubt stand behind Thoreau's wry observation to Harrison Blake that in reading Whitman "to be sure, sometimes I feel a little imposed upon."[21] The nature of that imposition is no less characteristic for the way in which open pleas for recognition go hand in hand with paranoid fears of misrepresentation. It is as if the "intimate anonymity" of "Crossing Brooklyn Ferry" had splintered into two styles of address: where in one moment the text represents an open space for invitation and integration in the next it becomes a zone of prohibition and outright exclusion. Being alternately the object of solicitation or the object of distrust, Whitman's reader is led to confront the odd fact that he is by turns indispensable (everything turns on your existence, you must be called forth) and expendable (this discourse generates itself, it will confuse you, you will not comprehend it). "The man," notes Hart Crane, "is both distant and near."[22]

More overtly wary than democratic, more nervous than fraternal, a poem like "Whoever You Are Now Holding Me in Hand" chronicles a strange courtship of teasing seductions and balked encounters. Ironically nominated as "the candidates for my love," his camerados will perhaps take rueful comfort from those lines in "Song of Myself" that speak of the poet as "curious what will come next, / Both in and out of the game, watching and wondering at it." Of course, it may be objected that, like most diffident lovers, Whitman is indeed only playing games here, that his repudiation of the reader is merely designed to produce the same effect as his desire to reach him. Whether it be gestures toward inclusion or exclusion, in other words, the idea of pursuit is paramount. Defying his listener to "fetch me at first," Whitman goads him to continue the search. Or, taking this objection a step further, one may note that the kind of confidence games here on display are hardly unprecedented, as anyone who has been beguiled by works as dissimilar as *Paradise Lost, Benito Cereno,* or *Pale Fire* will be quick to testify and as recent forays in reader-response criticism have amply documented. These fictions play on our sympathy through a cycle of enchantment and disenchantment, alternatively seducing and reeducating the expectations of their audience. Yet the insights we derive from such vicissitudes are more likely than not the *results* of reading, secured and reconstructed through the careful interpretive practice of inference and retrospection. In Whitman—to repeat my earlier contention—we do not infer this predicament but confront it. The veiled tensions we are accustomed to speak of between author and reader here overtake and openly monopolize the poem's concerns. The prominence of such tensions, moreover, should be enough to cast doubt on those who prefer to see Whitman's "elusiveness" as part of a coy game of pursuit. Catching us by surprise, "Whoever You Are Now Holding Me in Hand" prides itself on announcing that it will not yield to a similar fate. The poem intends to put its auditor not only on guard but on trial. Hence the willful ambiguity of the line "But these leaves conning you con at peril," whose lack of punctuation raises the wholly relevant question of what grammatical role Whitman's pronoun is playing. Is it nominative or accusative? The agent of action or its object? In the latter alternatives we must be prepared to entertain not simply the possibility of deception ("these leaves conning you . . .") but the prospect of a more disturbing reversal. Being conned instead of conning, being read instead of reading, Whitman's "you" is conceived as the object of scrutiny rather than its agent. Such a condition is the antithesis of the self-reflexive, for this verse is anything but a poem-about-poetry. Rather than testing the authority or legitimacy of its own fictions, the poem rigorously throws such questions back upon us. Venturing interpretive judgments, Whitman wishes to impress upon us, is somewhat like committing oneself to an interminable shell game where the critic is poised before a meaning "which you may guess at many times and not hit" and which affords results that are "uncertain, perhaps destructive." The point to be stressed is that critical response is not thereby annulled, subverted, overthrown, manipulated, or transcended. It is, rather, something the poet is overwhelmingly anxious to make secondary.

"*Leaves of Grass,*" observes Mitchell Breitwieser, "calls attention to itself as writing at the same time that it mounts the ruse of spoken conversation."[23] In poems which fluctuate so pointedly between invitation and resistance and whose recipients shift so unpredictably between the roles of accomplice and adversary, we are well-advised to keep both impulses in mind. Held before us, in effect, is neither shield nor greeting but an ongoing clash between both stances, leaving us with what Ashbery calls in "Self-Portrait in a Convex Mirror" (his own meditation on the entrapments of the beholder), "the shield of a greeting."[24] No doubt purely personal factors play an important part in these antagonisms, especially in light of what we know of Whitman's wretched family background, his tormented sexual development, and the decades of silence and contempt that welcomed so many editions of his *Leaves.* Yet pinning down his "you, whoever you are" to a specific person or group (parent, lover, or readership) is likely to be a misguided undertaking, not unlike the forlorn hope that could we ascertain the identity of "W. H." we would possess the key that unlocks Shakespeare's heart. From a broader perspective, Fredric Jameson suggests a more promising line of approach, one that usefully supplements our own inquiry into these texts, in the course of speaking on the long-standing "attempt to devise a foolproof mechanism for the exclusion of undesirable responses to a given literary utterance." Any such fail-safe system is of course to be deemed "impossible," though Jameson does cite the pertinent example of generic categories, which he describes as "essentially literary *institutions,* or social contracts between a writer and a specific public" whose "perceptual signals . . . specify the use of a particular cultural artifact."[25] Such remarks help clarify why the "shield of a greeting" offered in Mill's fictive contract, where extremes of invitation and resistance are aligned into a mutually sustaining relationship, is a good deal more stable than comparable extremes in Whitman, for while Mill speaks on behalf of some three hundred years of accepted conventions, the hopeful "begetter of a new offspring out of literature" clearly does not. Although it is certainly the case that many texts in *Leaves of Grass* draw upon various literary kinds in an oblique but recognizably deliberate fashion (as "Song of Myself" does with respect to the epic, "Out of the Cradle Endlessly Rocking" with respect to the ode, or "When Lilacs Last in the Dooryard Bloom'd" with respect to the pastoral elegy), such traditions are treated with the circumspection we would expect from an author who believed them to be hopelessly compromised by the taint of "feudalism" which had marked the most glorious achievements in British poetry from Shakespeare to Tennyson. Moving away from those "literary institutions" whose function is "to specify the use of a particular cultural artifact" serves the purpose of making the drama of consent an evolving, active principle internal to the poem's construction. The difficulty that remains, of course, is that withdrawing such generic contracts, no less than withdrawing political contracts, merely foregrounds an urgency over what might "avail" to replace them lest "the text in question [be] abandoned to a drifting multiplicity of uses,"[26] as Jameson phrases it and as a text like "Whoever You Are Now Holding Me in Hand" clearly apprehends. To this we can add the corollary danger that the text, by overspecifying the conditions of its reception, merely falls back upon the "agonistic instruments" it had intended to obviate. It is a measure of the special ambivalence of Whitman's project, as well as the honesty of his temperament, that his addresses no more pretend to make up the rules of exchange as they go along than they presume to do away with them. We instead find them halted uncertainly between both options, simultaneously extending the promise of conversational intimacy at the same time they are driven to insist upon a textual authority that barricades itself against all scrutiny.

The taut juxtaposition between proximity and distance, while not always pressed to the dramatic extremes evident in "Whoever You Are Now Holding Me in Hand," does provide an index of Whitman's own quandaries in being both in and out of the game of the social discourse, at once an engaged participant in the play of dialogue his verse records and the transcendent embodiment of that dialogue. By way of rounding out this discussion of Whitman's quarrel with reading, I want to pause over this latter role, for alongside Whitman's essays in "reader engagement" there exists the dream of utter disengagement, the stance of a speaker who can boast "Apart from the pulling and hauling stands what I am, / Stands amused, complacent, compassionating, idle, unitary." There is in fact some warrant for believing that Whitman consciously intended to alternate solicitations to the reader with an more "indirect" mode of speech. A preliminary indication of this is supplied in the the following journal entry: "But all converging sooner or later into the clear monotonous voice, equable as water—sometimes direct address to you, the hearer, without a pause afterward, as if an answer is expected. Then perhaps for many minutes total abstraction and travelling to other fields, the vocalism limpid, inspired, no account made of the material place, the audience, but only that other more spiritual world in which the speaker is roaming." "Total abstraction" introduces a new element, one which, as C. Carroll Hollis notes, provides a concise rationale for the celebrated catalogs, whose cascading flood of metonymic details subsumes the identities of poet and audience alike. Before we accept the adequacy of this self-analysis, though, it should be observed that some of it is plagiarized from one Charles Murray Nairne, Professor of Rhetoric at Columbia University.[27] The debt is in itself negligible, but it does suggest the image of the poet turned commentator seeking retrospectively to codify the rules of his composition with a decisiveness his verse belies. A more cautiously mediated approach to "total abstraction" occurs in the following remarkable conceit, which appears in Whitman's artistic manifesto, "A Song of the Rolling Earth":

> Of the interminable sisters,
> Of the ceaseless cotillions of sisters,
> Of the centripetal and centrifugal sisters, the elder
>   and younger sisters,
> The beautiful sister we know dances on with the rest.
>
> With her ample back toward every beholder,
> With the fascinations of youth and the equal
>   fascinations of age,
> Sits she whom I too love like the rest, sits
>   undisturb'd,
> Holding up in her hand what has the character of a
>   mirror, while her eyes glance back from it,
> Glance as she sits, inviting none, denying none,
> Holding a mirror day and night tirelessly before her
>   own face.
>
>   (*CRE*, p. 221)

Formally, these lines are perfectly in keeping with the poem's controlling conceit, catapulting as they do the figure of the rolling earth heavenward into a dance with its sister planets. Tonally, they mark a shift from the opening and closing sections of the poem, which rely heavily upon appeals to "you," by moving away from a fixation on the beholder to a fascination with the act of beholding itself. "Holding a mirror day and night tirelessly before her own face," Whitman's beautiful sister adumbrates an image of self-absorption so complete as to negate acknowledgment of all beholders. What this in turn precludes is of course the pretense of direct address: "with her ample back toward every beholder," the earth can only be described rather than summoned, evoked rather than invoked.

"The deeper the remoteness which a glance has to overcome, the stronger will be the spell that is apt to emanate from that gaze," remarks Walter Benjamin in his analysis of the "regard familier" in the lyrics of Baudelaire, another man of the crowd who sought out passing moments of intimacy in the amorphous mass. Adding further that "in eyes that stare with a mirror-like blankness [this] remoteness remains complete," Benjamin suggests that "inapproachability is in fact a primary quality of the ceremonial image,"[28] a quality that plainly animates this portrait of sisterly planets and their stately procession. Whitman's "beautiful sister," his own familial Muse whose imperturbable poise often appears in his verse, likewise incarnates an aura of absolute disinterest. Neither unknown nor unknowable she is simply indifferent to being known. "Inviting none, denying none," she is by necessity a figure to be defined through negation. In this her characterization echoes that of "Liberty" in the 1855 Preface: "Liberty relies upon itself, invites no one, promises nothing, sits in calmness and light, is positive and composed, and knows no discouragement" (*PW* 2:417). Possessed in their self-possessiveness, "Liberty" and the rolling earth can know no discouragement because each concept has been purged of any transitive function. Just as each self-subsisting entity "never invites and never refuses," so each displays an utter insensibility to outside influences. These are plainly idealizations of "remoteness" and implicit within them we can detect the efforts of a poet bent on extricating himself from the more crippling duplicities of the fictional contract. It is no longer possible to speak of a rhetorical *exchange* here since this is expressly what Whitman's figures of indifference have been designed to make irrelevant. "Ever regardful of others, ever regardless of others," they somehow stand outside the arena of the linguistic marketplace without repudiating it. As such, they shift attention away from a poetry obsessed with strategies of containment in favor of a vision of complete self-containment: "Outline sketch of a superb calm character, his emotions complete in himself irrespective (indifferent) of whether his friendship, etc. are returned or not . . . his analogy the earth complete in itself enfolding itself all processes of growth effusing life and power for hidden purposes" (*UPP* 2:96).

Lest it seem as though we are on the verge of stealing the Good

Gray Poet back into the very aesthetic we have been measuring him against, it should be noted that Mill's "impersonality" and Whitman's "total abstraction" bear only superficial resemblances. The disinterestedness Mill takes to be a conventional poetic stance has become in Whitman the subject of an impossibly extreme idealization. His "superb calm character," elsewhere familiar to us as "Me Impertube" or as the "Me Myself," is neither a persona nor a voice but a supernatural hero of erotic self-sufficiency. Oblivious to all compacts and absolved of all dependencies, it expresses the fantasy of a self-enclosed writing triumphantly indifferent to the losses of reading. Needless to say, so extreme a reaction to the threat of betrayal only argues its persistence and, as we may suspect, Whitman's determination to renounce acknowledgment of all beholders often turns out to be a self-defeating enterprise. There can be no question, for example, that once a state of self-absorption is *asserted* it is no longer a state of self-absorption but becomes something else. In the hands of Whitman it becomes, particularly in his weaker moments, a fetish. Take by way of illustration the rhapsodic "One Hour to Madness and Joy," whose "tender and savage achings" reach fever pitch in the closing stanza: "O something unprov'd! something in a trance! / To escape utterly from others' anchors and holds! / To drive free! to love free! to dash reckless and dangerous! / To court destruction with taunts, with invitations . . . To rise thither with my inebriate soul! / To be lost if it must be so!" (*CRE*, p. 106). The problem here—one that asserts itself with depressing regularity in texts written after 1865—is that the speaker has pledged himself to the vain task of *willing* himself into a paroxysm of "total abstraction." The overwrought hysteria of the rapture owes less to the ecstasies of abandonment than to the speaker's half-hearted pursuit of them, resulting in the same kind of furious wheel spinning that makes reading a "visionary" poem like "Passage to India" (1871)—with its chronic, frenzied entreaties to "Steer forth, O my soul" while it in fact goes nowhere—such a dismal experience:

> O we can wait no longer,
> We too take ship O soul,
> Joyous we too launch out on trackless seas
> Fearless for unknown shores on waves of ecstasy to sail.
> . . . .
> Passage, immediate passage! the blood burns in my
>   veins!

Away O soul! hoist instantly the anchor!
Cut the hawsers—haul out—shake out every sail.
. . . .
Sail forth—steer for the deep waters only,
Reckless O soul, exploring, I with thee, and thou with me.
(*CRE*, p. 418, 420, 421)

Appeals like these remain safely locked into the cycle of redundancy they would otherwise seem to deplore. An unwitting burlesque of ecstasy, they exemplify that "mad prepense of pseudo-poetry" that Coleridge excoriates as "the startling *hysteric* of weakness overexerting itself, which bursts upon the unprepared reader in sundry odes and apostrophes to abstract terms."[29] To this severe judgment we may add, questions of "weakness" aside, that the strain of Whitman's peculiar "overexertions" also have their source in an unrelenting conservatism that will not allow the poet "to be surprised out of his propriety," however desperately he may appear to desire it. What we see acted out, as we have seen acted out with varying degrees of intensity throughout this discussion, is the crisis of solipsism in reverse: not the spectacle of a self absorbed in the splendid labyrinth of its own perceptions but the quandary of a poet who cannot forgo the suspicion that his world is all spectacle. "To be lost if it must be so" describes the consternation of a would-be Orpheus hedging his bets, not unlike the would-be quester of Frost's "Into My Own," who tantalizes himself with anticipations of a perilous, visionary journey which he is perpetually about to take and therefore never will. The more feverishly a transcendence "beyond others' anchors and holds" is pursued, the more transparent it becomes that any such relief will not be forthcoming.

"You must forget yourself in your ideas," scolded Henry James in a petulant review of *Drum-Taps*, "you must be *possessed*, and you must strive to possess your possession." Aggravated to the point of exasperation by "wanton eccentricities" and "monstrous attitudes," James may have been the first and was certainly not the last to voice his dismay over a poetry that, by refusing the state of self-forgetfulness which "art, above all things, requires," openly calls upon a nation of kindred spirits. For James, such overtures are unpardonable because they do not simply transgress the generic contract ("an offence against art") but are crudely manipulative of our presence—"a little nursery game," as he puts it, "'of open your mouth and shut your eyes.'"[30] And yet, of all the difficulties besetting his second-person poetry, it

must be said that manipulation is the *least* prominent, as becomes
evident once these texts are measured against the cagey maneuvering
of omniscient authority present in, say, *Benito Cereno* or *The Scarlet
Letter*. Honoring the demand for aesthetic distance so ardently upheld by James, the narrative voices of Melville and Hawthorne obey a
virtually ritualistic movement of assertion and denial which simultaneously excites and subverts expectation, simultaneously advances
and discredits meaning. If we find a similar dynamic taken to magni-
fied and exacerbated extremes in Whitman's apostrophes, that is in
part owing to their principled aversion to such ironic control. More
nervous than manipulative, the tensions that accrue from the competition for meaning between listener and speaker are, more fundamentally, the product of a basic conflict in his *Leaves* between the longing
to abolish all mediations in the social discourse by offering a poetry
"before preaching and law" and the consternation that ensues over the
withdrawal of such mediations. As a measure of his own conservative
radicalism, Whitman is not only unwilling but unable to assent to the
fiction of the beholder's "nonexistence," for it is at this point apparent
that keeping his eyes on the listener entails for him both the promise
of a free exchange of communication and an indication of its fragility.
For reasons that have less to do with temperamental insecurity or
artistic carelessness and more to do with the quandaries of a representative who would be all things to all people, Whitman's "shield of a
greeting" bespeaks the pressures peculiar to this role and the necessary
tensions that accompany it.

Of course, it can always be said that any writer's conception of an
audience must remain hypothetical by default. After all, it was Henry
James himself who maintained that the author "makes his readers very
much as he makes his characters."[31] On these grounds, the breadth of
invention reaches beyond the printed page, with the reader made over
into another construct of the imagination. The writer's power over
"you" is accordingly absolute and inconsequential; or rather, absolute
because it is inconsequential. However devoted he may be to freeing
up or revising the process of exchange, in one fundamental sense the
addressee only comes into existence by virtue of the poet's fiat:

> Not forgetting either the chance that you
> Might want to revise this version of what is
> The only real one, it might be that
> No real relation exists between my wish for you

To return and the movement of your arms and legs.
But my inability to accept this fact
Annihilates it. Thus
My power over you is absolute.
You exist only in me and on account of me
And my features reflect this proved compactness.[32]

Ashbery's deft mind games charmingly remind us of the teasing seductiveness usually emphasized in Whitman's dealings with his camerados. If the preceding pages have for the most part minimized this playfulness, that is not because it forms an inessential or irrelevant dimension to this verse. Yet it does offer a partial view of Whitman's motives. And while he would in all likelihood have acknowledged the truism that "the writer's audience is always a fiction," what must strike us is how compellingly vivid his sense of "you, whoever you are" remains throughout the overtures here discussed. Assailed though he was by the terrible doubt of appearances, he never had cause to doubt the existence of his interlocutors. What he seeks from his verse is not the "proved compactness" of a voice inviolate in its fictional supremacy (the modernist version of James's triumphant, unbounded aestheticism) but rather a proven "compact" of fraternity. Having reviewed some of the essential features of this quest, I wish now to shift the terms of comparison to more native grounds by exploring Whitman's relation to the figure who most influenced him.

2

Lessons of the Master

ONE WAY TO PUT Whitman's quarrel with reading more fully in
perspective is to recall that *Leaves of Grass* often implies the careful
reading of a literary "master" of its own. The debt to Emerson is of
course pervasive and has been amply documented by literary historians.[1] Most obvious among these debts is Emerson's call for a
national benefactor (poet, scholar, reformer) whose charismatic
power of speech would triumph over division by restoring authenticity to "the whole man." In Emerson, Whitman found "the original,
true Captain who put to sea, intuitive, positive, rendering the first
report," a report that aimed too at the reconstitution of the social
contract through the enjoyment of "an original relation" between the
self and its neglected divinity. As in *Leaves of Grass,* reclaiming the
integrity of this relation meant reacting against a polity whose mind-
lessness had shrunk nature to a mere commodity; whose discourse
had prostrated itself before reified abstractions of its own devising;
and whose members had relinquished the vitalizing myth of "the
whole man" for a body politic which, now "subdivided and peddled
out," had "suffered amputation from the trunk" and had left in its
wake "so many walking monsters,—a good finger, a neck, a stomach,
an elbow, but never a man" (*W* 1:83). To the degree that the pressing
issue in question was not the fraudulence of the state so much as the
lamentable fact that its constituents had defrauded themselves of their
own power over such a construct, Emerson came before his countrymen, as he certainly came before Whitman, to "bring what you
much need, yet always have." So it is that the poet was "to stand
among partial men for the complete man, and apprise us not of his
wealth but of the common wealth" (*W* 3:5). Hearing this summons as
though it were a personal mandate, an undistinguished carpenter,
journalist, and hack writer of sentimental lyrics and lurid melodramas
was, as the story goes, brought to a boil.

My reason for introducing Emerson into the discussion at this stage is not, however, to tally lines of influence, invaluable as these were for the younger poet. Discussion of their relationship has drawn upon any number of perspectives, ranging from the simpleminded pairing of the bard of the body and the seer of the soul to Harold Bloom's more intricate drama of oppressed latecomer struggling under the shadow of a crippling precursor. Though it will be necessary to come back to the subject of influence and its anxieties later, what I have primarily in mind for the pages that follow is the rather different concern of juxtaposing two competing models of consensus; for while both figures are dedicated to the common task of awakening the dormant will of their readership, each draws upon divergent and, as I shall be suggesting, ultimately antithetical means to forward that cause. In the case of Whitman, those means essentially begin and end with adherence to "the profound lesson of reception" realized in a speech of unbounded inclusiveness capable of uniting the many and the one without dependence on a preestablished hierarchy of sacrifice and exclusion. Judging from what we have seen so far of his "hymns of you," however, neither the dream of inclusion nor a surreptitious principle of exclusion best characterizes these solicitations but a vivid oscillation between the two extremes, often leaving their "ties to others" locked into an inflexible, albeit precarious, standoff. In the case of Emerson, an entirely different approach is taken toward these same issues, one that begins with the assumption that the entanglements of inclusion and exclusion are not simply the risks any representative speech must run but are in principle inevitable to it. So regarded, the competition for power between author and reader, no less a central preoccupation for Emerson than for Whitman, is less a cause for consternation than a subject to be diagnosed, a subject his essays are forever bringing to light, brooding upon, and annotating. At bottom, Emerson's stance toward all forms of exchange, whether political, literary, or cultural, was ironic: liberation produces its own enslavements, which in turn engender the need for further liberation, which produces further enslavement. In a world where "nothing is got for nothing," as Emerson tells us in "Compensation," no release from this circularity is obtainable and no "lesson of reception," however profound, can escape its workings. For this reason, we find Emerson actively embracing as indispensable those "agonistic instruments" that Whitman hopes to overcome, so much so, in fact, that the consensual paradigms promulgated by Emerson's writing—the "Universal Mind," the "Oversoul," "Reason"—do thrive in open and explicit ways on a rigorous hierarchy of sacrifice and exclusion. As his meditations on the fate of his representative men insistently reveal, at the heart of Emerson's conception of union there prevails a retributive scale of justice or what can be called a law of betrayal: whoever aims to speak for the general interest perforce corrupts that interest; whoever seeks to join the many and the one invariably violates these terms.

Emerson, in other words, was not the representative man that he called for. Rather, the "antagonizing mind" that speaks through his essays presents itself to us as the exemplary *reader* of all claims to representativeness—at once the advocate, guardian, and arbiter of a transcendent unanimity possessing all and possessed by no one. Instead of suffering the law of betrayal he analyzes its workings, with the result that the dream of universality—the myth of "the whole man"—is held to be forever inviolate precisely because it is forever deferred. Whitman's "true original Captain who put out to sea" can in this respect be recognized as a latter-day Jeremiah whose vision, as Sacvan Bercovitch has remarked more generally, "[feeds] on the distance between promise and fact."[2] For the author of *Leaves of Grass*, who did believe himself to be the representative man that Emerson called for, failure to close that distance signified a failure of poetry itself. For him, the purpose of writing was not to regulate an archetypal totality but bring it into being—to "send no agent or medium, to offer no representative of value, but offer the value itself" (*CRE*, p. 212). It becomes in turn appropriate to ask: is a commonality of interests imaginable beyond recourse to expectation, unfulfillment, and anxiety? Or would this vision merely fall prey to the sacrifices that Emerson takes to be unavoidable? Taking stock of these questions should shed light not only on the different stances of both writers but on the kind of tradition from which Whitman was attempting—with equivocal results—to emerge.

What is an Emersonian reading? What are its assumptions and ambitions? In seeking to answer such questions we are directly faced with difficulties, for the first thing to be said about Emerson on the issue of reading is that he considers it to be less an activity than a stigma. At his own insistence true reading can only be a contradiction in terms since the ultimate aim of reading is to teach us its impertinence. What he urges of "the student of history" he asks no less of his listener at large; that he learn "to esteem his own life the text, and books the commentary." "The muse of history," he adds, "will utter oracles, as never to those who do not respect themselves. I have no expectation that any man will read history aright who thinks that what was done in a remote age, by men whose names have resounded far, has any deeper sense than what he is doing today" (*W* 2:8). Such acts of self-respect (of "seeing back," through the past, articulations of ourselves) translate history into a medium of self-interpretation. So conceived, they also transform acts of reading into self-reading, inasmuch as what the reader ideally recovers from the texts of the past is nothing less than vestiges of a subliminal power within the self. "In every work of genius," runs that inexhaustible aphorism from "Self Reliance," "we recognize our own rejected thoughts; they come back to us with a certain alienated majesty" (*W,* 2:39–40). Hence the pressing task is not at all to read the great author but to reclaim him as ourselves. Hence, too, the deeply tautological character of Emersonian reading: it seeks to confirm in others what we already possess. Thoreau, coming at the issue from the opposite direction, expresses the force of this tautology still more severely. "The works of the great poets," he remarks in the chapter on "Reading" from *Walden,* "have never yet been read by mankind, for only great poets can read them."[3]

It is not enough, then, merely to say that Emerson sought to free reading from the bonds of passive reception or that he called for a more empathetic identification between writer and reader. He wishes to efface the distinction between writer and reader altogether. For what the reader confronts in every work of genius is not the writer's text but the concealed writer within that text: himself. The appeal of those works lies hidden in their whispered confidence that "it is you talking just as much as myself . . . I act as the tongue of you, / It was tied in your mouth . . . in mine it begins to be loosened." That appeal failing, reading is tantamount to a defeat or flawed recognition; the reader remains fixed in his role, eclipsed by an author who has somehow written the *reader's* text, whose unreclaimed thoughts "come back" at him with the alien majesty of his own rejected muse. Longinus, speaking as a critical expositor of the sublime tradition, notes that in reading the great poet "we come to believe that we have created what we have only heard."[4] Emerson, speaking as a hopeful exponent of the same tradition, defies that demystification by insisting to the contrary that our curse is such that we have come only to hear what we have in fact created. "The youth, intoxicated with his admiration of the hero, fails to see that it is only a projection of his own soul" (*W* 1:49). Understanding that the hero does not speak *to* us but speaks *through* us compels the realization that the otherness of texts is largely a delusion, fostered by a lack of "self-trust." From this it follows that Emerson's aim is not simply to revoke contractual obligations to the past but to assail the guiding premise of the fictional contract itself, for once his quester begins to conceive of reading as a reciprocal exchange—an interaction between two parties—he is lost. (The same principle can be seen at work with respect to Emerson's performance as a stylist within his own essays, whose rhetorical eccentricities leave us, as Stanley Cavell has suggested, "at liberty to discover whether he belongs to us or we to him." Cavell also goes on to remark insightfully of Emerson's prose that "it does not require us."5 Needless to say, the same cannot be said of Whitman.)

Still, a distinctive methodology emerges from Emerson on reading, and certain salient procedures can be described. Reading for the lusters, as Emerson did, meant above all severing authorial agency from textual meaning. The inspiration we take from great men, he reminds us time and again, is not, properly speaking, their own. "When we are exalted by ideas," he observes in a characteristic aside, "we do not owe this to Plato, but to the idea, to which Plato was also debtor" (*W* 4:21). Contending that we owe no debt to Plato but to the idea to which Plato himself is debtor allows him to broaden the disparity between the man of genius (the agent) and the idea of genius (the higher significance), with the latter simultaneously inciting and exceeding the efforts of the former to embrace it. Evidently Emerson *could* know the difference between the dancer and the dance, for everything in his account of the reader's sublime turns on that knowing. The distinction stands behind his familiar habit of evoking the felicities of the sublime moment as an irresistible force or oceanic influx "on which [the hero] can draw, by unlocking at all risks, his human doors, and suffering the ethereal tides to roll and circulate through him; then he is caught up into the life of the Universe, his speech is thunder, his thought is law, and his words are universally intelligible as the plants and animals" (*W* 2:46). Through such acts of "abandonment" the hero serves as a medium of divine impressions. His virtue inheres in his "self-trust," though it is essentially a blind trust, for while his "words are universally intelligible," the source that inspires his eloquence is not. Character, Emerson tells us in the essay of that name, is distinguished by "a reserved force that acts directly and without means"; it discharges a "certain undemonstrable force . . . by whose impulses the man is guided but whose counsel he cannot impart" (*W* 3:89–90). The "substantial man" wields an "occult power" which may be worshiped, reviled, or ignored, but never understood. Greatness is perforce "an obedience to a secret impulse," an impulse (or more accurately, a compulsion) that is conveyed surreptitiously. Greatness for this reason manifests itself to the Emersonian reader most authentically when it is *betrayed*. "Great men have always confided themselves childlike to the genius of their age, betraying their perception that the absolutely trustworthy was seated at their heart, working through their hands, predominating in all their being" (*W* 2:47). Such confidence is fortified by the aegis of the "Universal Mind" or "Oversoul" that "lies under the under-most garments of Nature and betrays its source in the Universal Spirit" (*W* 1:44).

Having effectually swept aside authorial intent, the Emersonian reader is at leisure to celebrate the virtues of genius as "a sort of self-existent poetry" that endlessly renews the promise of refreshed possibility. Yet Emerson's interest in this rhetoric of betrayal answers a far more pragmatic purpose as well, a purpose that he is not at all loath to exploit. For if the truth of genius, strictly speaking, articulates itself, if it is true that "all things betray the same calculated profusion," and if the soul is indeed "superior to its knowledge, wiser than any of its works," then it follows that "the great poet makes us feel our own wealth, and then we think less of his compositions. His best communication is to teach us to despise all that he has done. Shakespeare carries a wealth which beggars his own. . . . The inspiration which utters itself in Hamlet or Lear would utter things as good from day to day forever" ("The Oversoul," *W* 2:289). Thus the fortuitous economy of the reader's sublime: in beggaring his own wealth Shakespeare apprises us of our own. Despising all that he has done, we become "porous to thought" and to that inspiration which "utters itself" through him.

Two prevailing expectations, at once discrete and interrelated, inform Emerson's method of "reading." We pass from the glory of genius which betrays itself through its spokesmen to the fate of self-betrayal that looms over the careers of these spokesmen. If the first phase affirms the efficacy of genius in its most expansive mode, the second is clearly a defensive maneuver, designed to protect against the perils of overinfluence. This dialectic has a long and eventful history in Emerson's thought, and while this is not the place to follow out its evolution, a final illustration of its workings may be in order. My text is Emerson's chapter on Plato in *Representative Men*, that volume in which what I have called the rhetoric of betrayal is most prominently

(and, I think, most predictably) on display. (It was also the last published work by Emerson to see print before the first edition of *Leaves of
Grass*.) Emerson credits his subject with a number of accomplishments, but his most sustained appreciation is devoted to "Plato's
balanced soul . . . [which is] perceptive of the two elements" (*W*
4:54). The philosopher imported into Western civilization "the infinitude of the Asiatic Soul," and so fused "the unity of Asia with the
detail of Europe" (*W* 4:54). These may be somewhat fuzzy distinctions, but what interests Emerson most is Plato's quintessential
representativeness. His "sentences contain the culture of nations;
these are the fountainheads of literatures." Characteristically, the emphasis from the outset of the essay falls upon Plato's talent for opening
himself up to a "range of speculation" unparalleled in Western
thought. His catholicity is such that "He absorbed the learning of his
times," and like "every giant soul . . . consumed his own
times . . . tak[ing] up into himself all arts, sciences, all knowables as
his food" (*W* 4:39, 49). Synthesis, assimilation, and unity are the
keynotes of the essay.

The tribute continues for some forty pages until Emerson draws up
rather abruptly near the end to cite "two defects" in Plato's thought.
First, Plato overvalues the intellect and therefore lacks vitality. Second, Plato's interests were too diffuse—he lacks a system. Passing
over the implicit contradiction between these two "defects" for the
moment, let us pause briefly on the first complaint. Plato's dialogues
"have not, what is no doubt incident to this regnancy of intellect,—
the vital authority which the screams of the prophets and the sermons
of unlettered Arabs and Jews possess" (*W* 4:76). Whatever the ultimate validity of this charge may be, it can only sound odd coming as it
does on the heels of Emerson's celebration of Plato's "daring imagination," which is to be "apprehended by an original mind in the exercise
of its original power." Indeed, Plato merits our homage precisely
because he integrates "the freest abandonment . . . with the precision
of a geometer" (*W* 4:57). "He never writes in ecstasy, or catches us up
in poetic rapture," Emerson notes admiringly; his dialogues instead
combine a daring creativity with scrupulous discrimination. The second "defect" is more curious still. The Greek "has not a system,"
Emerson avers; "he attempted a theory of the universe, and his theory
is not complete or self-evident" (*W* 4:76). Emerson, in effect, finds a
deficiency within a deficiency: if Plato suffers from an excessive intellect, it nevertheless would appear that his intellect was not rigorous

enough. "One man thinks he means this, and another that; he has said one thing in one place, and the reverse of it in another place" (*W* 4:76). As if to compound our confusion Emerson then proceeds in the next paragraph to lament that Plato, far from simply lacking a system, was too imperial in his systematizing: "it shall be the world passed through the mind of Plato,—nothing less. Every atom shall have the Platonic tinge; every atom, every relation or quality you knew before, you shall know again and find here, but now ordered; not nature, but art" (*W* 4:77).

Running up against contradictions is a familiar experience for students of Emerson, and it takes some dexterity not to get entangled in them. But in this case the paradoxes are not the result of philosophic density or a simple fondness for contraries; they are a preparation for what we can now recognize to be a distinctive pattern. The genius that betrays itself through Plato's discourse returns to lord over Plato's self-betrayal. The very terms of praise thus provide the basis for indictment. Emerson begins his enconium by extolling Plato as the "fountainhead of literatures"; he ends it by declaring that the world has become nothing but a "mammoth morsel" for his prodigious appetite. His ambition to "consume his own times" prompts Emerson to envision a countersacrifice wherein the eater becomes the eaten.

> He has clapped copyright on the world. This is the ambition of individualism. But the mouthful proves too large. *Boa constrictor* has good will to eat it, but he is foiled. He falls abroad in the attempt; and biting, gets strangled: the bitten world holds the biter fast by his own teeth. There he perishes: unconquered nature lives on and forgets him. So it fares with all: so must it fare with Plato. (*W* 4:77)

So it also fares with Swedenborg, whose "perverted" visions soon come to foster "a dangerous discord with himself" to so vicious a degree that he "makes war on his own mind . . . and on all occasions traduces and blasphemes it" (*W* 4:131). So it fares with Shakespeare, who prostitutes "his genius for the public amusement" and suffers himself to remain a mere entertainer—"the master of the revels of mankind" (*W* 4:216, 218). So it fares with Napoleon who, for all the magnificence of his cunning and brutality, is victimized by an "absolute egotism" that is not only "deadly to all others" but "was in principle suicidal" (*W* 4:257). (It was not for nothing that Carlyle, while expressing admiration for *Representative Men,* added a note of qualification in a letter to its author by saying "I generally dissented a little about the *end* of all these Essays . . .")⁶ The list could go on, but it is enough to see that the rhetoric of betrayal not only glorifies a knowledge without a knower; it calls, more severely still, for a knowledge at the *expense* of a knower. Unconquered nature does indeed live on, acting—to borrow a phrase from "Circles"—as "at once the inspirer and condemner of every success." As Emerson's visionary company is sacrificed on the altar of their own excesses, so too does the unconquered reader live on, dispatching his representatives to oblivion. Thus Plato becomes, in Emerson's mordant wordplay, his own "fare," an epitaph whose laconic finality is reminiscent of the "capital negation" which attends the death of Satan in Stevens's "Esthetique du Mal," a negation all the more devastating, we may recall, because "It had nothing of the Julian thunder-cloud: / The assassin flash and rumble . . . He was denied."⁷

Denial alone, however, is not the exclusive aim of these readings. Because the soul that is always "impatient of masters" is also impatient *for* them, it requires other "victims of vanity" to carry the cycle of worship, enthrallment, and retribution "on and forever onward." "In vain the wheels of tendency will not stop," proclaims Emerson in the opening essay of *Representative Men* as he enjoins his listeners to "be another: not thyself, but a Platonist; not a soul, but a Christian; not a naturalist, but a Cartesian; not a poet, but a Shakesperian" (*W* 4:29–30). In a world where every hero is by definition an overreacher who "strives to grow and exclude and to exclude and grow, to the extremities of the universe" and where "every benefactor becomes so easily a malefactor only by continuation of his activity into places where it is not due" (*W* 4:25–26), the task of the self-reliant reader is not to break free of this vicious circularity but to observe its workings by letting it work upon him. Seeing how the master becomes a slave at last to his own "tyrannizing unity" allows the quester to reject him and seek other models, where the same cycle will be repeated. This unending pattern of conflict Emerson calls "Rotation . . . or, the law of Nature"; in less rarefied terms we can recognize it to be a faithful extension of the practices of the American jeremiad. In his compelling account of this mode, Sacvan Bercovitch draws our attention to the common trait of the jeremiad to keep before its listener a chronic state of crisis (here in the threat of self-betrayal) while bringing to pass no decisive change in the status quo. Or, in Emerson's most pointed formulation of the Transcendental quest: "I am Defeated all the time, yet to Victory I am born," an aphorism which, by invoking despair as the occasion for still greater exhortation, embraces a ceaseless revolution in consciousness whose primary outcome is to keep the "wheels of tendency" forever in circular motion. Anxiety, discord, and alienation accordingly work to fortify allegiance to an archetypal "union of all minds," which is intimately knowable and necessarily out of reach, like the "splendid nobody" mentioned in a journal entry by Emerson who, "hiding himself like God in deluges of light . . . disappears the moment we go to celebrate him."[8]

Emerson, I suggested earlier, was not the representative man that he called for. For him, unanimity cannot occupy the same ground as any given discourse that would attempt to embrace it; those who controvert this law by presuming to speak on behalf of the power of universality suffer the appointed retribution. Whitman, in turn, did aspire to the title of "liberating god" as defined by Emerson in "The Poet," and, notwithstanding his misgivings over what the push of reading might or might not accomplish, did believe that verse could successfully embody that timeless "common platform" where all the particulars of its world could meet. In view of these ambitions it is not altogether surprising that most of the adverse commentary on *Leaves of Grass* should essentially repeat the kind of critique mounted in *Representative Men;* one thinks, for example, of D. H. Lawrence's acid sketch of the Good Gray Poet as yet another *boa constrictor* whose rage for imaginative conquest mercilessly disgorges itself upon and finally levels everything in its path. Emerson's representative suicides accordingly reappear in the guise of what Lawrence tags "post-mortem effects."[9] As with nearly everything that Lawrence says of Whitman, these reservations are both overblown and acute, and I shall want to return to them later in this chapter. First, however, it is useful to bring forward the more obvious and less worrisome fact that Whitman was plainly swayed by the more charismatic and capacious "uses of great men" prized in Emerson's meditations on genius, *Leaves of Grass* being among other things incontestably the most exuberant testament on record to the pleasures of that "fluid and attaching character" whose "instant conductors . . . seize every object and lead it harmlessly through me" (*CRE,* 57). In keeping with the Emersonian celebration of power ceaselessly betrayed through its spokesmen, the self styled as the "free channel" of expression comes to life by inviting the manifold objects of its sense to converge upon and course through it: "through me the long dumb voices . . . through me the afflatus surging and surging, through me the current and index" (*CRE*, p. 52). Rather than being obliterated by this process of exchange, the self ideally incarnates the medium of exchange itself; current and index alike, it moves between the "influx and efflux" or give and take of betrayal in a cycle of possession and dispossession.

Yet it is the second, though by no means secondary, sense of this term that calls for further attention. Certainly premonitions of betrayal hover over many of Whitman's invocations to "you, whoever you are": hence the insistence that there is no way around him, that his words itch at our ears until we understand him, that none shall escape him and none shall wish to escape him; hence the corresponding disclaimers that he will surely elude our grasp, that the push of reading has been foreseen by his ordaining, that he is a force to be reckoned with at the same time he reminds us that any such reckoning will certainly be futile. Hence, too, the familiar edict that his verse distills an air of "indirection" so as to secure the greatest possible freedom of inference for the reader, a notion expressed so programmatically as to belie an abiding unease with any such freedom. Betraying all things, he would be betrayed by no one. And yet, it is also important to add that fears this pronounced do not fall under the framework of a controlling rhetorical paradigm; Whitman is not "asserting consensus through anxiety," nor is he "using promise and threat alike to inspire (or enforce) generational rededication."[10] Where promise and threat come together in his poetry, it is more likely to be self-interfering (to recall Burke's phrase) rather than mutually enabling. By contrast, when the author of *Representative Men* declares "the more we are drawn, the more we are repelled" (*W*, 4:27), the antagonisms implied in his statement, by entering into what appears to be a causative relationship, readily enter as well into the system of identification and counteridentification that guides his reading at large, where submission and revolt are joined together in perpetual partnership. In Whitman the antagonisms of reading persist as geniune antagonisms: tensions of the kind looked at in the previous chapter between invitation and resistance, attraction and repulsion, are not accommodated to and finally recontained by a prevailing "ritual of socialization," nor are they made instrumental to its workings. It would indeed appear that such anxieties acquire added prominence to the degree that *Leaves of Grass* wishes to obviate such "rituals of consensus."[11] So it is that the very vicissitudes so vividly *described* by Emerson—the plight of the representative hero who, in releasing the collective will of his readership, also enslaves it; whose ends are sabotaged by the rhetorical means at his disposal; and who discovers himself to have transgressed the shadowy line between consensus and coercion—reappear in *Leaves of Grass* as vicissitudes to be confronted and acted out.

This need not imply that all manifestations of anxiety in Emerson are subordinated to one changeless masterplot, particularly once we take into consideration the thinly disguised fact that each of his totalitarian overreachers variously externalizes in order to defend against the "ambition of individualism" in Emerson himself, a defense all the more urgent in view of his stipulation that such ambition is both essential and suicidal. As Whitman correctly remarked, Emersonianism breeds the giant that destroys itself, a fact that would occasion some dismay for the implied master of *Representative Men* who declares "So it fares with all." Yet even if we were to develop such preliminary qualifications further, they would not finally obscure a central difference between these two authors. For *Leaves of Grass* reopens to inquiry precisely what a text like *Representative Men* takes to be a closed issue. Is there a form of unanimity possible which would not be profaned or violated in the moment of its announcement? Would its authority be established primarily by its power of retribution and revenge? Would it be an ideal that remains inalienable only insofar as it remains unobtainable? With these questions in mind, the author of "A Song for Occupations" asks "Will the whole come back, then? . . . Will you seek afar off?" He does not do so in order to induce consternation over the loss of a forsaken totality or to hold out the promise of one day recapturing it. "I do not affirm that what you see beyond is futile, I do not advise you to stop," he explains, yet neither does he wish to consider the "enclosing purports" of union as something evermore about to be be. On the contrary, "happiness, knowledge" are to be welcomed "not in another place but this place, not for another hour but this hour." The concluding lines of the poem, graced with all the "wit and wisdom" justly admired by Emerson, seek to make good on this claim:

> When the psalm sings instead of the singer,
> When the script preaches instead of the preacher,
> When the pulpit descends and goes instead of the
>   carver that carved the supporting desk,
> When I can touch the body of books by night or day,
>   and they can touch my body back again,
> When a university course convinces like a slumbering
>   woman and child convince,

> When the minted gold in the vault smiles like the
>   night watchman's daughter,
> When warantee deeds loafe in the chairs opposite and
>   are my friendly companions,
> I intend to reach them my hand, and make as much of
>   them as I do of men and women like you.
>   ("A Song for Occupations," *CRE,* p. 218–19)

These lines speak to the imperative of retrieving the subject, of resituating value within the assertion of human agency. In fact, they do not merely advocate this imperative but work through it so that by the time we reach the poet's final vow the antithesis between those reified icons of everyday life (the psalm, script, or pulpit) and those enslaved by them (singer, preacher, or carver) has already begun to melt away under the sensualizing charm of his similes. Smiling gold and friendly warantee deeds, in being reinvested with the "touch" of human proximity, bring near to fulfillment the pledge the poet is in the process of delivering. Whitman too takes aim at the alienated majesty of misplaced worship, though what initiates this projected recovery is importantly nothing other than the "reach" of the poem's intentions. He too defends against the severance of act and agency, but does so without recourse to a supervening order of archetypes (the "Universal Mind," the "Oversoul") or to a discourse of re-crimination and promise:

> Whovever you are! Motion and reflection are
>   especially for you,
> The divine ship sails the divine sea for you . . .
> The song is to the singer, and comes back most to him,
> The teaching is to the teacher, and comes back most to
>   him,
> The murder is to the murderer, and comes back most to
>   him,
> The theft is to the thief, and comes back most to him,
> The love is to the lover, and comes back most to him,
> The gift is to the giver, and comes back most to him,
> The oration is to the orator, the acting is to the
>   actor and actress, not the audience,
> And no man understands any greatness or goodness but
>   his own, or the indication of his own.
>   ("A Song of the Rolling Earth," *CRE,* p. 223)

Whitman's desire to move outside the jeremiad tradition is scarcely explained by a lack of familiarity with its workings. When the "divine literatus" serves notice at the outset of *Democratic Vistas* that "the United States are destined either to surmount the gorgeous history of feudalism, or else prove the most tremendous failure of time" (*PW* 2:363), he establishes himself as still another keeper of the Republican flame who embraces "the priceless value of our political institutions" while railing against the backsliding, perversions, and "heart-weary-ing postponements" these have fallen prey to. (Appropriately for this mode as well, his stance allows for withering attacks on the headlong commercialism of "our materialistic and vulgar American democracy" at the same time that it precludes starker examination of the prevailing order; as he notes early on, "I shall use the words America and democ-racy as convertible terms" [*PW* 2:363].) While *Democratic Vistas,* composed in the aftermath of the Civil War, came fairly late in Whit-man's career, other appearances of the jeremiad tradition can be traced as far back as "A Boston Ballad," a satire written written one year before the first edition of *Leaves of Grass* which summons the fathers of the Revolutionary War in order to survey the degeneration of a nation prostituted by the passage of the Fugitive Slave Law. Yet these are for the most part the proverbial exceptions that prove the rule. By tem-perament if not by design, *Leaves of Grass* is purposeful in its resistance to a rhetoric of affirmation by way of castigation, even to the point of implying that this procedure has worn itself out. "Master," affirmed the poet in an open letter to Emerson that formed the preface for the 1856 edition of *Leaves,* "I am a man who has perfect faith." For Whitman that faith entailed, among other things, "knowing the per-fect fitness and equanimity of things." Inasmuch as "there was never any more inception than there is now . . . and will never be any more perfection than there is now" (*CRE,* p. 30), things as they are acquire sanctity by the sheer fact of their existence, without need of further justification. "The moth and the fish-eggs are in their place, / The bright suns I see and the dark suns I cannot see are in their place, / The palpable is in its place and the impalpable is in its place" (*CRE,* p. 45) In a world where "the unshakable order of the universe" is duly accepted, where "no specification is necessary . . . to add or subtract or divide is in vain" (*PW* 2:454), it is idle to suppose oneself "defeated all the time" yet to "Victory" forever born, this being precisely the state of affairs the evangelist of "perfect faith" hopes to dispel. Affir-mations which are apt to strike the reader as flat-footed or impossibly trite in their serenity may no doubt be construed as such, yet they also bear witness to a continuing desire to eliminate anxiety from expectation. "I do not know what is untried and afterward," confesses the "kosmos" of "Song of Myself," pondering an uncharted future, "but I know it will in its turn prove sufficient and cannot fail" (*CRE*, p. 79). We are to set our minds at ease. Not custom, lecture, admonition, encouragement, or dispute is wanted, only the "lull" or "hum" of a preestablished harmony excelling "all art and argument of the earth." "Sauntering the pavement thus, or crossing the ceaseless ferry, faces and faces and faces, I see them, and complain not, and am content with all" ("Faces," *CRE*, p. 464).

By virtue of this inexhaustible magnaminity, the poet hopes to put back into human circulation values otherwise deferred or alienated in those forms of exchange that regulate society at large, that lock away the gold in the vault and the psalm in the pulpit. To "reach" these by hand is to imagine a discourse able to bring to pass what it calls for, "to see nothing anywhere but what you may reach it and pass it . . . to see no being, not God's or any, but you also go thither, / To see no possession but you may possess it . . ." (*CRE*, p. 156). Possessiveness this indiscriminate may call to mind Emerson's rapacious representatives, though it can be noted, in ways that have already been touched on, that whatever accrues to the self is, for Whitman, to be freely dispensed by it. The possessing hand is also a prodigal hand, one whose affluence is measured by its capacity for unending expenditure. "You shall not heap up what is call'd riches," counsels the speaker of "Song of the Open Road"; "you shall scatter with lavish hand all you earn or achieve" (*CRE*, p. 156). Poems are accordingly to be considered offerings or tokens of gratitude bequeathed to a nation whose "impalpable sustenance" fills them as they in return fill it, thereby acting out what is elsewhere called in "Song of Myself" a "perpetual payment of perpetual loan." As Lewis Hyde has remarked in his sensitive discussion of the "gifted self" in *Leaves of Grass*, "the self that identifies with a cycle of gifts takes its own activity as its identity—not the reception of objects, not the bestowal of particular contents, but the entire process, the respiration, the give-and-take of sympathy and pride."[12] From this standpoint, there can be inferred a sensitivity to the same concerns over the specter of a "tyrannizing unity" voiced by *Representative Men*, though what Emerson takes to be a transgressive exercise of will on the part of the hero Whitman is at pains to circumvent by insisting that his verse does not favor one side of a given transaction (neither owner nor owned; creditor nor debtor) but travels between both positions so as to incarnate the dynamic of giving and receiving itself. Because ownership has no final resting place in the course of undergoing constant recirculation, it ideally remains immune to the threat of expropriation, whether this threat derives from speaker or listener. By "enjoying all without labor or purchase, abstracting the feast yet not abstracting one particle of it," each enjoys a freestanding relation to the whole without being bound to, or falsely appropriating, any one element within that totality (*CRE*, p. 156).

Assimilating the debts of the imagination to an ongoing cycle of reception and bestowal, denying anxiety to anticipation, praising things as they are without reference to a transcendent principle of justice—each of these gestures remains faithful to the project of forwarding a mutual accord of interests that will not disappear the moment we go to celebrate them. Still, even if we were to go on to delineate comparable attitudes and ambitions informing the "man of perfect faith," it would be careless to suppose that the two models for union sponsored by Whitman and Emerson—the one celebratory, comic, and immanent; the other admonitory, retributive, and deferred—were in any categorical sense absolute in their differences, as if they occupied entirely separate realms whose traits admitted no interaction. When Hyde, intent on upholding precisely such a contrast, defines the "eros power" of gifts which ideally fuse the body politic in a sympathetic concord of giving and taking against the "logos power" of "law, authority, competition, hierarchy," and so forth,[13] he speaks on behalf of a dichotomy that has more than ample warrant in *Leaves of Grass,* but he does so with a measure of confidence in the stability of these terms that Whitman cannot unreservedly endorse. Not least among the concerns we have seen expressed in his "hymns of you" is the apprehension that the acquiring "I" may itself be reduced to an acquisition, one whose words drift from the "touch" of human intentionality and become expropriated goods or mere "portable property." Where the fear of such expropriation is especially manifest, when it becomes necessary to declare "Camerado, this is no book, who touches this touches a man," a conflict emerges between the task of restoring value to the community at large and that of defending against responses which threaten to distort or falsify the speaker's intentions. By way of sharpening our sense of the tension here involved, we can recall that for Emerson's self-reliant reader the threat of expropriation is in fact no threat at all but something he thrives on by learning to exploit. The great man striving "to grow and

exclude, and to exclude and grow, to the extremities of the universe"
becomes finally a partial man, one who makes of any enjoyment of the
whole a subjugation of it. Out of this failed attempt at appropriation
by the representative who "carries a wealth that beggars his own," the
reader is in turn seized by the uncanny return of his "own rejected
thoughts," that influx of discovered power that Emerson calls in the
essay on "History" the "unceasing succession of brisk shocks of surprise," now cut loose from all "barbarous homages." Whitman is of
course pledged to a similar task of liberation, though it remains a
matter of some consternation for him whether this should entail deference to "a power so great that the potentate is nothing" (*W* 4:23).
The following poem, bearing the simple inscription "To You," bespeaks such a consternation by making vivid the conflict between
releasing the authority of "you" and preserving the authority of the
"I." First published in the same edition (1856) that was prefaced by
an open letter to Emerson, the poem provides grounds for believing
that in this case Whitman did have a specific respondent in mind for
his generic "you, whoever you are":

> Whoever you are, now I place my hand upon you, that
>   you be my poem,
> I whisper with my lips close to your ear,
> I have loved many women and men, but I love none
>   better than you,
> O I have been dilatory and dumb,
> I should have made my way straight to you long ago,
> I should have blabbed nothing but you, I should have
>   chanted nothing but you.
> I will leave all and come and make the hymns of you,
> None has understood you, but I understand you,
> None has done justice to you, you have not done
>   justice to yourself,
> None but has found you imperfect, I only find no
>   imperfection in you,
> None but would subordinate you, I only am he who will
>   never consent to subordinate you,
> I only am he who places over you no master, owner,
>   better, God, beyond what waits intrinsically in
>   yourself.
>   (*CRE*, p. 233)

"None has done justice to you, you have not done justice to yourself": one could not ask for a more disarming summary of the gospel of Self-Reliance as well as the jeremiad rhetoric that mobilizes it—disarming both for the perspicuous fidelity of this translation and its wholly disabling effects. It is no longer conceivable for the reader to come upon this address with the aim of drawing from it the unreclaimed majesty of his own rejected genius for the simple reason that Whitman has already called upon him to do so. The uncanny influx of *discovered* power cherished by Emerson Whitman here brandishes as an explicit theme, so that the furtive luster of the master's speech, like the latent power of his questers, is brought forward and domesticated. Rather than finding himself in the self-consuming authority of the representative's text, the reader is found and, by poetic fiat, textualized: "I place my hand upon you, that you be my poem." The magnificent presumption of this placing, rivaled only by the wonderful hypocrisy of the passage as a whole, initiates a call for a democratic equivalence of potential which "I only" is nevertheless commissioned to actualize. The paradoxical effect, unmistakable with the final lines, is to render the authority of that "I" all the more irresistible in the act of abjuring it. Setting no master, owner, or God over "you," the speaker plays something of all these parts, thereby reinscribing the inalienable "reach" of his intentions. In the last chapter of *Pragmatism*, William James quotes this "fine and moving poem" as exemplary of that genre of literature that "encourages fidelity to ourselves," yet it is not too captious to say that the scale of gains is in this instance balanced to favor fidelity to the poet, just as it is no surprise to discover that by the time we reach the poem's conclusion the promised deliverance of that "which waits intrinsically in yourself" is emphatically overshadowed by the heroic perseverance of the deliverer: "I track you through your windings and turnings. . . . the hopples fall from your ankles, you find an unfailing sufficiency."[14]

Awakening the dormant will of the second person—the slumbering "glory of you"—here amounts to paralyzing it. In his parodic internalization of the lessons of self-reliance, the remorseless liberator stalking us in "our windings and turnings" embraces the notion of "inner divinity" with a fervor that effectively cripples its emergence. While the irony of the poem is presumably unintended, its very prominence deepens our sense of Whitman's continued resistance to the retributions of reading, his unspoken insistence that he does *not* carry a wealth that beggars his own. Such resistance deserves further consideration, especially when measured against the prevailing wisdom that guides most accounts of the importance of the beholder in Whitman's verse. I refer to the view which regards his auditor as an intratextual participant or accomplice whose mission is not simply to derive significances but to cooperate and in some sense complete the poem's creation. "I round and finish little," explains Whitman in *A Backward Glance;* "the reader will always have his or her part to do, just as much as I have had mine. I seek less to state or display any theme or thought, and more to bring you, reader, into the atmosphere of the theme or thought—there to pursue your flight" (*PW* 2:725). Inasmuch as "the process of reading is not a half-sleep but, in the highest sense an exercise, a gymnast's struggle," the democratic listener is "to do something for himself, must be on the alert, must himself or herself indeed construct the poem . . . the text furnishing the hints, the clue, the start or framework" (*PW* 2:425). From these formulations it is only a short leap to the widely shared belief that "Whitman aimed not simply to create a poet and then a god, but to assist at the creation of the poetic and god-like in every reader."[15] This manner of speaking has become so ingrained in discussions of *Leaves of Grass* that special effort is required to reassess its premises. One need not accuse Whitman of outright duplicity in order to sense how easily assisting at the creation of the poetic and divine in every reader can imply obstructing it, particularly when that reader is likely to deplore any such aid as an anathema. "We do not quite forgive the giver," comments Emerson in his brief meditation on "Gifts" in the *Second Series* of *Essays.* Giving is unforgivable because it incurs dependency, and "we wish to be self-sustained." "You cannot give anything to a magnanimous person," he complains; "after you have served him he at once puts you in debt by his magnanimity" (*W* 3:88, 89). Such qualms bring to light the scandal of generosity—a kind of *potlatch,* as the French writer Georges Bataille describes it, which "excludes all bargaining and, in general, is constituted by a considerable gift of riches, offered openly and with the goal of humiliating, defying, and obligating a rival."[16] The "lavish hand" establishes the superiority of its wealth by its prodigality, thereby stunning its recipients with a munificence so boundless that the possibility of response is preempted, the kind of unanswerable munificence on view when the poet declares "I myself am not one who bestows nothing on any man or woman, / For I bestow upon any man or woman the entrance to all the gifts of the universe" ("To the Rich Givers," *CRE,* p. 273). And, of course, when the gift in question is nothing less than our own identity, then the adage that "the gift is to the giver, and comes back most to him" acquires disquieting implications. Thus we are invited to travel down the open road of self-discovery, but only so long as there is no doubt about who initiates our progress: "Whoever you are come forth! . . . you must not stay sleeping and dallying there in the house though you built it . . . Out of the dark confinement! Out from behind the screen! It is useless to protest, I know all and expose it" ("Song of the Open Road," *CRE*, p. 157).

"You see," explained Whitman to Horace Traubel while musing over his "various feelings" toward Emerson, "I both blaspheme and worship" (*WWC* 4:152). Given the baffling paradox of coming to terms with the influence of a writer who urges a flight from all influences, this report will seem more inevitable than perverse. In later years, when he began to fret over the issue of influence publicly, it is true that Whitman repudiated his mentor altogether. Responding with ill-concealed irritation to a query from a correspondent in 1887, he wrote: "It is of no importance whether I had read Emerson's writings before starting L of G. The fact happens to be positively that I had *not*. . . . If I were to unbosom to you in the matter I should say that I never cared so very much for E's writings" (*CORR* 4:69–70). Five years earlier, though, he contradicted this denial in *Notes Left Over*, likening his passion for Emerson to an adolescent crush ("Emerson-on-the-brain," he called it) which came and went. Then again, he reasoned, the problem of "E's writings" was no problem at all, since "the best of Emersonianism is, it breeds the giant that destroys itself. . . . No teacher ever taught, that has prepared for his pupil's setting up independently" (*PW* 2:517–18). Yet, as the poet who asks "I teach straying from me, yet who can stray from me?" recognized, casting off Emerson's legacy could not be much different from emulating it, since both came to the same thing. In view of this double bind, it is unlikely that Whitman would find solace in a "pact" or "truce" of the kind drawn up by Ezra Pound in the course of addressing his literary forbear; too many "various feelings" stood between master and follower for the latter to declare without irony "let there be commerce between us."[17] With simple acceptance no more desirable a response than outright denial, it in turn becomes clear why Whitman should be pressed to combine the two, making slavish adherence to "the best of Emersonianism" an occasion for ventriloquizing it. Decrying a life of "subordination" thereby offers a means of prolonging it; sponsoring the "glory of you" a way of containing it. In this respect, his readers do indeed confront the majesty of their own rejected thoughts, a majesty which, as a final glance at "To You" makes vivid, is brought back to them in thinly disguised accents of mockery. The result is worship and blasphemy with a vengeance:

> O I could sing such grandeurs and glories about you!
> You have not known what you are, you have slumbered
>   upon yourself all your life,
> Your eyelids have been the same as closed most of the
>   time,
> What you have done returns in mockeries,
> (Your thrift, knowledge, prayers, if they do not
>   return in mockeries, what is their return?)
>
> The mockeries are not you,
> Underneath and within them I see you lurk,
> I pursue you where none else has pursued you,
> Silence, the desk, the flippant expression, the night,
>   the accustom'd routine, if these conceal you from
>   others or from yourself, they do not conceal you
>   from me . . .
>   ("To You," *CRE*, p. 234)

Such facile inversions, it is by now needless to add, accomplish little beyond enforcing an impasse between speaker and addressee they otherwise purport to transcend. In fact, it remains doubtful whether they accomplish even that, for like most parodic discourses this too cannot escape the more disheartening irony that the adversary it privately mocks is also the adversary it most resembles. Disarming the feared usurper in the text—"whoever you are"—requires an aggressive act or usurpation in return, one which relies on silencing the listener's voice so as to empower the poet's own—"tied in your mouth, in mine it begins to loosen." A spirit of competition and hierarchy is no less discernible in the "shield of a greeting" here offered than in the Emersonian motto that best describes it: "the more we are drawn, the more we are repelled." Insofar as containing the will of the self-reliant reader proceeds by replicating the practices of that reader, the distance between Whitman's worshipful blasphemy and that encountered in *Representative Men* will appear negligible. This being the case, we are, along with Whitman, thrown back on the familiar paradox: the master who makes liberation from all "barbarous homages" possible thereby makes his centrality inescapable.

Yet Emerson alone is scarcely responsible for inventing this dilemma, one which would indeed appear unavoidable in any form of address that proposes to "bring what you much need, yet always have." In a broader sense, the paradoxical interdependency of freedom and oppression evident in the crude and somewhat self-defeating tactics of a poem like "To You" is not sufficiently explained as a mere aberration or a local clash of wills contending for imaginative priority. Rather, the point to be stressed is that such a paradox does not simply pose an obstacle to Whitman's pursuit of the "free sense" of acknowledgment but in an elementary way sustains that pursuit. Thus the unnerving slippage of the autocratic and the democratic in the texts we have been discussing, a slippage that has never been far from being a source of unease for readers of *Leaves of Grass*. What renders these terms problematic is not, of course, that they stand in opposition but their readiness to declare themselves leagued in collusion, the kind of collusion on view in the 1855 Preface when Whitman writes: "Of all mankind the poet is the equable man." Inasmuch as the promised effacement of all distinctions here supplies the basis for one, we are presented with that oxymoronic creature, the poet as most equable man. Under a similar logic we are also informed further on in the Preface that just as the American bard is "hungry for equals night and day," he is also, as "the most affluent man," one that "confronts all the shows that he sees by equivalents out of the stronger wealth of himself" (*PW* 2:446). The power to abolish all differences, in sum, establishes the power of the poet's difference. The egalitarian and the authoritarian are thus mutually constituted, where the latter does not stand *behind* the former in a condition of potential subversion but subsists *beside* it in an ongoing relation of adjacency. This of course is not Whitman's way of conceiving it, and everything in his stance as the Answerer—"the equalizer of his age and land"—implies a vehement denial of the kind of thinking present in Roman Jakobson's sharply drawn distinction that "poetry of the second person . . . is either supplicatory or exhortative depending on whether the first person is subordinated to the second one or the second to the first."[18] Yet vows such as "I only am he who will never consent to subordinate you," however well-intentioned or benign, plainly perpetuate a sense

of subordination by their very act of retracting it—a complication
that lends an added twist to Jakobson's formulation but does not
refute it. The Lawgiver cannot legislate away his own authority without exercising it, and in this strict sense it hardly matters if the poet
seeks an accord of shared interests that will not disappear the moment
they are announced, for this will occur anyway. The "equable man"
accordingly discovers himself embroiled in the same perversity of
logic that besets Rousseau's notion that "whoever refuses to obey the
general will shall be constrained to do so by the whole body, which
means nothing other than that he shall be forced to be free"[19]—an
apparent paradox elaborated at greater length in the following paragraph, which begins by restating a central premise of the democratic
compact and ends by revealing its necessary counterpart:

> The messages of great poets to each man and women are, Come
> to us on equal terms. Only then can you understand us. We are
> no better than you, What we enclose you enclose, What we
> enjoy, you may enjoy. Did you suppose that there could only be
> one Supreme? We affirm there can be unnumbered Supremes,
> and that one does not countervail another any more than one
> eyesight countervails another . . . and that men can be good or
> grand of the consciousness of their supremacy within them.
> What do you think is the grandeur of storms and dismember-
> ments and the deadliest battles and wrecks and the wildest fury
> of the elements and the power of the sea and the motion of
> nature and of the throes of human desires and dignity and hate
> and love? It is something in the soul which says, Rage on, Whirl
> on, I tread here and everywhere, Master of the spasms of the sky,
> and of the shatter of the sea, Master of nature and passion and
> death, And of all terror and pain. (1855 Preface, *PW* 2:445–46;
> Whitman's ellipsis)

Democratic sympathy breeds its own violence, the convulsions of
dismemberments and furies which trade in equal terms for despotic
commands and which make apparent that the rageful aggression of
the soul does not merely compromise the offering of equality but
comprises, engenders, and otherwise fuels it. Various critics have, it is
true, sought to recast this aggression in a less forbidding light, some
by falling back on the notion of Whitman assisting at the creation of
the poetic and godlike in all (the Master in every reader), others by
pointing to his care in maintaining a "democratic balance" between

"egalitarian faith" and "egocentric proclivities" (a world of freely contending Masters).[20] Of all the ways of upholding the integrity of Whitman's democratization of the sublime, though, one imagines these to be less than reassuring, mostly because a structure of dominance and submission will persist not simply *despite* the poet's protests to the contrary but *because* of them. Bad faith or a case of self-interest masquerading under the guise of a disinterested generality is in any case not the real issue here; it is, rather, the more fundamental sense insisted on by Emerson that any claim to representative speech— "what I assume, you shall assume"—is in some measure a transgressive act. And where this transgression is felt to be especially overbearing, where it is sensed that sanction for the poet's speech demands a suppression of our own, we then confront the same violence in uniformity that provokes Santayana's recoil at the "barbaric" leveler of sensibilities in *Leaves of Grass;* that produces Lawrence's unforgettable cartoon of Walt hurtling down the open road in his "great fierce poetic machine" shrieking "ALLNESS" while happily "oblivious to the corpses underneath the wheels"; or that informs Pablo Neruda's ambivalent homage to "the first totalitarian poet."[21]

There is an element of truth in these assessments, and I do not see how any serious appraisal of Whitman's quest for "indissoluble compacts" can afford to wish them away. There is no future in trying to factor out the democratic altruist from the democratic egotist where both lie together as intimately as the "measureless pride" and immeasurable "sympathy" of the bard who "has lain close betwixt both" (*PW* 2:443). For this same reason, however, it should be clear that stigmatizing Whitman's demagoguery carries little more authority than endeavoring to rescue him from it, since both responses take the relation of the autocrat and democrat to be governed by a law of contradiction, the one functioning as the prohibitive limit or negation of the other, as if a line could be drawn between the two, marking off deviation from norm, as if indeed the issue at hand were at best a lapse of vigilance on the part of "the equable man" and at worst a marauding, uncontainable lust for power. A more reflective view on these matters can profit from Bataille's assertion that "respect is really nothing other than a devious route taken by violence. On the one hand respect keeps order in a sphere where violence is forbidden [while] on the other it makes it possible for violence to erupt incongruously in fields where it has ceased to be permissible."[22] How to escape this alliance by devising a colloquy of boundless respect removed from all dissension defines, in turn, Whitman's ideal—a discourse which, like the song of the rolling earth, "does not argue . . . scream, haste, persuade, threaten. promise, / Makes no discriminations, closes nothing, shuts none out" (*CRE*, p. 221). Yet what is to be noticed at this point is that the more the dialectic of respect and violence is construed as a polarity (as is evident in the strenuous pains taken by the poet to insist that it is only through an absolute equivalence of relationship that he can be understood, or in the efforts of his commentators to preserve a gap between "eros power" and "logos power" or "egalitarian faith" and "egocentric proclivities"), the greater the inducement to violence, be it in the unleashed fury of the master of "passion and death, and of all terror and all pain" or in the oppressive magnanimity of a speaker who, determined to rouse the slumbering "glory of you," casts his auditors in the uncomfortable role of the hapless Jim to Whitman's Tom Sawyer, the latter zealously absorbed in the farcical mission of "setting a free man free."

In his own gloss on the sentences from Bataille cited above, Tony Tanner ventures a paraphrase directly applicable to our purposes: "contracts *create* transgressions; the two are inseparable, and the one would have no meaning without the other."[23] That his paraphrase reads in turn like a paraphrase of *Representative Men* is entirely appropriate for a work where preserving connections among the whole requires, under the sanction of "Nature's law," attention to how this totality is necessarily perverted or blasphemed. "The Muse herself betrays her son," writes Emerson, in full acceptance of the circularity Tanner speaks of. Dismayed by this logic and the system of justice it enforces, Whitman's "profound lesson of reception" seeks its truth, as we have seen, "before preaching and law." That his vision can have the result of engendering the violence it was meant to cure does not, however, invalidate his quest, any more than it brings to light a massive case of self-delusion. The very prominence of the ironies we have been tracing—where the more vehemently subordination is denied the more acutely it is felt; the more insistently the dualism of contract and transgression is thought to be transcended the more intimate its alliance—need not be ascribed to misapplied logic or simple naïveté. Such ironies instead make vivid the extraordinary pressures implicitly brought to bear on Whitman's construction of the "equable man," one whose categorical insistence on an absolute equality of exchange ("I shall be even with you and you shall be even with me") and whose compulsive reminder that his sentences issue from our lips not only frustrates his own apparent intentions but bears witness to the pressing need to literalize communicative bonds, to assert rather than simply assume the achievement of consensus. So extreme a devotion to "equal terms" argues the utter evanescence of that concept, and it is in this context that we can best apply Kenneth Burke's observation that "if men were not far apart there would be no need for the rhetoritician to proclaim their unity"[24] to the proclamations of the "better President" of *Leaves of Grass*, whose lunging embrace of the reader is compelled by similar apprehensions. As we attend to the enmity and strife so eloquently conveyed in the act of being so zealously banished by these overtures, we cannot fail to hear in them as well an unsuspected poignance, as in these parting lines from "Song of the Open Road":

> Camerado, I give you my hand!
> I give you my love more precious than money,
> I give you myself before preaching or law;
> Will you give me yourself? Will you come travel with
>   me?
> Shall we stick by each other as long as we live?

3

Unbetrayable Replies

AT ONE POINT IN HER STUDY of revolutions in the modern age
Hannah Arendt draws attention to the belief widely shared among the
Founding Fathers that winning the war of rebellion against British
tyranny signified "the first act" only in what was to be the larger
drama of securing American independence.[1] Beyond the sheer ordeal
of military struggle and long-awaited triumph lay the equally formidable and equally daunting task of constituting the Republic's
newfound freedom, the essential requirement for converting a mere
rebellion into a genuine revolution. Something of the same sense of
priority holds true for *Leaves of Grass,* which does not rest content with
proclamations of a ground-breaking originality but stakes its claim on
our attention in seeking out the conditions and structure favorable
to a redeemed solidarity, with its "free sense at last." The drama is
not over once imaginative independence is declared, since that declaration demands in turn still further stages of deliberation in promised
fulfillment of poetry's—and, by extension, America's—"unfinished
business." While not necessarily false, the picture of the American
Adam sauntering down the open road is deceptive so far as it encourages us to believe that what Whitman most needed from poetry was
the assurance of a self-fathering authority free from the afflictions of
personal and cultural belatedness. Heeding Emerson's call "to build
therefore your own world," Whitman understood it as a point of
departure, not an end in itself. Perhaps this is one reason why the topic
of literary inheritance, so much a subject of anxious meditation in
Emerson, Thoreau, and Hawthorne, excites comparatively little
alarm in Whitman, whose first words to the public of 1855 reveal a
determination to get beyond such tiresome oppositions as that between New World freshness and Old World tradition: "America does
not repel the past or what it has produced under its forms or amid

other politics or the idea of castes or the old religions . . . accepts the lesson with calmness . . . is not so impatient as has been supposed" (*PW* 2:434).

The project of constituting freedom is on the other hand apt to generate tensions of its own, as *Leaves of Grass* and its invocations to the reader attest. Modern historians have tended to construe this tension along the lines of a conceptual antagonism between liberty and regulation until the very phrase "constituting freedom" begins to look like a contradiction in terms—thus the common perception that the passage of the United States Constitution marks in its own right a reactionary or even counterrevolutionary episode in the nation's history. Arendt is no doubt correct to attack such views for their reliance upon a peculiarly modernist dogma which restricts liberty to a negative value merely, as if the concept of freedom were intrinsically hostile to social definition. Acknowledging the justice of her criticism should not, however, lead us to conclude that discussions of the value and significance of constitution-making have not attracted markedly divided opinions: one example occurs in the opening pages of *Common Sense,* where Paine celebrates national compacts as the indispensable instrument for overthrowing despotisms of the past and thereby creating the body politic anew at the same time that he stigmatizes these instruments as tokens of corruption, another among many "badges of lost innocence" in a fallen world. Where from one standpoint constitutions reverse time, from another they testify to its irreversibility. A somewhat different version of this same ambivalence informs the following definition, which appears in one of Whitman's reading notes to Rousseau's *The Social Contract:*

> The honest and novel bargain of government palpably assumes that the contracting parties meet on exactly the same level as of a fresh and open affair, where each man [is] without any distinction whatever . . . and the debatable points not affected by previous ties.[2]

Whitman here joins Locke and Rousseau in disputing the Hobbesian claim that citizenship requires, tacitly or otherwise, the alienation of all rights. Interestingly, though, in the course of defending the merits of the contract Whitman renders it superfluous: this "honest and novel bargain" has nothing to do with bringing consensus into being but simply *confirms* one that already exists. Useful as it may be in settling local grievances, contractual agreement is but a supplementary form which has evolved from a precontractual covenant that guarantees absolute equality. This covenant is at any rate what "government palpably assumes," though it would seem that the more compelling feature of this definition rests on the ideal assumption that one kind of (contractual) agreement could be merged into another more basic agreement. The effect of this merger is to place the contract outside the bounds of critical discussion, to regard it in fact not as a contract at all but as the *result* of one long since accomplished. As with Mill's definition of poetry, preserving the authenticity of the terms of exchange here depends on ruling the concept of exchange out of existence.

Likewise conceived after the model of "a fresh and open affair," the poetry of *Leaves of Grass* envisions its own colloquy of equals who "meet on exactly the same level." Yet, unlike the definition cited above, it also implies a far more alert understanding of the difficulties involved in the pursuit of such goals, just as it confronts with considerably more candor the difficulties involved in the retroactive desire to subsume contractual agreements under the rubric of self-evident principles. This latter stratagem is by no means unique: Daniel Webster, who cherished a devotion to the Union no less "mystical" than Whitman's, made his reputation on the Senate floor by insisting (against Calhoun and his followers) that the Constitution was not in fact a contract between the states at all but "the result of a contract." In his own attempt to situate this *"fundamental law"* outside the bounds of critical discussion, Webster maintained that the founders' document was "not the agreement but something created by the agreement, and something which, when created, has a new character, and acts by its own authority." By reason of this special difference—the contract which is "something" more than a contract—"the agreement itself is merged in its own accomplishment."[3]

Though Whitman's Unionism did not lead him down the road of political compromise, the impulse to articulate an accord whose authority would be irrevocably sealed in the moment of its accomplishment remained essentially the same. In his role as Answerer the poet of course intended to make that accomplishment visible by presenting himself as the conjunctive medium for the social discourse—the connective link through whose utterance speak "the many long dumb voices" and through whose reach there is offered "the pass-key of hearts." But impinging on that role is also the tremendous strain of sustaining that mediating voice, one whose embrace of the reader combines impossible demands for intimacy with equally impossible demands for absolute equality. Having witnessed how this "shield of a greeting" informs Whitman's solicitations in a number of different texts, I want now to turn to a longer and better-known poem, "The Sleepers," in order to suggest how this crisis of mediation in the synthesizing persona of the Answerer has further bearing on the crisis of Union at large. That these two subjects—personal trauma and collective tragedy—are only tentatively brought together in the course of the drama reveals, to my mind, its deepest source of interest. First appearing in the 1855 edition of *Leaves,* "The Sleepers" is also, as I shall be suggesting, a transitional poem, one which draws upon the original burst of creativity from "Song of Myself" to be discussed in Part 2 and which looks ahead to the spate of "Chants Democratic" we have just explored.

Long considered a forerunner to the stream of consciousness technique in modernist fiction, "The Sleepers" is often said to represent the hallucinations of a mind at sleep. But it would be more accurate to say that this is what the poem does and does not want to become, without quite making up its mind. On the strain of this irresolution the drama of the first half of the poem is poised. Though we are initially afforded a glimpse of a speaker "wandering and confused, lost to myself, ill-assorted and contradictory," the opening section hardly plunges us into the phantasmagoria of the poet's psyche. Rather than the poet dreaming we come upon the poet dreaming of other dreamers dreaming: "I dream in my dream all the other dreams of the dreamers." A kind of subjectivity is being intimated here, but one which, typically enough, feels most comfortable under the aegis of a larger intersubjectivity, as if the phrase "I dream" could not stand alone. But this is a presumption the poem does not sponsor so much as punish. While the author claims to be "lost to myself," it is immediately clear that his disorientation is the result neither of his "vision" nor of his immersion in the visions of his sleepers. With their studied use of anaphora ("The wretched features of ennuyees, the white features of corpses, the livid faces of drunkards"), symploce ("The female that loves unrequited sleeps, / The male that loves unrequited sleeps"), and interrogation ("And the murder'd person, how does he sleep?"), the opening lines project a self-enclosed world that accentuates the isolation of a witness who cannot quite blend into the dreamscape, however intimate his proximity. "I stand in the dark with drooping eyes by the worstsuffering and most helpless, / I pass my hands to and fro soothingly a few inches from them." While such furtive gestures of consolation, which anticipate the ministrations of "The Wound-Dresser," identify Whitman's stance to be that of a purposeful forgetting, they also candidly expose the cross-purposes behind it. If the transferred epithet ("drooping eyes") of the first line hints at identification, this is promptly qualified against the carefully measured distance preserved in the second. Far from being "lost to myself," the poet, if he has lost anything, has lost his most familiar rhetorical pose. As the only poem in the 1855 edition which does not begin by calling on its auditors, "The Sleepers" blankets Whitman's "you, whoever you are" under the cover of a darkness that "pervades and enfolds" a phantom audience. Denied the opportunity for address, the poet confronts a still life of inarticulate figures who neither invite nor refuse.

In consternation over its awareness that it is neither complete within itself nor to be consolidated through its "ties to others," the roaming "I" finds itself cast adrift in an ontological limbo, where "it is neither ground nor sea." Ground and sea specify the two principle sites of *Leaves of Grass*, encompassing the "competent loam" of "Song of Myself" as well as the elegiac plangencies of the *Sea-Drift* lyrics. But here the poet has his aptest analogue in the specter of the moon which "comes floundering through the drifts." "Pausing, gazing, bending, and stopping," he is groping for some kind of entrance into a text not clearly his own. Although a breakthrough is proclaimed in line twenty-six ("Now I pierce through the darkness"), the next twenty lines pass on to a random exposition of multiple roles that are discarded as soon as they are named: "I am dance . . . I am the everlaughing . . . I am the actor, the actress, the voter, the politician, / The emigrant and the exile." Acting the actor, representing the representative, embracing the displaced personae of emigrant and exile: such overtures keep the drama of identification at a double remove, bespeaking again the restless maneuverings of a spectator who craves relation while hoping to evade the perils of entrapment. The exaggerated juxtapositions (murderer and married couple, drunkard and infant, emigrant and exile) throughout the first section further emphasize a world closed off to all mediations, particularly those informing the "equal terms" of the poet. To be sure, there are moments when we overhear the promptings of someone bent on persuading himself that he does belong: "Well do they do their jobs, these journeymen divine, / Only from me they can hide nothing and would not if they could." He reverts momentarily to the bravura of Democratic Redeemer, the equable "boss" who commands "Out from behind the screen! / It is useless to protest, I know all and expose it!" But now the tyrannous liberator who unmasks all resistances must itself be resisted; the "cunning covers" of his "journeymen divine," like the "cunning covers" of the text, are lifted to "signify me," not the slumbering glories of you. As yet, however, his fantasy of inclusion among this company of "blackguards" is merely anecdotal, a stolen moment of intimacy that underscores the chameleonlike spirit of the bard who remains as fleeting and evanescent as any of the characters on the page. The "common ground" is no ground; or rather, it is a "shadowy shore" whose boundaries seem at once enigmatic and impenetrable.

The semiconscious revery of the first forty-five lines cannot be inhabited, yet the poet has no other place to go. As an onlooker he must now become an interloper, and the scene of trespass coincides with the poem's first formal petition to the darkness. Figuring himself as "she who adorn'd herself and folded her hair expectantly" while awaiting my "truant lover," Whitman at last ventures upon a threshold: "double yourself and receive me darkness, / Receive me and my lover too, he will not let me go without him." Though we are initially presented with three presences (lady, lover, darkness), they quickly become interchangeable for the simple reason that Whitman is both wooer and wooed, both the Mariana-like maiden awaiting erotic release and the truant lover who steals into the scene. The ensuing autoerotic fantasy results in what is no doubt the most well known passage that Whitman marked for deletion in later editions:

O hotcheeked and blushing! O foolish hectic!
O for pity's sake, no one must see me now! . . . my
        clothes were stolen while I was abed,
Now I am thrust forth, where shall I run?

Pier that I saw dimly last night when I looked from
        the windows,
Pier out from the main, let me catch myself with you
        and stay . . . I will not chafe you;
I feel ashamed to go naked about the world,
And am curious to know where my feet stand . . . and
        what is this flooding me, childhood or manhood . . .
        and the hunger that crosses the bridge between.

> The cloth laps a first sweet eating and drinking,
> Laps life-swelling yolks . . . laps ear of rose-corn,
>   milky and just ripened:
> The white teeth stay, and the boss-tooth advances in
>   darkness,
> And liquor is spilled on lips and bosoms by touching
>   glasses, and the best liquor afterward.

Various readings of "The Sleepers" have profitably explored its oedipal strife, here manifest in the confused slippage between an overt and predatory phallicism and images of a more infantile, regressive attachment.[4] The "bridge between" the child and the man eludes sure definition, and at the end of his night sea-journey Whitman will attempt to harmonize these roles in his covenant with the maternal night. At this point, however, it is evident that the poet's puzzlement over such transitional states of being is in a broader sense symptomatic of the baffled and tenuously drawn transitions that characterize the poem as a whole. Rudely "thrust forth" into what has become a groundless place, the poet's effort at situating himself remains uncertain, precarious. Thus, while the gleefully overstated hysteria of the opening lines, written as if to caricature the speaker's panic over venturing into the text, insists on an utter nakedness before the world, the presence of the "I" by the end of this fantasy is virtually eclipsed by metonymic constructions ("life-swelling yolks"; "white teeth"; "the boss-tooth") that eerily take on a life of their own. We move precipitously from the extremes of self-exposure to self-effacement with no foothold between, from the "foolish hectic" thrust forth upon the stage to an invisible voyeur who savors his own erotic delights. Although this rift between the participant and the observer cannot be said to trigger the kind of violent schizophrenia imagined in one journal entry describing the "wise man [who] observes himself with the nicety of an enemy or a spy, and looks on his own wishes as betrayers (*UPP*, 2:94), it does suggest that what is at stake for Whitman is not simply the eruption of these wishes but the quandary of contextualizing or placing them within a secure framework.

Neither entirely in nor out of the game, Whitman's vignette continues to highlight the paradoxical position of an "I" who is both overspecified and secondary, both at the center of the story and inconsequential to it. Of course, these extremes are more related than opposed, and the next section (two) sharpens our sense of their connection by giving it a name: "Perfume and youth course through, and I am their wake." Of the double meaning suggested in Whitman's pun, the first confirms what we have already witnessed: the passage of selfhood from signifying presence to signified trace—a ghostly wake or washed-up drift stricken from the float that holds the "I" in suspension. Yet acting the "wake" to his own fading creations is for Whitman also a passing away, and in fulfillment of his wordplay the speaker soon discovers himself to be the helpless attendant to his own death scene. The magnificent portrait of the "beautiful swimmer swimming naked through the eddies of the sea," the centerpiece of the text, is transparently a self-portrait, one that most immediately recalls the naked swimmer drifting from the pier and that more distantly recalls the proud persona of "Song of Myself" who pledges "Now I shall be to you a bold swimmer, / To jump in the midst of the sea [and] rise again." Needless to say, Whitman's "courageous giant" does not rise again; on the contrary, the vividness of his evocation owes its force to the zeal with which his sacrifice is recorded. It is not enough that "the brave corpse" be borne "swiftly and out of sight"; he is "baffled, bang'd, and bruis'd . . . the slapping eddies are spotted with his blood . . . they roll him, swing him, turn him, / His beautiful body is borne in the circling eddies, it is continually bruis'd on the rocks." Such ecstatic cruelty speaks to the ongoing demand for atonement; as with the hot-cheeked and foolish hectic, the sheer act of venturing forth and the unbearable condition of presence to the world this entails brings a swift and severe penalty. Only now unqualified shame yields to unqualified rage given full vent through the displaced fury of the sea and its "red-trickled waves" and "slapping eddies." A certain prevenient anxiety can be deduced from the vehemence of this sacrifice, for the unstated logic of the scene would appear to be that it is preferable to drive home the futility of self-assertion now than see it betrayed by others. Having no one else to turn to, Whitman turns on the drifting corpse of himself, insinuating an alter ego into the poem which he can then slaughter in his imagination. So doing, he can at least hope to be the reader, not simply the unwitting victim, of his own effacement.

The "beautiful gigantic swimmer" whose "brave corpse" is borne "swiftly . . . out of sight" may distantly recall the corpse of the past mentioned in the first paragraph of the 1855 Preface which is "borne from the eating and sleeping rooms of the house . . . [as] it waits a little while in the door" in anticipation of the "the stalwart and well-shaped heir who approaches" (*PW* 2:434). Yet the more exact analogue for Whitman's Promethean overreacher, no sooner seen than slain, can be found in Emerson's band of thwarted representatives sacrificed at the shrine of unanimity from which they take their identity. It would indeed appear as though the complicity between a representative heroism and the transgressive impropriety this role invariably entails has not been dispelled but wound to a keener pitch, here evidenced in the skittish movement of a self whose only means of integrating himself within the drama is to come before us as a violent intruder upon the scene or an impotent bystander to this violence. To reflect on this dualism is to note further how intimately the anxiety of betrayal continues to shape Whitman's text, for in the preemptive martyring of his "courageous giant" we see writ large the same apprehensions besetting the synthesizing voice of "Crossing Brooklyn Ferry" who, by releasing the push of our reading, is also concerned to exempt himself from its judgments.

The question that remains to be considered at this stage in the poem is whether the act of *foretelling* such retributions can provide a means of *forestalling* them. In essence, this is the course pursued by *Representative Men*, whose visionaries are putatively esteemed for shadowing forth the unclaimed majesty of rejected genius but whose suicidal careers supply Emerson with the grounds for measuring his distance from them, not so much that he might recover this alien majesty but that he might keep it alienated. As I have argued, Plato's self-defeat not only exemplifies the inextricable alliance between contract and transgression that governs Emerson's vision of consensus but contains its violence, thereby allowing his biographer to propound Nature's universal "law" while somehow standing beyond it. Would Whitman's alter ego, doomed for no other reason than his own impulse to swim, serve a similar function? Certainly, in broad outline, "The Sleepers" wants badly to locate a "bridge between" sacrifice and a more inclusive vision of union, as is suggested in its difficult movement from the disjointed hallucinations of the grave ("A shroud I see and I am the shroud, I wrap a body and lie in the coffin") to affirmations of a resurrected Eden ("the diverse shall be no less diverse, but they shall flow and unite—they unite now" [*CRE*, pp. 427, 432]). And we know elsewhere from *Leaves of Grass* that death is its author's favored catalyst for transformation whereby the local constraints of individuality are shed and a more rarefied generality attained: thus the hero of "Song of Myself," abstracted from a particular time and place, bequeaths himself to grow from the grass he loves at the end of his epic so as to filter and fiber our blood, just as he had earlier driven himself to the brink of extinction, his windpipe throttled in the fakes of death, until he is "let up again" to a widened vision "to feel the puzzle of puzzles, / And that we call being" (*CRE*, p. 56). Yet "The Sleepers" retreats from these phoenixlike sublimations. No transcendence follows the slaying of its author's second self. Still less does this sacrifice serve to assuage the premonitions of betrayal, which will only broaden in implication before they are surmounted. With an integrity too seldom acknowledged in accounts of this poem, Whitman catches himself up; quick to deny that the staging of his own death scene offers release from the world of his text even as he implies the longing that it might do so, he begins the section directly following the execution of the naked swimmer with cautious deliberation:

> I turn but do not extricate myself,
> Confused, a past-reading, another, but with darkness
> yet.

(CRE, p. 428)

As he nears the midpoint of his journey, the only assertion of will left to the speaker is paradoxically to hold fast to his own will-less state, to utter "myself" even as he knows that this is as yet an abstraction that cannot be predicated.

With these pivotal lines Whitman ends the first phase of his descent. To be "confused, a past-reading, another, but with darkness yet" is to reach a final stage in the dismantling of his most familiar persona, with the hero of consensus commissioned to bind and reconstitute our divergent readings now ceding to his starker antitype in the form of "a past-reading"—the self as a blank screen which mutely receives history's manifold tragedies. "I cannot aid with my wringing fingers," he explains in the aftermath of still more drownings, in this case from a shipwreck, "I can but rush to the surf and let it drench me and freeze upon me" (*CRE*, p. 429). As the futile heroism of the battered swimmer passes into these futile gestures of assistance, the stance of entranced passivity evoked previously begins to develop into a central theme with the next three sections (four, five, and six). From the "wringing fingers" of the spectator on shore in section four to Washington's witnessing of the slaughter of his troops, the abrupt departure of "the red squaw" from the homestead of the poet's mother, and the impotent wrath of Lucifer's "sorrowful terrible heir," each vignette isolates figures utterly helpless to avert the loss and abandonment they are called upon to behold. With this continued emphasis on the devastation of betrayal, Whitman at last approaches a "bridge between" private and public discord, though it is important to note directly how this expanded frame of reference is accompanied by a further contraction of identity. Throughout this dream sequence his function as "a past-reading" dictates his complete effacement from the scene, as if the very attempt to broaden the significance of his materials demanded an increased distancing of the "I." The closer Whitman moves toward a vision of social violence and disintegration the more apparent becomes his resolve to remain a medium for this conflict, not its mediator.

The withdrawal of a mediating center of consciousness has of course been the true subject of this poem all along, yet it is only when Whitman is able to relate the disorientation resulting from this withdrawal to the crisis of Union at large that his poem can begin to realize the full measure of its implications. To the extent that these "past-readings" portray the dissolution of a community or the shattering of familial bonds, their admonitory import is self-evident. In the first of these Washington stands less as a model of stoic fortitude for the post-Revolutionary generation to emulate than an exemplary mourner who "cannot repress the weeping drops" as "the slaughter of the southern braves [is] confided to him by their parents" (*CRE*, p. 429). A world where parents and leaders helplessly congregate to behold the butchery of their children foreshadows the world of *Drum-Taps* some ten years later, where Washington in fact makes another appearance in much the same manner. It is no doubt in this mood of darkened anticipation that "The Sleepers" begins by including among its dimly perceived forms of "ennuyees" and "onanists" the "white features of corpses [and] the gash'd bodies on battle-fields" (*CRE*, p. 424). The classic image of Washington dreading disunion and warning his descendants against the horrors of fratricidal war plainly informs Whitman's lithograph, so much so that its portentous overtones cloud his subsequent evocation of the postwar disbanding of the victorious army ("The same at last and at last when peace is declared"), where tears again are shed at the general's parting.

The next section, the sixth, moves away from the scenes of violent death that have hung over this portion of the poem, although it too has as its central subject the impermanence of social attachment.

Washington's disbanding army oddly dissolves into the still more peculiar visit of "a red squaw" to the "old homestead," where she no sooner wins the lasting affection of Whitman's mother than she departs. In keeping with the experience of dreams, Whitman's impassive narration continues to underscore the seemingly gratuitous, motiveless nature of these betrayals; as with swimmer, shipwreck, or slaughtered troops, no attempt is made to explain or evaluate the significance of this random loss, which is consequently made to appear all the more irreversible and meaningless. He neither glorifies nor condemns his mother's sudden infatuation but fixes intently on her desolation in a manner almost as clipped and laconic as the story itself. Highlighting his mother's inconsolable response to the desertion of the Indian woman, he notes that "all the week she thought of her, she watch'd for her many a month, / She remember'd her many a winter and many a summer," but the beloved visitor "never came nor was heard of there again" (*CRE*, p. 430). To this image of fruitless expectancy Whitman appends another portrait in the same section ostensibly intended to elaborate further on the theme of abandonment; yet it is one which considerably alters the direction and continuity of the poem by now including the "I" as an active agent who suddenly assumes the voice of a slave crying out for vengeance against a white master:

> Now Lucifer was not dead . . . or if he was I am his
>   sorrowful terrible heir;
> I have been wronged . . . I am oppressed . . . I hate
>   him that oppresses me,
> I will either destroy him, or he shall release me.
>
> Damn him! how he does defile me,
> How he informs against my brother and sister and takes
>   pay for their blood,
> How he laughs when I look down the bend after the
>   steamboat that carries away my woman.
>
> Now the vast dusk bulk that is the whale's bulk . . .
>   it seems mine,
> Warily, sportsman! though I lie so sleepy and
>   sluggish, my tap is death.[5]

Years later, after he had witnessed his nation barely survive a civil war, Whitman was moved to strike out this astonishing outburst, a deletion approved by most commentators on the grounds that the fierceness of tone swerves too violently from the larger design of the poem. That line of reasoning is not implausible, yet one imagines that the very power of this monologue to violate aesthetic propriety is significant in its own right, for in yoking together the impotence of grief and a destructive vengefulness that have so far traveled down parallel but entirely disparate paths, the slave not only promises to fuse both these emotional strands but, in doing so, threatens to shatter the fragile equilibrium of the poem as a whole. The archetypal rebel, Lucifer's "heir" most obviously embodies another portent of disunion in his bitter vow either to destroy or be released; and his insurrectionary fervor, a common enough topic of anxiety in 1855, takes on added force in view of the tacit contrast between two kinds of aspirations for freedom that Whitman has set before us, one involving a pious commemoration of Revolutionary sacrifice one section earlier, the other concerning the enraged defiance of the slave. In the previous sketch, Whitman had profiled a benevolent father figure who parts from his family with a display of comradely affection; in the present, he impersonates a son who, sundered from his family, pledges revenge against his oppressor. The effect is to make vivid, if only momentarily, the irremediable antagonism between national myth and contemporary strife, as though the present were not simply disconnected from that mythological time but had turned accusingly against it in order to reveal its central flaw in the crime of slavery.

When placed against comparable renditions of this subject by Longfellow, Whittier, or Stowe, Whitman's portrait remains unparalleled in its jarring intensity. Its only contemporary rival is to be found in the portrayal of Babo in *Benito Cereno*, also published in 1855 and similarly concerned to intimate the explosive alliance between oppression and revenge. And yet, much in the same way that Melville's arch narrator is, strictly speaking, no more to be identified with Babo's demonic stratagem than with Delano's obtuse credulity but is careful to a fault in holding himself aloof from both figures, so Whitman reveals a similar diffidence in his presentation. While his subsequent retraction of this episode from *Leaves of Grass* probably stems from the aesthetic and political conservatism of advancing years, one cannot fail to note that the passage, even as it stands in the original text, is easily overlooked among the other visions. So far from emphasizing its explosive force, the form of "The Sleepers" tends to camouflage Lucifer's wrath: because it directly succeeds the cryptic story of the Indian woman, his portrait is made to appear as a mere sequel to the prior vignette—another parable of shattered ties whose more compelling repercussions are virtually lost in the grief-stricken maze of "The Sleepers." Such gestures of containment are worth stressing if only because we do in fact know that Whitman originally conceived this monologue to be something more than an afterthought, for at least two journal entries antedating the appearance of the first edition of his *Leaves* contain preliminary sketches of this aggrieved figure, one beginning with the crude but memorable revelation that

> I am curse: a negro thinks me;
> You cannot speak for yourself, negro;
> I lend him my own tongue;
> I dart like a snake from your mouth.[6]

Such ventriloquism most immediately reminds us of the bravura voice in "Song of Myself" who proclaims "It is you talking just as much as myself, I act as the tongue of you, / Tied in your mouth in mine it begins to be loosen'd" (*CRE*, p. 85). Yet just as we had occasion to note that the authority for that voice is in some measure dependent on the silencing of our own, so it becomes evident that Whitman's surge of sympathetic identification is here predicated on a recognition of the slave's quintessential helplessness. His convulsive rage offset by impotent grief, the slave perfectly crystallizes the clash of interests discernible in Whitman's simultaneous effort to expose the collapse of personal and social coherence at the same time he diffuses these apprehensions by muffling them in the scattered hallucinations of the night. If the opening sections of the poem had depicted the viscissitudes of a speaker who alternately fears being consumed by the presence of others or hopelessly estranged from them, these later sections deepen this complexity by calling attention to the mixed motives of a speaker who undertakes "at curious removes and indirections" to intimate the collapse of the social order without becoming engulfed by it. In this respect, the paralysis of the dream state provides "The Sleepers" with its own "shield of a greeting": it is the enabling medium for the poet's cautious exploration of the historical dimensions of his journey and it is the necessary screen that precludes a more sustained examination of those dimensions.

Whitman cannot allow his vision to end on so irresolute a note, and the protracted coda of the last two sections accordingly regathers his dispersed audience as dawn appears on the horizon, "an amour of the light and air." Suddenly and rather inexplicably raised to an omniscient height that the poem has so far refused him, the speaker witnesses the homecoming of his sleepers and affirms that all is well. Every wound is healed, every ill cured. "The beautiful lost swimmer . . . the red squaw . . . he that is wrong'd," all these and more— "every one between this and them in the dark"—they are all "averaged now—one is no better than the other" (*CRE*, p. 431). Having guided his nation through the enervating ordeal of disconnection and death, Whitman is now prepared, with ritualistic propriety, to preside over a new dispensation, announcing that "everything in the dim light is beautiful, / The wildest and bloodiest is over and all is peace." Needless to say, these proclamations of cosmic harmony do little more than bring the drama full circle, and as we overhear Whitman murmuring "the soul is always beautiful, / The universe is duly in order, every thing is in its place . . . the diverse shall be no less diverse, but they shall flow and unite—they unite now" (*CRE*, p. 432), we may suspect that he has emerged from the world of dreams only to relapse into deeper fantasies. Yet however forced these assurances may be, their insistence nevertheless derives from an urgency that is all the more poignant for being unintended. Curiously, the closer the poem draws toward a vision of restored union, the more tendentious and artificial its structure becomes; as the sleepers "flow hand in hand over the whole earth from east to west" in the final section, the rhetoric begins to take on an increasingly schematic appearance. The Asiatic is paired with the African, European with American, learned with unlearned, male with female, father with son, mother with daughter— chiastic constructions abound as scholar responds to teacher and teacher answers scholar; the slave master, the master slave; insane sane; sound unsound. Such elaborate counterpointing, meant to seem magisterial while it in fact sounds only contrived, bears witness to a demand for order sufficiently anxious for us to surmise that these serene pairings remain haunted by the violent discord they are meant to lay to rest. As we have seen elsewhere, it is not enough that the conditions for consent be inferred; they must be stated and confirmed: the poet who gathers his exiles and fugitives and swears "they are averaged now—one is no better than the other, / The night and sleep have liken'd and restored them" (*CRE*, p. 431) suggests his essential kinship with the "president of regulation" in the 1855 Preface whose impossible calls for an absolute equivalence of relations ("come to us on equal terms, only then can you understand us") concede in their extremity the absolute evanescence of that union. The labored, overdeveloped symmetry of father and son, learned and unlearned, master and slave likewise attest to the same burden, where the quest to consolidate the bonds of community is overtaken by the pressing imperative to literalize them, to stipulate rather than simply intuit an achieved solidarity.

The weakness of this concluding catalog is not entirely uncharacteristic of other moments of weakness in *Leaves of Grass*, which are almost always the result of a rigid formalism and not chaotic abandon. With the closing apostrophe to the night, however, the focus comes back to the poet himself, who makes explicit in the form of a question the fear that has been implicit throughout:

> I too pass from the night,
> I stay a while away O night, but I return to you again
>   and love you.
>
> Why should I be afraid to trust myself to you?
> I am not afraid, I have been well brought forward by
>   you,
> I love the rich running day, but I do not desert her
>   in whom I lay so long,
> I know not how I came of you and I know not where I go
>   with you, but I know I came well and shall go well.
>
> I will stop only a time with the night, and rise
>   betimes,
> I will duly pass the day O my mother, and duly return
>   to you.

As the legalistic emphasis on "duly" suggests, the longing for a covenant binding "I" and "you" also returns, though in a manner that does not anticipate an ecstatic merging of writer and reader but imagines a precarious venture predicated on "trust." After so many lines chronicling severed relations and thwarted allegiances, the pledge not to "desert her in whom I lay so long" is altogether fitting, even if this is promptly weighed against an unseen past and an equally unforeseeable future. As if it too were another momentary attachment no longer sufficient to his needs, Whitman leaves behind his nighttime aesthetic of the "beautiful" and its orderly and unreal flow of linked opposites; instead, the last two lines subtly call to mind the solicitude of someone concerned to placate two contrary states of mind as he passes from the disintegrative anarchy of the night to the pastoral negligence of "the rich running day." One's parting impression is of a temporary interlude or moment of appeasement that is destined to be short-lived.

"The Sleepers" may be counted as something of an anomaly among Whitman's major texts in that it stands virtually alone in confronting with any degree of explicitness the incipient collapse of his sacrosanct "National Identity." That even this explicitness is severely muted by the deflections and distortions of the dream state bespeaks the essential ambivalence of a project devised both to intimate and contain this feared collapse but which can be said to accomplish neither of these objectives satisfactorily, left suspended as it is between each of these imperatives. Far from integrating the impotent and uncomprehending beholder who haunts the body of the text with the magisterial figure who supervises the homecoming and restoration of his sleepers at its conclusion, the poem's baffled development tends to make the discrepancy between these roles especially visible. Yet what we might ordinarily consider an aesthetic flaw also defines the central burden of Whitman's sleep chasings, a burden made all the more vivid through the tentative elaboration of isolated scenes and characters which are brought into explosive yet blurred relation and whose significance is held at a point of implied but veiled conflict, as in the case of Washington's pious grief and Lucifer's undying wrath. What sets "The Sleepers" apart from the arcane allegory of stillborn desires and narcissistic obsessions it is usually taken to represent lies in just these expressive contortions of form which search restlessly for some common denominator or principle of "averaging" (night, sleep, death, grief) to liken and restore a splintered community. By no means a piece of trenchant sociological analysis, the poem and its mosaic of tenuously attached episodes nevertheless remains compelling in its effort to yoke the crisis of Union together with the crisis of mediation, each brought together and condensed upon the narrative voice or "past-reading" who does not appear to have composed this text so much as set himself the enervating task of collecting and reconciling its disparate and discordant energies.

In order to affix standards of taste to the full range of aesthetic experience, some determining ground of judgment or basis of agreement must first be present. If estimates of the "beautiful" are to retain their integrity and transcend the vagaries of subjective response, they necessarily involve an appeal to certain "universal laws" whose validity applies to one and all. Such is the line of inquiry pursued by Kant in his *Critique of Judgement*. Familiar though his argument is in its concern to divorce appreciation of the beautiful from any taint of local interests, it is instructive to note that Kant is at the same time careful to insist that any claim to universality in aesthetic judgments is "an idea *only*," for such a judgment "does not *postulate* the agreement of every one. . . . it only *imputes* this agreement to every one, not from concepts, but from the concurrence of others."[7] In effect, what Kant terms "the universal voice" necessary for aesthetic evaluation is to be counted as a working *assumption* and nothing more, this owing to the simple fact that there can be "no rule according to which anyone is compelled to recognize anything as beautiful." The process of reaching agreement on the beautiful can only be provisional, never prescriptive. In fact, to the extent that "proofs are of no avail whatever for determining the judgment of taste," unanimity on these matters is utterly insusceptible to empirical demonstration even if it is being continually assumed. Always in the background but forever beyond the reach of scrutiny, the achievement of consensus is to be taken on faith.[8]

And this Whitman cannot do. Not a premise to rest upon but an arduous struggle to act out, the process of securing consent throughout his "hymns of you," as indeed throughout *Leaves of Grass*, repeatedly suggests that whatever is shareable in human experience has become attenuated to so extreme a degree that what is required can no longer be the mere *assumption* of a "universal voice" but its lasting, unarguable confirmation. Even when he is moved to embrace his own version of "the beautiful," as in the coda to "The Sleepers," this glorification of the aesthetic coexists uncomfortably beside proclamations of peace and communion whose formulaic insistence implicitly calls into question, as we have seen, the sufficiency of art's power of reconciliation. The point to be stressed here is not that the author of *Leaves of Grass* boldly departs from the more conventional definitions of art to be found in thinkers like Mill or Kant, for the common understanding of art as providing a timeless *locus communis* exempt from the competition of local interests and rising above the clash of ideologies exemplifies, after all, precisely the ambition that the figure of the Answerer purports to incarnate and totalize. It is instead the extremity to which these received opinions are taken that accounts for the singularity of *Leaves of Grass*, where the virtues of

what Kant calls art's "universal standpoint" and what Whitman elsewhere venerates as "one primary, broad, universal, common platform" are the more urgently coveted in this verse the more they are
suspected to have lost their power of persuasion. And perhaps it is this
urgency, more than any topical prophecies forecasting the fate of the
house divided, that best allows us to gauge the dimensions of the
historical crisis which *Leaves of Grass* so guardedly strives to deflect and
diffuse. The self-frustrating, self-interfering imperative both to intimate a tacit compact of living fraternity *and* to verify this union
beyond all doubt, of seeking to prove what must remain unprovable,
will continue to deepen in intensity before it relents, as I now hope to
show in turning to Whitman's longest and most ambitious poem, also
published, along with "The Sleepers," in 1855.

PART 2

"ORGANIC COMPACTS"
The Conception of
"Free Growth"

*I*n the early 1840s—during the period when Emerson brought out his *Second Series* of *Essays,* when Poe was composing some of his most enduring short stories, when Hawthorne, recovering from Brook Farm, issued the second edition of *Twice Told Tales,* and when Melville set out for the South Seas—an obscure Brooklyn printer was busily versifying sermons on the folly of Pride and Fame. "Ambition," to take one typically awful example, recounts the predicament of an melancholy youth who dreamily ponders "the chances of his future life." Fired by the "burning and glowing coal Ambition," he wonders "shall I, in time to come, be great and famed?" A reply is promptly heard from a "wild and mystical phantom," who proceeds to berate the dreamer's "weak and childish soul" for daring to presume that "thou shalt build a name / And come to have nations know / What conscious might dwells in thy brain." Importantly, the specter is willing to concede that "some will win the envied goal," but asks tauntingly "who shall ever fix upon thee their reverent glance?" Crushed and "sick at heart," the devastated youth is left in silence to overlook the ruins of his "lofty aspirations [and] visions fair."[1]

The parable is at best an improbable prelude to the career of a poet who would some ten years later be "jetting the stuff of far more arrogant republics." How the wretched youth of "Ambition" became the genius of *Leaves of Grass* is of course one of the enduring mysteries of the American Renaissance. While one of Whitman's first admirers saluted him "at the beginning of a great career," he would also remark that "it must have had a long foreground somewhere for such a start."[2] Sharing Emerson's bafflement, scholars have ventured a number of scenarios to fill out that foreground: a passionate love affair in New Orleans, a mystical seizure, the impact of Carlyle, Emerson, or George Sand.[3] But the hypotheses are at best speculative and nothing can be satisfactorily documented. As if to tantalize future researchers, Whitman would in later years decree that "it were useless to read [*Leaves of Grass*] without carefully tallying that prepatory background," though his "crude and boyish pieces"—as he called them—rudely call that background into question. Rather than looking ahead to a poet or poetry to come, "Ambition" points forward to nothing at all; rather than setting out on the open road the bard finds himself stalled in a dead end, caught between the Transcendentalist's yearning for "grandeur, love, and power" and the self-accusatory derision such yearnings foster. Surveying the cryptic remains of Whitman's "go-befores and embyrons," one biographer asks in resignation "why go before 1855 to explain the birth of *Leaves of Grass?* The attempt is doomed to failure."[4]

Yet however much the conditions leading to Whitman's self-proclaimed emergence as "the begetter of a new offspring out of literature" remain obscure, the reason for our continued interest in them does not. To isolate and analyze the genesis of a poetic career answers the familiar desire to extrapolate a governing narrative for that career, with its salient "turning points," moments of crisis, and careful distribution of beginning, middle, and end. Could we grasp that catalytic event responsible for transforming "Mr. Walter Whitman Jr., journeyman printer" into "Walt Whitman, one of the roughs, a kosmos," we could take possession of the story of a life and, in doing so, confer upon it a measure of legitimacy. "Greatness is the other word for development," writes Whitman in an early journal entry; animated by the conviction that "something long preparing and formless is arrived and formed in you," he remarks elsewhere that "it is not to diffuse you that you were born . . . it is to identify you" (*CRE,* p. 438). Still, one need not read far into *Leaves of Grass* before discerning that its author is no less perplexed or obsessed than his commentators over the ambiguous "birth" of his texts. While D. H. Lawrence hailed Whitman as "our great post-mortem poet . . . the poet of the soul's last shout and shriek, on the confines of death,"[5] it is difficult to think of a poet more visibly absorbed in and distressed by the enigma of his poetry's provenance and growth. Thus in "Scented Herbage of My Breast" the author struggles to articulate the poem he knows to be within him but which, unaccountably, will not "sprout." He begins by expostulating his "tomb-leaves, body leaves, growing up above me, above death," beseeching them to "tell in your own way the heart that is under you." But his appeals are fruitless—his "taller, sweeter leaves" remain obstinately silent—and the poet, now "stifled and choked," can do nothing but renounce that scented herbage: "emblematic and capricious blades I leave you, now you serve me not, / I will say what I have to say by itself." Thrown back on his own utterances, Whitman proceeds in a grander, more prophetic mode, now raising "immortal reverberations through the States" and offering himself "as an example to take permanent shape and will through the States" (*CRE*, p. 113–15).

"Scented Herbage" is a popular piece for the anthologies and most readers, following Lawrence, will recall the closing apostrophe to death, whose "real reality . . . perhaps will dissipate this entire show of appearance." And yet the negative identification between the willful muteness of the leaves and the poet's "stifled and choked" utterance is too striking to be incidental. What begins as an implementing metaphor to evoke an unlabored reciprocity between the leaves of the earth and the leaves of Whitman's text—"scented herbage from my breast, / Leaves from you I glean, I write"—soon breaks down. By a curious reversal, the very metaphor introduced to objectify the poem's genesis comes to *thwart* that ambition, and if Whitman's "capricious blades" are "emblematic," it would appear to be in their failure—or perhaps refusal—to dramatize this evolution.[6] As the imperatives midway through the lyric mount in exasperation ("Grow up taller, sweeter leaves"; "Spring away"; "Do not fold yourselves"), it is plain that the concept of growth cannot be considered simply a premise to build on but a vexing question that forcibly obtrudes upon and threatens to paralyze the poem's concerns. In the concluding lines Whitman of course sweeps beyond this deadlock by adopting the guise of prophet who raises "immortal reverberations," but only at the expense of formally renouncing what had been the poem's initial impetus—soliciting the growth of voice out of the "faint tinged" roots of his creation. The developmental impasse afflicting the stricken youth of "Ambition" has not been entirely left behind.

Our previous discussion of Whitman's "hymns of you" had emphasized the poet's quest to reconstitute the social discourse of his world, to bring to pass a colloquy of speaker and listener sufficient to triumph over the divisions of time and place. As apostrophe turns inward, now making its author an anxious interrogator of his leaves, such concerns persist, only now with the identity of "you" shifting from the reader to speech itself. In each case what is being sought by the summoning voice of the poet is a responsive voice in kind which would complete and make legitimate a desired circuit of exchange. To this extent, a parallel may be observed between the dream of spontaneous assent that impels Whitman's overtures to "you, whoever you are" and the dream of spontaneous growth that motivates his appeals to these "taller, sweeter leaves." But in each case too we have ample reason to suspect that such ideals are precarious in the extreme, for just as Whitman's second-person poetry may often reveal a decisive standoff so we find a similar impasse between the poet and his "emblematic and capricious blades" that no longer serve. Doubtless a more local reading of "Scented Herbage" would need to take other factors contributing to this stalemate into account, especially in view of its conflation of "the faint-tinged roots" of sexuality with death, a coupling that is very nearly a matter of course in *Leaves of Grass*. Yet so far as it may be taken as a paradigmatic case, the peculiar deadlock between speaker and his speech illustrates larger quandaries besetting this "begetter of a new offspring out of literature." Foremost among these involves an unmistakable split in attitude between the urge to justify the conditions of the poem's development and the sudden decision to retract this effort as Whitman ascends, without transition, to the platform of democratic bard "promulging" his immortal reverberations. No less strangely than that ubiquitous reader whose presence cannot be taken for granted but must be called forth, here growth cannot be silently presumed but must be actively witnessed—in this case confirmed and corroborated by sight ("Grow up there taller, sweeter leaves that I may see you"). Perversely enough, however, the more frantic the demand for some outward criterion capable of verifying development, the keener the frustration: evidently, the poem cannot decide whether it wants to put the sanction for its utterance before or behind it, whether, that is to say, the terms for validating the emergence of its representative hero are to be fleshed out in the course of composition or whether this issue need not be taken up at all. As the poem brings these questions to the surface without resolving them, we can reflect back upon Kant's notion that universality is unprovable even as it is always being assumed and the unease we have seen Whitman elsewhere exhibit over this truism.

How Whitman is drawn to call upon metaphors of growth to validate development, how he is moved to call off these overtures altogether, will be the point of departure for the discussions offered over the next three chapters. In them, my primary object of concern will be with that rambling monologue Whitman belatedly entitled "Song of Myself," though I shall also be ranging throughout the *Leaves* for pertinent parallels. "Rambling monologue" may seem a rather cavalier expression when measured against the considerable efforts of past commentators to extrapolate an overriding structure or, more modestly, some sort of developmental pattern, for Whitman's "barbaric yawp."[7] Yet over the length of time these attempts have proven to be no more persuasive (and no less plentiful) than comparable attempts to shed light on the mystery of the poet's "long foreground." There are, it would appear, as many narratives for "Song of Myself" as there are readers. Others have accordingly felt at leisure to waive questions of symmetry altogether; joining Whitman in tramping his "perpetual journey," "as endless as it is beginningless," they most prize a poem that scorns all formal constraints, decenters all centers, and scandalizes all comforts of closure. As I experience Whitman's "proto-epic," neither perspective (formalist or aformalist) has much to recommend it until they are brought together. "Song of Myself," that strange grab bag of lyric miscellany, dramatic monologue, historical closet drama, and epic cataloging, is a text which feels itself to be simultaneously groping after an organic myth of "free growth" even as it is oppressed by it. Just as its eternal vistas have an uncanny way of shrinking into sudden moments of deadlock, fixity, or outright paralysis, so do these moments have a way of repeating themselves that seems terrifyingly interminable to the poet. To speak of the poem's continuity is inevitably to encounter its discontinuities and, as I shall be suggesting, nowhere are those moments of discontinuity more discernible than in those occasions when the poet is brought to visualize the conception of his text—the autochthonous genesis of its "uttering tongues" or "aromatic leaves." That conception invariably marks a double, contradictory movement for Whitman: it promises to furnish incontrovertible "proof" for his leaves (their "undeniable growth") at the same time that it inflicts upon his rhetoric so heightened a sense of demand as to paralyze from the

outset the possibility for growth's emergence. "Chasing one
abortive conceit after another," scoffs *Democratic Vistas,* taking aim
at the decadence of foreign literary imports flooding the New
World. Yet something of the same can be said of a poem, lunging
forward by fits and starts, which compulsively circles back only to
draw away from the scene of its conception.

   In later years Whitman was fond of reminding his readers that
the leading impetus for *Leaves of Grass* was to exhibit "my own
physical, emotional, moral, intellectual, and aesthetic
Personality . . . and to exploit that Personality, identified with
place and date, in a far more candid and comprehensive sense than
any hitherto poem or book" (*PW* 2:714). But Whitman perceived
as well that any record of this "Personality" could only be as
successful as the discourse which articulated it. Not merely a
revision in the content of speech but a suitably revised style of
speaking was needed, for without realization of the latter
requirement the former would count for very little. Any treatment
of the better President cannot, accordingly, be complete without an
inquiry into the lineaments of his better discourse, one which alone
can tally and fuse a "series of peoples and States into the compact
organism of one nation." Through close attention to the form and
structure of "Song of Myself," I intend to outline not only the
salient objectives of that discourse but, as I have hinted, its equally
salient obstacles. In this special sense I shall be taking the song and
not simply the self as the central protagonist in a poem whose raw
and uncontainable exuberance thwarted the author's best efforts to
hit upon a satisfactory title for more than twenty years after it was
first composed. What I am particularly concerned to discover is
how Whitman's sense of the genesis and development of his leaves,
issues which periodically erupt as explicit topics of anxiety
throughout this poem, raises questions about the value and
legitimacy of poetry's "organic compacts." What authorizes these
songs? What is at stake in their investment in the ideal of "free
growth?" What defines and regulates the conditions for their
validation and perpetuation? These are as much Whitman's
questions as my own, and by way of providing a general overview
of their centrality for him I begin by considering his stance toward
language and what he hoped to bring to his "new American
expression."

4

Embryos and Skeletons

WHITMAN'S REFLECTIONS on the subject of language form an extended meditation sustained through the better part of his literary career. Thanks to the scholarly sleuthing of C. Carroll Hollis and others, we know that Whitman in all likelihood collaborated with William Swinton on the popular *Ramble Among Words* (1859), a pseudojournalistic tract combining linguistic analyses with prophetic outcries.[1] He also harbored vague designs for a new American dictionary and collected a number of notebooks on words, one of which was published posthumously by Traubel under the title *An American Primer*. These notebooks are scattered with references to grammarians, philologists, and lexicographers, including such familiar names as Webster, Horne Tooke, and Jacob Grimm as well as lesser known figures such as Christian Bunsen, Lindley Murray, Charles Murray Nairne, and Maximillian de Vere. Ascertaining the true scope of his learning is rather difficult, however. His reading seems more desultory than systematic and for the most part conveys the impression of a novice eager to catch up on the current scholarship without forsaking certain entrenched prejudices. As one would expect, Whitman finds in his research a good deal of murdering to dissect. "Drawing language into line by rigid grammatical rules," reads the first entry in his notebook on *Words*, "is the theory of the martinet applied to the most etherial [sic] processes of the spirit. . . . developments should be most encouraged, namely, in being *elliptical* and *idiomatic*" (*DB* 3:666–67). Typical in such assertions is the belief that language affords too "luxuriant" a "growth" to be tethered to a closed network of signs. It is an evolving organism or "living structure" where "words are not built in, but stand loose, and ready to go this way or that" (*DB* 3:723, 810). As a creature of his age Whitman would of course take a condescending view of mechanistic philosophies of composition and prefer to follow Emerson in extolling a metamorphic discourse of natural forms. Supplementing the Romantic animism that allowed Emerson to view Nature as a "vast trope," Whitman celebrates "the unspoken meanings of the earth" which "print cannot touch." And yet, such commonplaces notwithstanding, Whitman can hardly be considered a linguistic primitivist. His organicism did not seduce him, as it did Emerson and Thoreau on certain occasions, into a fruitless quest for the ultimate origin of expression. He startles us, in fact, with the blunt proclamation that *"Language cannot be Traced to First Origins.—*Of the first origins of language it is vain to treat, any more than of the origin of men and women, or of matter or of spirit. . . . Language makes chronology petty; it ante-dates all, and brings the farthest history close to the tips of our ears. No art, no power, no grammar, no combination of process can originate a language; it grows purely of itself, and incarnates everything."[2] It falls to the task of the poet to become a trans-lator or "joiner of tongues" who assimilates various linguistic inheritances (native slang, imported idioms, neologisms) and who grafts these onto his songs.

The closest Whitman comes to venturing an "impulse-source" for rhetoric is accordingly to be found with reference to another rhetoric. In "Slang in America" (published in 1885 but written well before this date), Whitman recommends slang as "a lawless germinal element" that thrives on "indirection," which he defines as "an attempt of common humanity to escape bald literalism and express itself illimitably, which in highest walks produces poets and poems, and doubtless in pre-historic times gave the start to, and perfected, the whole immense tangle of mythologies" (*PW* 2:572–73). Though it is said to "exist below all words and sentences, and behind all poetry," slang itself provides no bedrock to expression but characterizes language in "its ceaseless evolutions, its fossils, its numberless submerged layers and strata, the infinite go-before of the present" (*PW* 2:573, 577). The geological conceit, like the botanical figures he elsewhere draws upon, is no doubt felicitous for Whitman's purpose inasmuch as it allows him to get beyond the Lockean bias of regarding tropes as the mere dress or garb of thought. Because he deprecates a model of representation that demands an atomistic correspondence between word and thing ("bald literalism"), he is more apt to welcome rather than lament language's protean, promiscuous energy. (Compare "words . . . stand loose, ready to go this way or that" with Eliot's fastidious distress that "words . . . slip, slide, perish, / Decay with imprecision, will not stay in place, / Will not stay still.") Nostalgia for a potentially definitive or transparent relation to expression does not exert much sway in an essay like "Slang in America." Rather, coinages like "tap-root," "genesis-motive," "impulse-source," or "branch-idea"—strewn as they are throughout Whitman's prose—testify to a fascination with the transitive, engendering force in language itself, its "wholesome fermentation . . . of processes eternally active." In declining to hypothesize a first origin for speech, Whitman implies that language, insofar as it is self-sustaining, takes as its source nothing less than the dynamic of generation itself. "Grow[ing] purely of itself," language exemplifies its own principle of proliferation; a "mighty potentate," it is "indeed a sort of universal absorber, combiner, and conqueror" (*PW* 2:572).

There are, to be sure, occasions when speech may appear too aggrandizing a conqueror, when the "mighty potentate" may usurp the authority of the speaking "I." Whitman's lifelong campaign against what he once tagged "the *beauty disease*"—of a piece with his knee-jerk attacks on the verbal hedonism of Keats, Longfellow, Tennyson, and other "creamskimmers"—shows the Quaker plain stylist recoiling at an unseemly infatuation with the siren songs of mere rhetoric. Late in his life he also made the (rather disingenuous) confession that he has "not bothered much about style, form, etc.," asking instead nothing from his words "but negative advantages—they should never impede me, and never under any circumstances, or for their own purposes, assume any mastery over me" (*PW* 2:656). But such reservations are, as the title from which these remarks are taken tells us, "An Old Man's Rejoinder." When the author of "Song of the Open Road" exclaims in a parenthetical aside that "I and mine do not convince by similes, rhymes, or arguments, / We convince by our presence" (*CRE*, p. 155), he makes of himself a figure of voice impatient to overleap the constraints of representation altogether, just as the voice of "So Long" "spring[s] from these pages into your arms." Yet for a poet who so passionately believes that "greatness is the other word for development," such calls to presence are bound to seem especially melodramatic or unearned. Although Whitman could declare, sententiously enough, that "I myself make the only growth by which I can be appreciated" (*CRE*, p. 340), it is far more common for him to aver that the only possible validation for development is that which develops itself. Celebrating a discourse that "grows purely of itself" may be taken as Whitman's variant on the Keatsian imperative that the "creative must create itself." What counts for growth in such cases is of course its severance from the intentional designs of the author. In the process of decrying the "gaggery and gilt" of shopworn poeticisms, Whitman comments in the 1855 Preface that "the profit of rhyme is that it drops seeds of a sweeter and more luxuriant rhyme, and of uniformity that it conveys itself into its own roots in the ground out of sight. The rhyme and uniformity of perfect poems show the free growth of metrical laws and bud from them as unerringly and as loosely as lilacs or roses on a bush . . . and shed the perfume impalpable to form" (*PW* 2:443). As a number of scholars have remarked, this concise summary also shows the free influence of Samuel Taylor Coleridge. In 1847, Whitman reviewed a collection of Coleridge's literary criticism, where the aspiring poet was likely to have come across such dicta as "the organic form . . . shapes itself as it develops itself from within, and the fullness of its development is one and the same as the perfection of its outward form."[3] In this typically genetic correspondence between form and content, process and product, cause and effect, only the author is anomalous. Pater, setting the stage for future criticism, was distressed by this elision of identity and charged that Coleridge's naturalism was no less deterministic than the mechanical theories of creation it was meant to supplant. "The associative act in art or poetry," he observes disapprovingly, "is made to look like some blindly organic process of assimilation."[4] Much to his notoriety, however, Whitman considers this a process that can never be assimilative enough, and what Pater deplores as aesthetic abdication Whitman takes as a central command in his calling.

> Screaming electric, the atmosphere using,
> At random glancing, each as I notice absorbing,
> Swiftly on, but a little while alighting,
> Curious envelop'd messages delivering,
> Sparkles hot, seed ethereal down in the dirt dropping,
> Myself unknowing, my commission obeying, to question
>   it never daring,
> To ages and ages yet the growth of the seed leaving,
> To troops out of the war arising, they the tasks
>   I have set promulging,
> So I pass, a little time vocal, visible, contrary,
> Afterward a melodious echo, passionately bent for,
>   (death making me really undying,)
> The best of me then when no longer visible.
>   ("So Long," *CRE,* p. 505)

Swept along the current of these cascading participles, one subject evanescing into the next, the poet stands a rapt witness to a scene of conception, more called upon than calling. "The growth of the seed" is experienced as an exultant *leaving*, one which underscores a fantasy of regeneration—"to ages and ages yet"—resulting in an autogenetic dynamic of insemination and dissemination. What remains of "the best of me" is a waning figure of voice or "melodious echo," the shadow of a presence acutest at its vanishing. As the self dies into its songs, bequeathing itself to the lines of these leaves as one "disembodied, triumphant, and dead," it becomes that song's exemplary referent, reawakened ("decease calls me forth") with every act of reading. No transcendent, extratextual ground of authority is advanced in support of the poet's "seed ethereal" other than the knowledge of its perpetual rebegetting, just as for the author of the 1855 Preface "no result exists now without being from its long antecedent result, and that from its antecedent, and so backward without the farthest mentionable spot coming a bit nearer the beginning than any other spot."[5]

This is not to convert Whitman into a visionary precursor of Mallarmé proclaiming the Death of the Word. After all, in the excerpt from "So Long" cited above we are served notice "Camerado, this is no book, / Who touches this touches a man." No sooner does he issue this salute, however, than he disappears back behind the "screen" of his text, much in the same way that he will inter himself in the ground at the end of "Song of Myself" to "grow from the grass I love." To speak accurately of Whitman's stance toward language it is best to speak, as John Irwin suggests, of "an endlessly oscillating grounding"[6] of self and text, with neither claiming absolute priority over the other but forever exchanging places of ascendancy so that Whitman may by turns insist upon a categorical distinction between self and text while in other moments he may imagine each to be consubstantial with the other, as root to plant. Conceptually, this may be nonsense; more loosely understood, it is perfectly consistent with Whitman's characteristic desire to evoke a partnership of equal footing where speech is no more an implacable adversary to be vanquished than a passive instrument to be manipulated at will. Language instead becomes another interlocutor in the author's field of vision, and for this reason it is not as odd as it may initially seem that the 1855 Preface says of the democratic bard that "He swears to his art, I will not be meddlesome." Language too is an other before which oaths may be sworn and pacts ratified—indeed, as we shall see throughout "Song of Myself," it may be accosted, cajoled, exhorted, placated, accused no less vehemently than his "you, whoever you are." So much depends upon the notion that self and text are separate but equal constituencies since so much depends upon establishing a noncoercive dialogue between them, a dialogue whose purpose is to deliver not an array of fixed meanings but a style of "free growth" whose meanings expand "onward and forever outward." By 1855 the great epic of the republic had in a certain sense already been written—"The United States themselves are essentially the greatest poem" (*PW* 2:434); it is left for the "translator" or "joiner of tongues" to reproduce without artificially restructuring "its vast, seething mass of *materials*" (*PW* 2:460).

When we place this outlook of the poet beside that of his younger self, the newspaper editor of the 1840s, an instructive contrast comes into view. Writing in 1847 as a "strict constructionist," that editor gave vent to his indignation over those apologists for the Southern aristocracy who defended the planters and their evil institution by claiming the sanction of constitutional safeguards even though the Fathers "looked longingly" to the day when the practice of slavery would be abolished. "With dextrous but brazen logic," argued Whitman in referring to the South and its statesmen, "they profess to stand on the Constitution against a principle whose very existence dates from some of the most revered framers of that Constitution!"[7] Ingenious sophistries and "idle theories" combined to perpetrate recondite and perversely literal readings of the Fathers' text which were all the more unnerving for carrying a vague air of plausibility. This in any event is Whitman's account, though in hindsight it is apparent that the real dilemma has less to do with irresponsible distortions of the text than with a critical ambiguity built into the Constitution itself, where the word "slavery" is never mentioned. Wrangling over the concept of "perpetual Union," the fine points of state sovereignty, the question of the framers' intent on the subject of slavery, and still more arcane debates were the legacy of this indeterminacy. But as we turn from the "organic compacts" of the state to those of poetry, it is important to note that Whitman does not simply propose a solution to this problem by projecting an antithetical stance. Rather than opposing indeterminacy, his rhetoric undertakes to disarm it of portentous overtones. When Justice Joseph Story complained of "how easily men satisfy themselves that the Constitution is exactly what they wish it to be,"[8] he was thinking of interpretive anarchy;

when applied to *Leaves of Grass* his remark shifts from the status of an apprehension to a fairly succinct description of Whitman's "new American expression": "You shall no longer take things at second or third hand," he promises, "you shall not look through my eyes either, nor take things from me, / You shall listen to all sides and filter them from yourself" (*CRE*, p. 30). The reader's mission is not to ascertain significances in the text but to rewrite, supplement them, for "these are really the thoughts of all men and all ages and lands, they are not original with me, / If they are not yours as much as mine they are nothing, or next to nothing" (*CRE*, p. 45). The proliferation of varying and opposed inferences fatal to the intelligibility of one document indicates what the other thrives upon. What is most wanted by Whitman is not the certainty of meaning but its endless reproduction, as is reflected in his delight in likening linguistic energy to libidinal energy, the deathless renewal and scattering of his "seed ethereal."

Of course, perceiving the rationale for the poet's calling is no guarantee of its acceptance. A generation ago it was not uncommon for commentators to worry that Whitman's self-propagating poetic bordered on mindless anarchy, reveling as it seemed in "a spontaneous dance of self-determining and autonomous symbols," according to Feidelson, which denied "any brake on the transmutation of form." The danger posed by such "blind assimilation" was clear: it threatened to "destroy the concept of fixity and within it the concept of hierarchy" altogether, for "on this showing the poem can establish no scale of value because it is wholly fluid, changing its shape as it moves from point to point."9 But we have not come this far in our reading of Whitman merely to echo misgivings over his literary radicalism, particularly since we have elsewhere seen this mixed with a good deal of literary conservatism. With this reminder, it may be timely to recall that among the most hallowed assumptions of the organicist aesthetic none is so familiar as the notion that the poem does not so much seek to "establish a scale of value" as it lays such questions to rest by internalizing them. Shaping itself as it develops itself from within, each work is simultaneously the informing cause and the final result of an "inner" logic of evolution that incorporates its own "hierarchy" and "scale of value." In a world where the sheer process of creation is held to be indistinguishable from the product of that creation, organicism aims to repel any attempt to justify its dynamic in terms other than its own. Such is evidently the "profit" of "free growth," which is marked by a regressive or re-ductive movement ("conveys itself into its own roots in the ground out of sight") that turns the act of expression back into itself. "Perfect poems" achieve perfection by ceaselessly replenishing their originary source, their "natural laws" thereby generating not only the perpetual renewal of the poet's discourse but the terms of its authentication as well. Or, put somewhat differently, we could say that organicism aspires to collapse the distinction between *legitimacy* (the source of value that renders power authoritative) and *legitimation* (the ongoing task of establishing, upholding, or defending that value).[10] Not only, in effect, collapses this distinction but robs it of intelligibility: for inasmuch as justification is perceived as instrinsic to the poetic enterprise Whitman calls "indirection"—of "one subject endlessly escaping into the other," with no transcendent end in view—there can be no discrepancy between the act of positing value and the establishment of value itself. The process is its own validation. From this premise it is only a short step to the anti-intellectual shibboleth, incipient in all organicist assumptions and especially prominent in Whitman's thinking, that nothing persuades so well as that which exempts itself from the need for persuasion. "Logic and sermons never convince," the author of "Song of Myself" intones, "only what proves itself to every man and woman is so, / Only what nobody denies is so" (*CRE,* p. 58). Similar appeals to the power of self-evidence, as Irwin has most recently shown,[11] abound in *Leaves of Grass,* and what the poet says of the "soul" may apply with equal relevance to the aspirations of his writing as well: "No reasoning, no proof has established it, / Undeniable growth has established it" (*CRE,* p. 227).

The proof of the poet's calling, it would appear, is to eradicate the demand for proof altogether, to presume it, so to speak, out of existence. Organicism, we can surmise, is especially appealing to Whitman to the degree that it affords him a rhetoric of justification that denies its own status as such. If "only what proves itself is so" is indeed so, then it is clear that there can be no question of the poet setting out to defend or uphold his aesthetic since to do so would controvert its most cherished assumption. What distinguishes poetry from other forms of communication is that it does not move *toward* a condition of acknowledged legitimacy but settles the question of legitimacy itself. Just so, "the poet is no arguer . . . he is judgment. He judges not as a judge judges but as the sun falling upon a helpless thing" (*PW* 2:437). For the executive will of the Answerer there can be no provision for *acts* of judgment, since the habit of mind revealed in such examples is to regard proof as a state, not an action; a noun, not a verb; a definitive judgment already rendered rather than a decision-making process.[12] In the course of unveiling his dream of communication Whitman accordingly moves beyond a longing for referential stability to a vision of rhetoric so pure of interest as to be drained of any referential function whatever. I am thinking here of the "possessing words" of the earth which "cannot fail," whose very openness to all forms of experience, its "unfailing sufficiency," does not divide but unites. "The earth does not argue," we read in "Song of the Rolling Earth," "Is not pathetic, has no arrangements, / Does not scream, haste, persuade, threaten, promise, / Makes no discriminations, / Closes nothing, refuses nothing, shuts none out" (*CRE,* p. 221). With speech acts being rarefied into a realm of flawless receptivity, proof is effectively disengaged from all sense of dramtic contest. Instead, we return to the theme of *prevenience* touched on in our account of Whitman's "hymns of you," in which the fusion of speaker and listener is not merely solicited but actively described within the poem itself. "We understand, then, do we not?" murmurs the revenant of "Crossing Brooklyn Ferry," thereby fostering the illusion of a consensus already formed and a validation already secured. "The great laws take and effuse without argument," chants the speaker of "Who Learns My Lesson Complete" in a similar spirit, adding "I am of the same style."

It would be misleading, however, to suggest that Whitman merely assumes the privileges of self-evidence as his own, for there is also a particular structure or what could be called a strategy of displacement instrumental to the workings of that notion, a structure we can start to unfold by turning to a suggestive term used by Kenneth Burke in *A Rhetoric of Motives.* There Burke speaks of the "temporizing of essence," by which he means the habit of narratives to confer value or importance on a given theme or intention by defining these in terms of their origin (how they begin) or in terms of their fruition or fulfillment (how they end).[13] And this Whitman tells us he will not do; "Song of Myself," for example, starts off by thrusting aside "all talk of the beginning and the end," delighting instead in "urge and urge and urge, / Always the procreant urge of the world." But if we cannot speak of the "temporizing of essence" in *Leaves of Grass,* can we speak, retaining Burke's pun, of a "temporizing of proof?" In the circular dynamic of "free growth" we found every progression to be also a regression: each upward growth is also an inward growth, enriching the source even as it expands outward from it. The ideal result is a discourse at once complete in itself and infinitely reproducible, much as, in a broader sense, Whitman retained the same title for a volume which he ceaselessly supplemented and expanded upon for the better part of three decades. What this in turn implies is that the moment of validation for speech is always elsewhere: it recedes into the invisible regress of the past, with "each antecedent result" disclosing another "antecedent result" and still more behind that result, or it is projected forward into the horizonless vistas of the future, as when Whitman summons his "poets to come" to "justify me." Temporally speaking, in other words, the terms of legitimation are conceived as something presupposed ("the acme of things accomplished") or something awaiting future vindication ("the encloser of things to be"). In either case the essential motive remains the same: to expel proof from the present scene of writing, to position it before or beyond the immediate act of composition. With these temporal barriers secure, the text is free to "promulge" its Supreme Fiction that the process is its own validation, that it in effect requires no other principle of justification than abiding in a timeless present or experiential "now" which gains credibility, as John Lynen puts it, "in the event of us experiencing it."[14]

Our survey of Whitman's poetic thus brings us to two central impulses: the emulation of that "lawless germinal element" in language irreducible to the strictures of closure and a corresponding wish to foreclose the strictures of proof. Theoretically, each impulse should be mutually reinforcing; yielding to "afflatus surging and surging," the "outsetting bard" may thereby avail himself of those "elementary laws [that] never apologize" and, in doing so, serve notice that he need not "trouble [his] spirit to vindicate itself or be understood" (*CRE*, pp. 48, 50). Yet to state Whitman's ambition this way is to raise more problems than it resolves, and we should not be surprised to find that the suppression of "vindication"merely guarantees, as the last quotation suggests, a chronic preoccupation with it. In "Scented Herbage of My Breast," moreover, we noted how such preoccupations warp the chances for development itself. No sooner is the command for the poem to objectify its growth issued than voice, staggering under this directive, finds itself "stifled and choked." What results is a poem that is in jeopardy of discovering that it has ended in the moment it seeks to begin. No longer relegated to the margins of the text, proof breaks into the present and disrupts the opportunity for growth by playing, as it were, both ends against the middle. This is of course a prospect Whitman works strenuously to fight off as he goes on to chant "immortal reverberations" that scan an open-ended future. Yet the pattern remains striking: closure, because it is felt to have come too soon, will therefore not come at all. Various critics call to mind a roughly analogous pattern when speaking of "Song of Myself" as "a starting-out and a summing-up," an "embryo and epitome," a "culmination" as well as "epitaph."[15] Although these phrases are intended honorifically, directing our attention to "Song of Myself" as a distillation of themes, motifs, and structures that its author would continue to explore, they also evoke the burdens specific to Whitman's organicism, whose chief nemesis is not a formless metonymy (Pater's blind assimilation) but an extreme form of prolepsis that closes off the prospect for development before it can be elaborated. Thus Whitman, in advocating "the wholesome fermentation . . . of processes eternally active" in speech, says of slang that "*it gave the start to,* and *perfected,* the whole immense tangle of mythologies." As knowledge of first and last gets conflated, the emergence of "undeniable growth" may end at the moment of its inception, often leaving us with "the whole immense tangle" of "stifled and choked" energies that "Song of Myself" will threaten to become in its quest to restore credibility to self-evident truths.

The twenty-fourth section of "Song of Myself" finds the poet at daybreak, beholding "hefts of the moving world at innocent gambols." In one of the most splendidly audacious leaps in the poem, he goes on to envision sun and earth enjoying a kind of celestial orgasm; the sun at dawn putting "upward libidinous prongs" as "seas of bright juice suffuse heaven," while subsequent sunsets consummate the marriage of sun, earth, and sky at "the daily close of their junction." The figure of the sun as a supreme symbol of fertility is an old conceit, perhaps most familiar to Whitman from the Psalmist's metaphor of "the heavens declar[ing] the glory of God . . . in them He hath set a tent for the sun, / As a bridegroom coming out of his chambers." Yet it is a conceit that Whitman curiously refashions as he goes on to note that the sun's "prongs" wield a "heav'd challenge" and "mocking taunt," daring him to "see then whether you shall be master!" Whitman concedes that, "dazzling and tremendous," the "sunrise would kill me / If I could not now and always send sunrise out of me." Rather than elaborating on this boast, he next engages in an extended debate with "Speech," as the easy confidence of the poet "sending out" a fatal sunrise gives way to the frustrations of "letting out" a voice, until Speech itself erupts into the text to deliver its own "mocking taunt" and "heav'd challenge":

> We also ascend dazzling and tremendous as the sun,
> We found our own O my soul in the calm and cool of the
> daybreak.
>
> My voice goes after what my eyes cannot reach,
> With the twirl of my tongue I encompass worlds and
> volumes of worlds.
>
> Speech is the twin of my vision, it is unequal to
> measure itself,
> It provokes me forever, it says sarcastically,
> *Walt you contain enough, whey don't you let it out*
> *then?*
>
> (*CRE*, p. 55)

While one is initially struck by the sort of clownish grandstanding first emphasized by Richard Chase,[16] Whitman's histrionics only partially conceal a confused and rather confusing response to Speech. Though the twirl of the tongue is suggested to have outrun vision, unable to control or regulate itself, despite this expansiveness—or perhaps because of it—something blocks the speaker from expression—he can't "let it out." If articulation scorns all limits it also takes sardonic delight in exposing them. Clearly, Speech is not simply a twin to vision but a worrisome rival as well, and the remainder of the section (twenty-five) traces the poet's efforts to parry his opponent's sarcasms with taunts of his own:

> Come now I will not be tantalized, you conceive too
> much of articulation,
> Do you not know O speech how the buds beneath you are
> folded?
> Waiting in gloom, protected by frost,
> The dirt receding before my prophetical screams,
> I underlying causes to balance them at last,
> My knowledge, my live parts, it keeping tally with the
> meaning of all things,
> Happiness, (which whoever hears me let him or her set
> out in search of this day.)
>
> (*CRE*, p. 55)

Moving from the dazzling splendor of sunrise to the gloomy recesses of the soil, the poet momentarily pictures the imminence of a birth, those folded leaves prepared to sprout from the loam of speech. Impelled by the gathering momentum of the syntax ("waiting . . . receding . . . underlying"), we are drawn to anticipate some impending breakthrough, as if those rude "prophetical screams" were about to ripen into a finer tone. And yet Whitman's burgeoning conception is abruptly aborted; the image, like the soil, dissolves into the hazy abstraction of the last line, whose parenthetical aside trails off into an especially lame non sequitur. While "my knowledge" is paired with "my live parts," it is also notable that Whitman's participles are left dangling, unattached to a body or subject that might complete them. One's passing impression is of an utterance just beginning to emerge from the "gloom" of inarticulate energies and untranslated screams only to be strangely stunted.

Now it is of course precisely the aim of this encounter to outwit the presumed imperialism of Speech by redirecting attention to the eloquence buried beneath. Where Speech would conceive too much of articulation Whitman answers by conceiving too little. Jolted into the awareness that his words have turned on him, he wittily turns words against themselves. Acts of suppression become in turn a matter of declared policy as the poet now refuses "putting from me the best I am." "Writing and talk do not prove me" he flatly declares following his rejoinder to Speech, "I carry the plenum of proof and everything else in my face." Speech and self-presence are regarded to be hopelessly at odds, triggering what Regis Durand, commenting upon this exchange, terms a "sort of panic over the use of language," one whose unrestrained proliferation ("unequal to measure itself") threatens to obstruct bodily immediacy. The feared autonomy of the "mighty potentate" is indeed so oppressive that it goads Whitman into openly disregarding what deconstructive criticism has taught us to regard as a classic double bind: calling upon language to banish language. As the section closes by retreating into the defiance of silent rebuke ("with the hush of my lips I wholly confound the skeptic"), it is nevertheless clear, as Durand further notes, that "Whitman's argument, which is seemingly about speech and the individual voice is in fact already caught up in the logic of trace, repetition, and difference—in short, the logic of writing."[17]

Something, however, rings hollow in this impasse, whose very starkness ought to call its urgency into question. Even if we were to discount the evidence that the poet's sympathies on this matter lay elsewhere, it is rather clear that his "panic over the use of language" hardly surfaces as a repressed, disguised theme but is brought forward with a hectic, eye-catching prominence. The terms of the debate are too sharply if not too tendentiously drawn—so much so that the critic may want to ask whether this frontal assault on the bothersome mediations of "writing and talk" does not serve to mediate another, equally vexing conflict. When Speech first erupts into the text it is not accompanied by anxieties of self-effacement. Rather, it exposes to ridicule the embarrassment of an overcharged plenitude ("you contain enough"), its sarcasms thereby repeating, as we have noticed, the "heav'd challenge" and "mocking taunt" of the sun. What is the significance of this association? What, for that matter, is the significance of the relation between the libidinous discharge of the sun and the text's folded buds? To bring these questions together is in some sense already to answer them, for the more elementary logic linking these images is easily reconstructed: presumably the sun's nightly consummation with the earth would fertilize the poet's buried seed. But the connection does not come off—the histrionic quarrel with Speech intervenes so as to make the coupling of these images merely virtual. Thus while "my knowledge, my live parts" is meant to answer the challenge of the sun's "libidinous prongs," this is apparent only in retrospect. Whitman, in effect, transposes the aggressive rivalry with the sun onto a rivalry with Speech, as though the magnificent yet murderous potency of the sun could not be borne except through displacement. And yet, this displacement notwithstanding, as he goes on to proclaim "writing and talk do not *prove* me," that "I carry the plenum of *proof* and everything else in my face," his protests continue to reflect the degree to which the trials of the word take their impetus from the trial of legitimacy itself. As the section draws to a close, his landscape remains instinct with the "mocking taunt" of a master who derides the labor of a discourse struggling to affirm its difficult conception.[18]

The need to devalue language, to put it in its place, to disclaim all ties to identity, discloses in its exaggerated vehemence the consternation of a wish betrayed: would that Speech would conceive enough, that, in the heroics of its extra-vagance, it consume worlds and volumes of worlds. For like Thoreau, Whitman does not fear but fears *for* the extra-vagance of his expression, his angry denial that Speech cannot "conceive" the self here serving to mask the more primitive uncertainty as to whether it can conceive at all. Mocking Speech, he would also be mocking his own staggering, excessive faith in its powers. We have already touched on the profound ties between the authority of the poet's calling ("my commission obeying") and the reproductive power of the "mighty potentate" of language, declarations like "the known universe has one complete lover and that is the greatest poet" (*PW* 2:441) being only a milder variation on this theme. The demand for the virtues of the "spermatic word" can reach extremes that verge on self-parody, as when the author of "By Blue Ontario's Shore" "plung[es] my seminal muscle" into "ma femme Democracy" and watches "her serenely giving birth to immortal children" as he dreams of "her dilating form" (*CRE*, p. 354). But as in the task of dropping "seeds of more perfect poems" outlined in the definition of "free growth," Whitman's outlandish fantasy of violating Democracy is not without sobering qualifications. Although he announces in "Democratic Vistas," heralding the advent of a new American poetry, that "the throes of birth are upon us," two pages later he concedes that "America has yet morally and artistically originated nothing" (*PW* 2:393, 395). Democracy he finds to be indefinitely suspended in its "embryo condition," at once pregnant with unspoken promise and stranded in the womb—"Ah Mother, prolific and full in all besides, yet how long barren, barren?" Like the slumbering giants of greatness in Emerson's essays, democracy is "a word . . . which still sleeps, quite unawakened, notwithstanding the resonance and many angry tempests out of which its syllables have come, from pen or tongue" (*PW* 2:393). Rather than stipulating a designated meaning, democracy urgently stands in need of one—an urgency betrayed in the wrenched articulation of "prophetical screams" and "angry tempests."

We can hardly consider Whitman's fascination with the "free growth" of "perfect poems" in isolation from the anxiety that his verse, like the Democracy it strives to voice, is at once prolific and barren, at once burgeoning with vision and unable to be "let out." Voice itself is caught up in this frustrated dialectic, being evoked on the one hand as supremely potent, ungovernable force and on the other as a buried, virtual seed hovering at the threshold of articulation. It would be a mistake to construe this double role in terms of a stark, inflexible rivalry, with Speech subverting a more sacrosanct or "privileged" silence or with that silence simply outwitting the tyranny of Speech (for *that* is the interpretation Whitman all too anxiously would impress upon us). Rather, what requires further investigation

is the disabling intersection of these supposedly opposed forces—
where the overidealization of one occasions the balked delivery of the
other which in turn augments still more hyperbolic claims for Speech.
Some such reasoning as this will be helpful in accounting for the
peculiar fact that while *Leaves of Grass* abounds in allusions to beget-
ting, gestation, parturition, and other references to birth, there is
remarkably little consternation over the potential for the illicit, unauthorized, or illegitimate. While "Song of Myself" contains its share of
gothic encounters, no demonic offspring haunt its scenes of conception.[19] In fact, the poet's dread is more likely to fix upon miscarriages
rather than monstrosities, as in those "corpses shrunken and
shrivelled . . . dismal mannikens of abortions, still-births so small the
doctors preserved them in bottles," that he itemizes in an early journal
entry. Suggested here is more than premonitions of blighted promise—the distress of a Lycidas dead ere his prime. As Whitman goes on
in the same journal passage to sketch the fate of "the fullest muscular
health of some fine giant—more inert and blue and fit for the swiftest
burial—more awfully a corpse because a perfect shaped and affection-
ate youth" (*UPP* 2:84), we recognize in the emphasis of his compara-
tives the degree to which divisions between the prolific and the barren, the virile and the sterile, have become alarmingly blurred. Rather
than the nightmare of a self-excluding illegitimacy, Whitman's predicament is better (if somewhat more crudely) described as an impotent
potency. Containing enough, he contains too much and therefore too
little. While the poet knows the importance of conserving "the early
bloom" of his seed "in the ground out of sight," he also knows that
"to be ripe beyond further increase is to prepare to die." "Will you rot
your own fruit in yourself there?" admonishes a voice from "A Song
of the Rolling Earth," "will you squat and stifle?" (*CRE*, p. 220).
Under the duress of such questions even the curse of a monstrous
progeny would conceivably be a blessing.[20]

When Whitman describes *Leaves of Grass* as "a gigantic embryo or
skeleton . . . fit . . . for native models" (*CORR* 1:247), his choice of
metaphors is therefore instructive. If the first calls to mind the image
of a conception too long delayed, bloated to grotesque proportions,
the second evokes its necessary counterpart in the eerie specter of a
corpse. This disturbing commerce between overabundance and
death—an overabundance that *means* death—takes us back directly to
Whitman's proud rejoinder to the sun, whose dazzling rays "would
kill me / Could I not now and always send sun-rise out of me." But as I

have suggested this is precisely what does not happen, leaving the poet impotent before his own figure of potency. Such a distressing condition is not new to our study, for we have seen it used extensively in Whitman's "hymns of you" where the feared power of the beholder is rendered powerless in course of being admonished, with mock concern, not to let the fruit of his own genius rot within himself. But there the paradox of an impotent potency was exploited for satiric purposes, a defensive ploy to keep the Master at bay. The sun incarnates a mastery of a different sort, one which inverts the usual proceeding of apostrophic discourse by assuming the power of invocation over the poet. Scorning all rivals, it demands neither power nor worship but *proof*. "This delusional privilege of being able to gaze at the sun without being dazzled," writes Freud, is traditionally attributed "to the eagle, who as a dweller in the highest regions of the air, was brought into especially intimate relations with the heavens, with the sun, and with the lightning. We learn . . . moreover that the eagle puts his young to a test before recognizing them as his legitimate offspring. Unless they can succeed in looking at the sun without blinking, they are cast out of the eyrie."[21] Such a legend has obvious pertinence to a fledgling republic undergoing its own "test of lineage," and more than one early advocate for a native American literature did not hesitate to make use of its special resonance in the process of asking why "no sons of ether yet have spread their broad wings to the sky, like Jove's own eagle, to gaze undazzled at the sun or to perch at the top of Olympus and partake the banquet of the gods."[22] Why the author of "Song of Myself" would be especially sensitive to such a calling will be the subject of more detailed inquiry in the next chapter. Here it will suffice to point to the fateful complicity between Whitman's prolific barrenness and the foregrounding of the issue of proof itself, in which the outright suppression of the latter only intensifies and perpetuates the vexations of the former. To attempt to close off the question of "my final merit" induces a more drastic sense of foreclosure, leaving in its wake "prophetical screams" rather than a "barbaric yawp."

Section twenty-five, to be sure, has all the trademarks of an oedipal crisis, and the citation from Freud will recall the connection between blinding and castration anxiety, if the sun's "libidinous prongs" have not already done so. We need to know more, however, about why this crisis should be so directly sublimated into the apparent "rivalry" between voice and vision and what impact these dissensions may have on Whitman's rhetoric of consensus. The convergence of excess and deficiency evidently denotes an antagonism between representation and any structure of legitimation that would make the former "presentable." As the question of proof breaks through Whitman's text, we again encounter the same kind of confusion that gripped "Scented Herbage of My Breast": does the "final merit" for the poet's discourse come from within or from without? Is it a value conceived prior to or coterminous with the elaboration of the work? In the absence of a clear response to these questions, Whitman confronts the dawning of a voice that overcompletes and therefore threatens to defeat him. He submits to a trial of strength only then to declare its unimportance, thereby suggesting that if the ordeal of proof is, by virtue of its very persistence, an affront to his poem (for what is in need of proof may also be disproved), it is also something desperately craved.

Whitman will not invoke the sun because he wants to persuade us that he already radiates its power. He apostrophizes Speech instead, hopeful that there he will find a more amenable adversary. So rather than outstaring the sun he ends up, rather absurdly, outstaring his own expression: "I crowd your sleekest and best by simply looking toward you, / With the hush of my lips I wholly confound the skeptic" (*CRE,* p. 55). Yet the burden of proof may be suppressed but not eliminated, and further confirmation for my view of section twenty-five as a failed test may be found in the brutally masochistic gauntlet of the senses staged in sections twenty-six and twenty-eight, which Stephen Black properly identifies as "the most powerful cathartic experience" in the poem.[23] Having renounced voice, the poet's task is now to reclaim it, though not in the spirit of restitution so much as in the spirit of revenge. Reclaiming voice is of course what Whitman begins section twenty-six by saying he will not do: "Now I will do nothing but listen, / To accrue what I hear into this song, to let sounds contribute toward it." The pledge, as it happens, can only be short-lived, and the centrality of utterance reemerges, though with a gruesomely physical twist. Culminating in the spectacle of a "grand Opera," the scene comes to an abrupt halt as orchestra and chorus drive the poet into what seems uncontrolled frenzy:

> A tenor large and fresh as the creation fills me,
> The orbic flex of his mouth is pouring and filling me
> > full.
> I hear the train'd soprano (what work with hers is
> > this?)

The orchestra whirls me wider than Uranus flies,
It wrenches such ardors from me I did not know I
       possess'd them,
It sails me, I dab with bare feet, they are lick'd by the
       indolent waves,
I am cut by bitter and angry hail, I lose my breath,
Steep'd amid honey'd morphine, my windpipe throttled
       in fakes of death,
At length let up again to feel the puzzle of puzzles,
And that we call Being.

                                           (*CRE*, p. 56)

Choking on an excess of its own delights, the rhapsody surges with a redundant energy that does not simply vex the poet's creation but threatens to tear it apart. Though scene and personae have changed, the interaction between voice's superabundance and its subsequent wastage has not. One senses, moreover, that the pattern has become so familiar that the violence inflicted upon the throat is not unconsciously compelled but willfully solicited, as if the last possible chance for voice's presentation lay on the cutting edge of ecstasy. Perversely enough, release can only be obtained by restaging the scene of constriction (Speech's oppressive plenitude) that had necessitated the pressing demand for release in the first place. "Round and round we go," comments the speaker, catching breath, "and ever come back hither." Section twenty-eight pitches this circularity to still more remorseless lengths as we now come upon the poet "quivering to a new identity" via touch. Once again, the "instant conductors all over me" simultaneously consume and are consumed by their stimuli until the poet, raped by the "prurient provokers" of his touch, falls into hysteria—"I talk wildly, I have lost my wits." Once again he aggressively insists on his own passivity, surrendering to a fantasy of dismemberment by becoming a plot of pasture land besieged by a "herd" that "go and graze at the edges of me." Determined to "glow a moment at the extremest verge," his imagination again draws irresistibly toward perilous extremes only to be drawn up by voice's suffocation and a gasping plea for release: "you villain touch! What are you doing? . . . My breath is tight in its throat; / Unclench your floodgates! You are too much for me" (*CRE*, p. 58).

Analysis may well despair at keeping up with this convulsive pace, but then, as these sections make clear, such overreaching is manifestly prescribed by the claustrophic space in which voice finds itself trapped. The call to "unclench your floodgates," the figure of the throttled windpipe, the choked articulation of "my prophetical screams": these gestures, in seeking to break the enervating hold of an impoverishing plenitude, continue to confirm its sway. They form a staggered, self-interrupting narrative that, while too furtive to be called a declared theme, is too pronounced to be dissimulated. So far from constituting an evasion of the crisis of proof, Whitman's ravishment by listening and touch is better described as a furious attempt to internalize its workings. Rather than "sending out" the dawn's "libidinous prongs" the speaker, "strik[ing] what is hardly different from myself," "cut by bitter and angry hail," turns them upon himself with self-lacerating fury. Whitman's capitulation to the "red marauder" of his libido of course represents, in yet more desperately exhibitionistic terms, another such attempt at incorporation, with autoeroticism hoping to answer the sunrise's magnificent potency at the same time it recontains the latter's threat within its own terms as sense wars against sense. Again, what is most at stake for the poet is less a matter of proof's *significance* (what "meaning" it may portend, what retribution it may inflict) than of its *location* (where it is posited, what site, in relation to his text, it inhabits). From the stark assertion that "I carry the plenum of proof and everything else in my face" to our subsequent discovery that the "plenum of proof" may require nothing less than the brutal dismemberment of the poet's presence—now left a ravaged Orpheus before his senses—Whitman's text continues to search out the grounds of its "final merit."

Yet much as these trials of the senses seek retroactively to master, without quite catharting, the trial of proof against which they rage, it is at the same time important to note how these sections gesture toward some sort of accommodation. Against the antagonistic dualism previously discussed in Whitman's split view of utterance—the mighty potentate of Speech ranged against the "ethereal seed" of a more latent discourse—voice is now accorded a negative or purely reactive status. For all the headlong destructiveness that "wrenches such ardors from me I did not know I possess'd them," it is distinctly the image of voice's mutilation that chastens the poet's delirium and restores him to a calmer repose—"at length let up again." Stripped of semantic reference, it signifies nothing so much as a breathing space. And while the speaker's "throttled windpipe" is endowed with a physical immediacy presumably meant to be distinct from the symbolic domain of "writing and talk," it is worth noting that it betrays no nostalgia for a preexistent Logos stirring "beneath" the text, like the notoriously unspecified "timely utterance" which "brings relief" to Wordsworth's "Intimations Ode." A prohibitive limit more than an authorizing source, utterance here seeks to recapture its borderline sense of "utter-most." Establishing a cautionary boundary beyond which ecstasy cannot transgress without annihilating itself, it establishes a claim of possession on the body, bringing it back to the "puzzle" of self-consciousness. This movement to accommodation carries over to the brief coda forming section twenty-nine, where the traumatic hysteria of the foregoing episodes is momentarily allayed by a hopeful recompense:

> Blind loving wrestling touch, sheath'd hooded sharp-
> toothed touch!
> Did it make you ache so, leaving me?
>
> Parting track'd by arriving, perpetual payment of
> perpetual loan,
> Rich showering rain, and recompense richer afterward.
>
> Sprouts take and accumulate, stand by the curb
> prolific and vital,
> Landscapes projected masculine, full-sized and golden.
> (*CRE*, p. 58)

Here at last is the harvest anticipated but averted some four sections earlier in the bard's wrestling with the sun. It is a subdued climax, one which stages no epiphanic breakthrough but drifts unassumingly into a meditation on the problematic commerce of recompense and sacrifice, spending and being spent. Whitman pauses to sort out proof's intricate economy: as "the perpetual loan" involved in the body's fantasies of dismemberment incurs a "perpetual payment" in the nearly fatal expenditure of voice, so does "the recompense richer afterward" offset the treasonous "bribe" of the "fellow senses" who had conspired "to swap off with touch and go and graze at the edges of me."[24] Implicit in these muted parallels is the suggested discovery that "writing and talk" may do more than "witness and assist against" the reckless ventures of the imagination by salvaging such extravagance through their metaphors. Rather than proclaiming a victory for the self over language, Whitman's leaves stay within a vocabulary of metaphoric "indirection"; they quietly extend a chain of linked analogies (seed, bud, sprout, landscape) in the hope of merging with and substantiating that larger corpus, the text of "Song of Myself." In the flourishing of these sun-drenched landscapes, we glimpse the momentary retrieval of Whitman's organicism, with its promise of a rhetoric spontaneously regenerating itself anew, shaping itself from within as it develops from without.

And yet by now it is clear that in order to reclaim this vision the very design of the poem must pass through the ordeal of those convoluted turns and abrupt detours in development that make the dream of "free growth" seem a distant fantasy. One might view this discrepancy as a local failure to accommodate theory to practice, but more is at stake in these sections than a matter of flawed execution. Earlier we touched on Whitman's belief that literary expression is not just one discourse among many competing for authority but functions instead as that cynosure around which all other claims to value fall naturally into place. As he says of the Answerer, "he puts things in their attitudes" (*CRE,* p. 167). He does so not by recommending one truth over against another, since that would merely duplicate the kind of entrenched oppositions (past vs. present, abolitionist vs. slaveholder, many vs. one) he is anxious to dissolve. The special distinction of art, its "final merit," consists in carving out a space of cultural agreement which abolishes the need for confirmation, which succeeds simply by virtue of its success, just as the grass establishes its credibility simply by the fact of its indisputable growth. This privileging of aesthetic value—the value of all values—is of course entirely conventional,[25] but what should be noticed is how once again Whitman's adaptation exaggerates and strains such accepted truths to the breaking point. Thus the peculiar dilemma overtaking these sections, the circular dilemma of endeavoring to prove beyond all question the poet's transcendence of proof. What is initially thought to designate a domain of uncontested value experiences, in the course of being articulated within the poem, a reversal in significance so that it now is rendered the explicit subject of dispute. In this respect the charged ambivalence surrounding the assertion of proof may be linked to the tensions surrounding the project of consensus at large, most pointedly evident in Whitman's habit of subjecting to anxious scrutiny concepts otherwise glorified for their power to command spontaneous assent. Sections twenty-five through twenty-nine are exceptional only in the starkness with which they profile this irony, one which reappears under various guises, as I shall be suggesting, throughout the poem.

"Song of Myself" shares with other poems in *Leaves of Grass* a fundamental ambition, that of reconceiving the integrity of self-evident truths. While it may seem as though the foregoing sections lose sight of this essential priority in their struggle to fight off the frustrations of an impotent potency, we need only reemphasize the matter of *conception* in order to see the intimate relation between the restoration of self-evident truths and the poet's determination to coax a voice out of his leaves of grass. Lest we overlook the central importance of this connection, Whitman returns us to it in section thirty. "All truths wait in all things," he declares, "they neither hasten their own delivery nor resist it, / They do not need the obstetric forceps of the surgeon." The journal entry from which these lines are quarried is still more explicit in recalling the "folded buds" of section twenty-five:

> All truths lie waiting in all things. They neither urge the opening of themselves nor resist it. For their birth you need not the obstetric forceps of the surgeon. They unfold to you and emit themselves more fragrant than roses from living buds, whenever you fetch the sunrise moistened with spring rain. (*UPP* 2:80)

The embryo of "truths" is preternaturally self-motivated and yet strangely impassive, neither hastening nor resisting the delivery of a meaning still to be delivered. This is the dream of a discourse hoping to conceive itself without coercion, undisturbed by the compulsions of history or even the vagaries of personal choice. Like the song of the rolling earth which does not argue, persuade, hasten, refuse, shut out, it cannot exist within the poem, but rises, phantomlike, as its Platonic archetype, that ideal which exists beside, without being able fully to mask, the poem's "willful birthmarks" (*PW* 2:756).

5

Native Models

"THE NEWSPAPER IS SO FLEETING," Whitman once commented while musing over his career in journalism, "is so like a thing gone as quick as come; has no life so to speak; its birth and death coterminous" (*WWC* 4:2). While comparisons between *Leaves of Grass* and journalism abound—Emerson's quip about the *Bhagavad Gita* and the *New York Tribune* comes to mind—we have found reason to extend Whitman's analogy along more precise lines by noting how this co-presence of birth and death haunts the language of "Song of Myself," with its "prophetical screams" working their way to the surface only to be choked off at the moment of emergence. In view of this threatened foreclosure of beginning and end we can better understand why Whitman should be so irresistibly drawn to the parthenogenesis of self-evolving "truths" and other variants on the myth of "free growth": it defines the successful elaboration of a rhetoric which, in securing immediate conviction through its display of "undeniable growth," stands outside the need of argument or persuasive demonstration. In this way authority for his songs of the earth is, to paraphrase Wallace Stevens, not to be imposed but only discovered. But inasmuch as this notion of a self-willed, uncoerced genesis that neither hastens nor resists its delivery specifies a dream that both demands and defies representation, the pursuit of "free growth" and its self-evident truths seek a context for what cannot be contextualized, seek to affirm what can only be inferred. What results is a critical hiatus between the moment of conception and the moment of its accepted "proof," a hiatus which is in turn responsible for the nightmare of the prolifically barren or what section twenty-five reveals to be a condition of overcharged plenitude which, finding no outlet for its energies, threatens to degenerate into a poetic that "stagnates in its vitals, cowardly and rotten."[1]

It may be that the tensions that accrue from the hiatus between initial acts of founding and their fully verified legitimacy plague any form of representative speech seeking public acceptance. Certainly, this predicament applies to the state of the nation Whitman found himself addressing in 1855, for when the South did eventually withdraw from the Union, its gesture of defiance merely brought to a head a crisis in constitutional legitimacy which had been in evidence long before then. Although legislation from 1820 onward made it possible to sustain and patch together the Union on the basis of compromise over slavery, it also sustained and perpetuated a rupture in the social contract which only civil war, as it turned out, could remedy. Over the course of his presidency Lincoln came to interpret this crisis in legitimacy in terms of a moral hiatus between 1776 and 1789, between the Declaration of Independence with its guarantee of equality for "all men" and the Constitution with its notorious silence concerning this same stipulation. "Four score and seven years ago," the year of 1776, marked the true beginning of nationhood, one whose founding Lincoln likewise evoked as a virgin birth conceived in liberty and brought forth by the Founders, less the "fathers" of the new nation than its midwife. In this "recontracting of society on the basis of the Declaration as [the] fundamental charter,"[2] as one analyst describes this revisionary gesture, Lincoln anticipated the day when "this nation under God shall have a new birth of freedom"—a rebirth, in other words, which would at last close the gap between the original moment of the nation's founding and its final, incontestable legitimacy. Needless to say, executing this goal exacted a staggering price, as the thousands slain on the fields of Gettysburg attested.

Whitman's motive, as we have seen, was to settle the matter of legitimacy itself by cultivating a song where the impasse between creation and validation would be a nonexistent issue. As the better President, his would be the naturalized decree of the executive "who judges not as a judge judges but as the sun falling upon a helpless thing." From what we have seen so far of "Song of Myself," however, it would appear that it is Whitman himself who is the helpless thing the sun falls upon; and while he does not enlist the sacrifice of slain soldiers to defend his self-evident truths his own ordeal with proof does require throttled windpipes and suicidal ventures in frantic vindication of his calling. To this extent, both literary and political institutions share the common plight of devising a vocabulary of justification which is not revealed to be inadequate or self-incriminating the moment it is asserted.

While the specter of disunion obviously lent added urgency to

Whitman's quest, the importance of literary institutions should not be overlooked, particularly because Whitman's chosen method for "re-contracting" society relies so heavily on the belief that literature alone is best qualified to define and vindicate the essential worth of a people and its culture. As he writes in *Democratic Vistas,* "the central point in any nation, and that whence it is itself really sway'd the most, and whence it sways others, is its national literature, especially its arche-typal poems. Above all previous lands, a great original literature is surely to become the justification and reliance, (in some respects the sole reliance) of American democracy" (*PW* 2:365–66). In truth, "two or three really original American poets . . . would give more compaction and more moral identity, (the quality to-day most needed) to these States, than all its Constitutions, legislative and judicial ties" (*PW* 2:368). With this appeal for "national expressers" Whitman adds his voice to a long chorus of pleas for an indigenous literature "fit for native models" and beyond the reach of the courtly muses of Europe. As various voices grouped under the rubric of literary nationalism, that chorus reached its peak in the interval falling between the nation's founding and the advent of those writers said to constitute the American Renaissance. Because it forms something of a hiatus in its own right, this period is by all accounts held to be among the most dismal in American letters, a cultural wasteland barren of talent and devoid of genius. This is not only the twentieth-century view but a contemporaneous assessment, for, as the periodicals, pam-phlets, and fugitive essays of the first half of the nineteenth-century overwhelmingly attest, glorious predictions on the destined accom-plishments of a National American Literature routinely coincided with the pained recognition, by turns defiant and apologetic, that It had not yet arrived. As early as the turn of the century Fisher Ames could in characteristic fashion begin a meditation on the prospects for "American Literature" by questioning "whether we are equal to the Europeans or only a race of degenerate creoles," while one generation later visitor Harriet Martineau was moved to comment that "if the American mind be judged of by its literature, it may be pronounced to have no mind at all."[3]

Thus, over the same period that witnessed disputes concerning the constitutional legitimacy of the nation there also arose debate regard-ing its cultural legitimacy. Criticism today affirms that Whitman and a select handful of contemporaries were instrumental in laying this second controversy to rest; in the words of R. W. B. Lewis *Leaves of*

Grass provided "full poetic realization" to "the stored-up abundance of hope"[4] that accumulated over the decades-long struggle for literary distinction. This of course is a retrospective judgment which draws implicit support from the still more widespread belief that *Leaves of Grass* did not supplement or revise an established tradition in American poetry so much as single-handedly invented one. To a large extent, that belief is indisputable: there is no need to repeat, once again, that Walt Whitman is not Joel Barlow. Even so, there is perhaps a certain irony in crediting a work like "Song of Myself" with finally settling the issue of artistic legitimacy in the New World when that is a question so much at stake within the poem itself. More particularly, the intrinsically paradoxical act of openly asserting what must by definition be only inferred ("only what proves itself is so, only what nobody denies is so") not only specifies a quandary for Whitman's text but defines a long-standing dilemma among the many advocates for an "American Genius" who preceded him. If they too believed that "democracy can never prove itself beyond cavil until it founds and luxuriantly grows its own forms of art" (*PW* 2:365), they were also bound, like the author of "Song of Myself," to come up against the contradictions involved in mounting an *argument* for the virtues of self-evidence. The difficulty we have seen Whitman encounter in integrating his self-evident truths into "Song of Myself" has, in other words, a literary history of its own, one that considerably problematizes his hopeful division between those flawed instruments of sociability ("Constitutions, legislative and judicial ties") and the universal politics of "archetypal poems."

A brief inquiry into the procedures of literary nationalism can usefully detain us, then, not so much for suggesting a preview of better things to come but for dramatizing in its own right and on a more extensive scale the whole awkward business of undertaking to justify "that which has not yet come into existence."[5] No doubt it is this paradoxical imperative that stands behind the often circular and seemingly interminable debates that grip what Edwin Fussell describes, mock-heroically, as "The Age of Growing Discomfort and Inadequate Remedy": whether, for example, "Americanness" is best displayed through the treatment of strictly national subjects or whether it is best evinced by a thoroughgoing internationalism; whether we cannot have a genuine American literature until we have a genuine literary criticism to appraise it or whether that criticism will falter so long as it lacks models worthy of appraisal; whether genius will not emigrate to the New World so long as the country's epoch-making achievements are too imposing for the imagination or whether genius must surely languish so long as it remains bereft of a heritage of tradition rich enough to sustain it. As with any caricature, this oversimplifies a good deal. Still, it seems safe to generalize that amid the proliferating assessments of and proposed solutions to the scandal of "our cultural inferiority" each would-be prophet of the American genius shared the common plight of "trying to be midwife to the unborn homonculous."[6] With the onset of the 1840s—coeval with the first stirrings of Whitman's literary apprenticeship—such frustrations were becoming increasingly apparent and the subject was fast acquiring all the hallmarks of a public cliché: trite but inescapable, something of a bad joke but irresistibly calling for comment. During the same period it is perhaps inevitable that we should find a substantial weariness with, if not outright revulsion toward, "our figure of anticipation," a backlash illustrated in such works as Hawthorne's "The Great Stone Face," Poe's "How To Write A Blackwood Article," and Longfellow's *Kavanagh*. No doubt the *locus classicus* of this antinationalist trend remains James Russell Lowell's attack on "Nationality in Literature." First appearing in the *North American Review* in 1849, Lowell's essay is predominately parodic in spirit, scrupulously taking up so as to lampoon nationalism's stock divisions (imitation versus originality; Anglophilia versus Anglophobia), its stock imagery (the "cultivation" of culture; the "gestation" of genius), and its stock anxieties (shame, embarrassment, betrayal). He is as much amused by the craven deference paid by his countrymen to European reviewers as he is scornful of mindless demands for instant recognition, "as if [literature] were some school exercise in composition to be handed in by a certain day." Observing that "our criticism has oscillated between the two extremes of depreciation and over-praise," Lowell argues that the forty-year campaign for literary independence has proven to be not only futile but in many respects pernicious. "Literature survives," he claims, "not because of its nationality, but despite it."[7]

Yet Lowell's polemic, while astute in perceiving an ironic complicity between the widespread belief in the poverty of American letters and the impoverishing effects of nationalistic discourse, is also naive in assuming that once this complicity is identified it can be somehow dispensed with. For an element of antinationalism had always inhered in the balked procedures of a discourse which, in

Hamlet-like distress, could but "make mouths at the invisible event." Mounting a critique on literary nationalism, even by 1849, could only be an anachronistic enterprise, since that is a project carried out, with varying degrees of explicitness, in the pages of nationalism itself. Speaking on the "peculiar motives to intellectual exertion in America" twenty-five years before Lowell, Edward Everett catches himself up in the midst of his Phi Beta Kappa address with the reminder that "it is impossible to tell what garments our native muses will wear. To foretell our literature would be to create it." With that concession in hand there is little left for the orator to do but look back with fondness on the revolutionary exploits of the past and dismiss with contempt those cynical enough to brand his own prophecy "the chimerical imagination of a future indefinitely removed."[8] But Everett's disclaimer serves to project the skeptic within himself. Justification runs aground here not simply because there is no literature deemed worthy enough to justify (despite the recent work of Bryant, Cooper, or Irving, no American authors are cited by Everett); his speech also fights a rearguard action, defending itself against its own premises. In more explicit fashion E. T. Channing abjures readers of the *North American Review* in 1816 to "get out of the bad habit of dictating to great minds. . . . Genius is not willing to be interfered with and told how to work, where to travel and what to admire. And yet there are men who go so far as to hold up models for imitation and standards of taste." No less emphatically than Lowell, Channing suggests that the greatest obstacle to literary development may be found in the moment of its advocacy. Not foreign models alone are to be deplored, "we must also be shy of ourselves."[9] Some, to be sure, would take solace in affirming the modest proposal that "a national literature uniting all the requisites of excellence . . . has as yet perhaps not existed [and] it may be impossible to create such a one, but it is not therefore idle to aim at it."[10] Among the more prescient spokesmen, however, the gap between prophecy and accomplishment was too imposing to ignore. As often as not their writing stops short at the divide signaled in Nietzsche's uncompromising distinction: "of what is great one must either be silent or speak with greatness."[11] Enjoying neither luxury, they alternately longed for one or the other. Even so tireless a standard-bearer as William Cullen Bryant is moved to confess that "were our rewards to be bestowed only on what is intrinsically meritorious, merit alone would have any apology for appearing before the public."[12] To the degree that the only possible proof for the cultural legitimacy of the nation lay in the undeniable evidence of its results, nationalism confronts a double scandal: not only the mortifying "delinquency" of American letters but the corollary recognition that to defend imminence of genius was thereby to register the fact of its absence. Prophecy, too, required an apology for appearing before the public, since merely to issue yet another call for a "Majestic Literature, self-reared, self-sustaining, self-vindicated"[13] was from the outset to betray the cause. Or, as Fisher Ames expresses this predicament with disarming candor in the first paragraph of his early essay (1802), "it might, indeed, occur to our discretion that, as the only admissible proof of literary excellence is the measure of its effects, our national claims ought to be abandoned as worthless the moment they are found to need asserting."[14]

Against this background there is ushered in the figure of Emerson, expounding the private infinitude of the Central Man. Coming in the wake of a generation given to lamenting the folly of holding Homer up against Joel Barlow or Plato against Thomas Paine, it was of course Emerson's vocation to insist that our genius is more native than we think. To the chronic rejoinder that "a right perception of the genius of others is not genius," Emerson would simply strike out the negative, recovering the usurped "majesty of [his] own rejected thoughts" in "every work of genius." This does not mean that Emerson thereby proposes, in one stroke, to overthrow or transcend the massive inferiority complex known as literary nationalism. He insists on this impasse with a candor that allows him to economize on its grievances more effectively. "Self-Reliance" he succinctly defines as "precisely that secret to make your supposed deficiency redundancy. If I am true, the theory is, the very want of action, my very impotency, shall become a greater excellency than all skill and toil."[15] Discovering possibility where Nietzsche would see only impossibility, Emerson in effect undertakes to speak with greatness and be silent at the same time. In the very magnitude of individual incapacity he posits individual power, converting imaginative poverty into imaginative plenitude. One reason the transparent eyeball epiphany in *Nature* and the catatonic breakdown in the opening pages of "Experience" have gained such notoriety is because they are so rare; it is far more common for Emerson to view himself "a pensioner; not a cause but a surprised spectator" (*W* 2:268), one who surveys "the awful gap" between the "promise of power and the shabby performance." Such distancing holds true for even the most ringing of affirmations.

"Speak your latent conviction and it shall be the universal sense" is a sentence that does double duty, obeying even as it thematizes its own imperative. Emptied of content, the status of *Emerson's* "latent conviction" becomes synonymous with speaking on its behalf, thus precluding the need for further action. "Act if you like—but you do it at your own peril," he writes in *Representative Men*. "Men's actions are too strong for them. Show me a man who has acted, and who has not been a victim of his action" (*W* 4:266–67).[16] Every heart must also vibrate to that iron law: to invest one's words with the force of consequence, to shoot the gap from prophetic motive to living deed is a prelude to self-betrayal. Emersonian discourse, oppositely, will not fall prey to such betrayals, will not resign itself to the embarrassment of discovering its claims disproven the moment they are found to need asserting. Rather, as I suggested previously, he allegorizes this predicament by seeing it played out in the works of others. In what amounts to a remarkable transference, betrayal no longer identifies a threat impinging upon one's writing but is projected out and fully mastered in the aggressive act of reappropriation Emerson calls reading. Perusing the past masters, the self-reliant reader reads a fate which is the reverse of his own. Clinging fast to his poverty he finds in the deeds of genius a strength that weakens and finally enslaves. So it is said of Shakespeare that "he carries a wealth that beggars his own."

In undertaking to actualize "the great psalm of the Republic" Whitman, as we know, could rest content only in speaking *as*, not *of*, the Central Man. The poet's "every word . . . must tell in action." From an Emersonian standpoint the consequence is as predictable as it is devastating: a musclebound bard seized with "Buffalo strength [but] choked by Titanic abdomen."[17] What Emerson glorifies as redundant deficiency Whitman finds rendered back into the vexations of a deficient redundancy. So section twenty-five accosts a voice surcharged with a wealth that beggars the poet's own. While it would be irresponsible to reduce the complexity of any author's work by threading it through the camel's eye of literary nationalism, the contrast can certainly be made that most American writers of Whitman's generation accommodated the imperative of fame by ironizing it— Hawthorne's Ambitious Guest, Melville's Pierre and such megalomaniacs as William Wilson are each in their own way grotesque overreachers whose overblown quest for commemoration merely dooms them to madness, suicide, or simple oblivion. Whitman, too, had begun his poetic career stuck head first in this vein, joylessly churning out commentaries on "The Punishment of Pride," "Fame's Vanity," and, of course, "Ambition." Yet in forging an aesthetic "as generous and as worthy" as the country it was to depict, Whitman came to perceive the need for a rhetoric purified of "ignominious distinctions." What remained for him to devise, in turn, was a structure of expression capable of fending off the disabling interaction between excess and deficiency as well as the disrelation between demand and response this interaction suggests.

Before going on to explore the impact of these issues on "Song of Myself," it might be useful to stand back and take stock of Whitman's affiliations to the background just outlined. Needless to say, he counted himself a staunch advocate in the drive for cultural independence and from his editorial post across the East River voiced his support for the Young America movement sweeping Manhattan in the 1840s. Firmly persuaded that "the top-most proof of a race is its own born poetry" (*PW* 2:474), he devoted essays to this "*sine qua non*" throughout the half-century of his writing career. (As a late as 1891 he was responding to yet another request from the *North American Review* for a piece on "American National Literature.") Yet it is worth noting that the author of "Song of Myself" was more than aware of the hopeless impasse that nationalism had turned out to be.

> *Caution*—not to blaart constantly for Native American Models, literature, etc., and bluster out "nothing foreign." The best way to promulge native American models and literature is to supply such forcible and superb specimens of the same that will, by their own volition, move to the head of all and put foreign models in the second class.
>
> I think today it would be best *not at all* to bother with arguments against foreign models or to help American *models*—but just go on *supplying American models*. (*N & F*, p. 30)

"Song of Myself" is scrupulous in honoring the spirit of such an injunction: it is careful to downplay the long-existent topos of *translatio studii* or the "Westering of Genius" (this being reserved for "Facing West from California's Shores"); it incorporates tableaux from American history (the storming of the Alamo; the old sea fight) with enough casualness to distance it safely from Joel Barlow's epic disasters; it abandons teleological narratives of cultural progress for the plotless adventures of a "kosmos"; it rewrites epic categories by subsuming them under the shared mythology of a celebrating self.

By 1855, then, Whitman did not need to be reminded that "literature comes not when it is bidden," that "you cannot force its growth." We can take this to mean something more than the fact that there will be no hailing of Columbia in Whitman's song by gaining a clearer sense of his cautious treatment of apostrophe at large. Few passages in *Leaves of Grass* succeed quite so brilliantly in coming to terms with this precaution as the opening lines of "Song of Myself," which eschew the ritual of invocation for a simple performative, "I celebrate myself and sing myself." The subject/object dualism conventional to address is here conflated for what appears as an inextricable fusion between the "I" that speaks and the "I" that is spoken, as if being claimed no permanence beyond the immediate moment it is uttered into existence.[18] There seems, in addition, no specifiable center or locus for this singing self, for, in what we can now recognize as a characteristic trait of Whitman's "arrivings and partings," no sooner does voice invest the speaker than it is dispersed through the landscape as so many "words . . . loosed to the eddies of the wind." Words evoked in this way become stray interjections ("the belched words of speech"), passing reverberations ("echoes, ripples, buzzed whispers"), substances of sound and sight divorced from the abstractions of meaning and returned to the seductive power of a preverbal energy called the "lull" or "hum" of the soul's "valved voice." Their significance inheres in the random energies they release. The manner of speech is more epideitic than prophetic, content to luxuriate in the good fortune of "my respiration and inspiration . . . the play of shine and shade." Thus it is worthwhile to note that as section three goes on to draw up a host of polarities—"beginning and end," "learned and unlearned," "I and this mystery"—these antithetical pairings are not so much subsumed as suspended. His lines want us to know that they are willing to countenance difference without wishing to absolve it: "Out of the dimness opposite equals advance, / Always substance . . . always a knit of identity, always distinction, always a breed of life" (*CRE*, p. 31). To exclude nothing but exclusion, deny nothing but denial, allows the poet even to shrug aside, with a kind of wearied acknowledgment, the world-dividing logic of nationalism; it is enough for the time being to be told "showing the best and dividing it from the worst age vexes age."

The opening lines of "Song of Myself" continue to tantalize their ablest interpreters; so deeply assimilated have they become into the American grain that it is difficult now to imagine them as anything but inevitable. Part of that mystique, as I have intimated, indeed consists in the power of these lines to foster the impression that the work of prophecy *has already been done.* In the leisurely combination of engagement and withdrawal, liberation and restraint—both in and out of the game, leaning and loafing—utterance occupies a perspective unqualified by the demand for justification. His words are willing to risk obscurity in order to savor that imperturbability, for "to elaborate is no avail . . . learned and unlearned feel that it is so . . . while others discuss I am silent . . . I have no mockings and arguments, I witness and wait" (*CRE,* pp. 31, 32). The point would not be that words fall short of the experience they seek to capture (for example, the poet's experience is "mystical") but that nothing could be added to a knowledge (call it "the perfect fitness and equanimity of things") that is not already enjoyed. (In this respect, to be told that "Backward I see in my own days where I sweated through fog with linguists and contenders" merely corroborates an inference already induced.) Adding to this sense that "my acceptation and realization" have been accepted and realized in the moment of being spoken is Whitman's use of the time-honored device of the Homeric legend or *pars epica,* by which the God or Numen is made present to the narrative through a recitation of its genealogical attributes, thus skirting overt supplication.[19] Though dusted off briefly in the opening lines ("My tongue, every atom of my blood, form'd from this soil, this air, / Born here of parents born here from parents the same, and their parents the same"), the device receives its most extended treatment in the much-acclaimed "spiritual awakening," retrospectively told in the fifth section, where the soul's tongue is "plung'd to my bare-stript heart"

> Swiftly arose and spread around me the peace and
>   knowledge that pass all the argument of the earth,
> And I know that the hand of God is the promise of my
>   own,
> And I know that the spirit of God is the brother of my
>   own,
> And that all the men ever born are also my brothers,
>   and the women my sisters and lovers,
> And that a kelson of the creation is love,
> And limitless are the leaves stiff or drooping in the
>   fields,

> And brown ants in the little wells beneath them,
> And mossy scabs of the worm fence, heap'd stones,
> elder, mullein, and poke-weed.
>
> (*CRE*, p. 33)

Though the communion is said to surpass the earth, it seems fitting that we should be returned to its particularity. Though section five records what might be called a primal scene of voicing, its effect is not to hasten or individuate visionary powers but again to diffuse perception through the random, luminous commonplaces of the world.

"Not prophecy! NOT prophecy!" thunders William Carlos Williams, "no ideas but in things." If the verse discussed thus far hardly reaches so shrill a pitch, it does seek to mute the ambitious sweep of prophetic discourse by tracing out the metonymic deviations of "indirection." With respect to the latter scholarly opinion and the poet are in close agreement, for both see in the diffusion of Whitman's "limitless leaves" not only a "theme [which] is creative and has vista" but the distinguishing feature that sets "Walt Whitman, one of the roughs, a kosmos," apart from "the empty American parnassus" of his predecessors. In keeping with the prescription that "the great psalm of the Republic" is "to be indirect and not direct" most admirers properly extol "a strain of enthusiastic, receptive, indeterminate openness to experience which finds expression in a loose, unstructured form."[20] Under the terms of our discussion we could rephrase this to say, without too much forcing, that a poetics of indirection must consider itself to be neither a conversion nor an inversion of past values but something like a convocation of them. "Not to repel or destroy but to accept, fuse, rehabilitate" (*CRE*, p. 196) defines the "profound lesson of reception," an integrative, paratactic discourse (the rhetoric of "tallying") which, as we have seen, excludes nothing but exclusion. "Indirection" finds its calling in suspending evaluative acts altogether; it manifests its "indeterminate openness to experience" by abiding in a timeless present, thrusting aside "all talk of the beginning and the end." At the same time we have noted how "Song of Myself"'s "profound lesson of reception" is predicated on one essential exclusion: it situates the moment of proof before or beyond the present act of writing, variously thinking of it as antedating the text (poetic election being recast as a remembered event, the coupling of body and soul) or postdating it (awaiting future validation, as in the pledge to "stop this night and day with me and you shall possess the origin of all poems"). Yet what we have come to sense in our reading is the enormous strain of upholding such mediations, a strain evinced as the present shrinks into the fusions and confusions of beginning and end.

What is the direction of indirection? In posing this question under the guise of another ("What is the *grass?*"), Whitman responds with a series of propositions designed to show, as might be expected, that no (single) answer is possible. As with Ishmael's Leviathan, there are as many significances to Whitman's "uniform hieroglyphic" as there are consciousnesses to interpret it. Electing to "guess at" its multiple connotations, the speaker's tour de force combines a number of associations, ranging from the personal ("the flag of my disposition"), metaphysical ("the handkerchief of the Lord"), political ("sprouting alike in broad zones and narrow zones") to, lastly, a meditation on death ("the beautiful uncut hair of graves"):

> Tenderly will I use you curling grass,
> It may be you transpire from the breasts of young men,
> It may be if I had known them I would have loved them,
> It may be you are from old people, or from offspring
> taken soon out of their mothers' laps.
> And here you are the mothers' laps.
>
> This grass is very dark to be from the white heads of
> old mothers,
> Darker than the colorless beards of old men,
> Dark to come from under the faint red roofs of mouths.
>
> (*CRE*, p. 34)

Something of being "both in and out of the game" persists in this delicate revery, though at least one subtle change in emphasis is worth noting. For the first time in the poem voice is invested with a signifying force; as the speaker soon "perceive[s] after all so many uttering tongues" and remarks that "they do not come from the roofs of mouths for nothing," utterance takes on a prominence that extends beyond the subliminal resonance of a "lull" or "hum." Now hoping to "translate the hints" of the grave, the speaker exchanges the pose of receptivity for hermeneutic appeal. It is as if, in passing from the autoerotic communion of tongue and heart to the broader question of genealogy, Whitman is acknowledging that self-creation is not enough, that legitimation, to be true, requires sources of validation outside the self. What this source consists of is, unsurprisingly, the principle of reproduction, the power of his leaves to prevail over closure. Consequently, as the poet next discovers that the furtive "hints" of his leaves remain inscrutable, so far from lamenting this he presently launches into ringing affirmations of life outlasting the grave: "All goes onward and outward, nothing collapses":

> What do you think has become of the young and old men?
> And what do you think has become of the women and
>   children?
>
> They are alive and well somewhere,
> The smallest sprouts show there is really no death,
> And if ever there was it led forward life, and does
>   not wait at the end to arrest it,
> And ceas'd the moment life appear'd.

> (*CRE*, p. 34)

But what materializes out of this ceaseless regeneration of meaning is, paradoxically, meaning's fixation. Distinct from the accumulating sprouts of section twenty-nine, where the temptation to symbolize is carefully resisted, here we do find the poet editorializing on what "the smallest sprouts show." His protests notwithstanding, there is a sudden effort to "translate the hints" of "so many uttering tongues" and this effort is not without a discernible strain, as suggested in the tortuous anacoluthon of the last two lines cited above, whose congested phrasing, syntactical inversions, and confusing shifts of tense carry the reader anywhere but forward. The vision of unarrested flux staggers under the weight of sheer assertion.

Viewed from a broader perspective it is clear that the section registers a split between a mood of random, contented surmise and blunt, contentious expostulation. In "this inextricable hodge-podge you find at once beautiful phrases and silly gabble," charged one commentator eight years after Whitman's death in 1892; "tender imagination and insolent commonplace" collide so as to perpetrate "literary anarchy and a complete confusion of values."[21] Others have more recently deplored Whitman's "prophetic shrillness" at this stage in the poem,[22] though we need to go beyond simple condemnation and ask why such overinsistence occurs. That the section should be so divided against itself denotes, it might be said, a sudden rift between a poetry of diffusion whose signifier (the grass) ranges effortlessly through a field of significances and a poetry of reduction which seeks relief from such indeterminacy. Yet, as was noted in the discussion of the rivalry between the silent latency of "folded buds" and the tyrannies of "Speech," this view too swiftly polarizes what can be more profitably seen as a dialectic exchange. For what is striking about the end of section six is the way that it enacts what it appears to prohibit, the way it protests against reductiveness in a manifestly reductive fashion. The defiance of death and all terminations works to overdetermine indeterminacy. His lines, in effect, subvert what they cannot ultimately condone: a self-evolving chain of correspondences, "behavior lawless as snowflakes, words simple as grass . . . laughter and naivete." The wish for this diffusion cannot be sustained any more comfortably than the drive to uphold its significance can be resisted. Stranded somewhere between both impulses, the myth of "free growth" threatens to harden into dogma.

"To impose is not to discover," Stevens warned. And once the uncompromising force of *that* imposition nears consciousness we fend it off by cleaving all the more adamantly to possibility. Cleave to it, in effect, with a bitterness that seems to only further drain it of significance: "It is possible, possible, possible. It must be possible." The difficulty facing Steven's predecessor, more easily resolved in theory than practice, is both obvious and acute. How does one propound the ideology of "free growth" without betraying its principles? How does a discourse that forswears the categorization of all value establish its own? To trace out the evolution of section six is to witness Whitman's struggle to accommodate his text to, in Richard Poirier's succinct definition, an aesthetic "so devoted to the *activity* of creation that it denies finality to the result of that activity, its objects and formulations. Art is an action and not the product of an action."[23] As an attempt to characterize "the place of style in American literature," this readily names the central aspiration of indirection: that no element in the text predetermine the course of its outcome. Yet while Poirier's generalization can certainly stand as an accurate paraphrase of Whitman's *ambition* it remains an equivocal account of his *achievement*. The quest for a "style continually fluid, leading on to shapes not yet apprehended and never to be fixed,"[24] identifies the project "Song of Myself" is *pressed against,* here more prosecuted by than prosecuting. Peering into the ominous richness of the grave, Whitman sees not only the simulacrum of womb and tomb but their composite in the macabre figure of "offspring taken soon out of their mothers's laps." What appears to presage the quickening of a new birth suggests as well its simultaneous demise.[25] Halted at a threshold which may be no threshold at all, the development of Whitman's conceit, itself something of a stillbirth, gropes toward an imagined bodily totality but succeeds in listing the *disjecta membra* of the grave: breasts, heads, laps, mouths, and tongues. Swerving from this phantasmagoria the poet concludes that nothing may conclude, and in the stridency of these assertions we overhear the anxiety that has set them in motion. The nemesis of foreclosure—"and did not wait at the end to arrest it and *ceas'd the moment life appear'd*"—persists. As we noted in reference to "Scented Herbage of My Breast," closure, because it is feared to have come too soon, will therefore not come at all.

The American writer, observes Leslie Fiedler, "is forever *beginning*," which is of course another way of saying that the American writer neither begins nor ends but is endlessly doing both at the same time.[26] I have been arguing that the drama of the excluded middle takes on a special urgency in "Song of Myself" since it marks that moment when Whitman's text confronts its "final merit" or "plenum of proof." Something thought to have pressed before or beyond the margins of representation breaks back into the present moment of writing, shutting down the chances for free growth before they can be set in motion. Proof wreaks havoc on temporality not by unraveling the continuity between beginning and end (this Whitman has already claimed to have done) but by condensing these terms with a swiftness that elides any middle ground capable of sustaining indirection's "indeterminate openness to experience." Time will always be out of joint for the revelations of proof so far as it underwrites that value which, like the grave's "so many uttering tongues," must and must not be translated. Representation is not thereby defrauded of its claims to legitimacy so much as it is preempted by the knowledge that any such claim can have no *place* in this song. As discourse falters between the imperative for autochthonous growth ("just go on supplying native models") and the prohibition against coercion ("you cannot force its growth"), prolepsis consumes metonymy, disclosing the end of every quest in the moment of its inception. Clearly, there can be little advantage in devising ways to anticipate the onset of this crisis since anticipation—the specter of foreclosure—itself defines the nature of that crisis. Looking back on section three, we read:

I am satisfied—I see, dance, laugh, sing;
As the hugging and loving bed-fellow sleeps at my side
         through the night, and withdraws at the peep of day
         with stealthy tread,

Leaving me baskets cover'd with white towels swelling
    the house with their plenty,

Shall I postpone my acceptation and realization and
    scream at my eyes,
That they turn from gazing after and down the road,
And forthwith cipher and show me to a cent,
Exactly the value of one and exactly the value of two,
    and which is ahead?

                               (*CRE,* pp. 31–32)

Much as this asks to be read as yet another instance of the kind of
good-humored histrionics displayed in Whitman's expostulation with
"Speech," there is genuine panic in it as well. We see the cross-
purposes at once: value, to be secured, must be banished; its sanction
will be its disappearance—"in the ground out of sight." This is not of
course the explicit burden of Whitman's mocking question, whose
satire we may imagine to be leveled at Lowell's witless crew of na-
tionalists impatiently clamoring for cultural vindication, "as if it were
some school exercise to be handed in by a certain day." And yet, as the
fiercely overwrought denunciation called down upon the eyes attests,
Whitman too wants not only proof but ocular proof. The godly
insemination swelling the house with its plenty—perhaps harking
back to the "houses and rooms" of the opening page or ahead to "the
faint red roofs of mouths"—again lays bare the collusion between
prolepsis and proof. Characteristically, postponement is not equated
with the mere deferral of action but a kind of fast-forwarding of vision
that prefigures the outcome of the journey before it has gotten under
way. Voice screaming at vision is in this context scarcely distinguishable from vision berating Speech, each gesture standing as a self-
reproach against the fetishizing of "proof," the overvaluation of "value."

    Later editions saw fit to drop the explicit reference to "God" as that
"hugging and loving bed-fellow" who steals away at daybreak,
though this deletion should not entirely obscure awareness of the
topos being toyed with in this vignette. The petition to draw down a
God from the heavens so as to authorize and guide the poet's calling
has a rich heritage in English prophetic tradition. So Milton calls on
his muse ("Descend from Heaven, Urania") as another loving bed-
fellow who "visit'st my slumbers nightly" and who is requested "still
govern thou my song . . . when morn purples the east." This "har-

rowing of the skies" persists through various odes of the eighteenth century and certain Romantic lyrics with enough prominence to be labeled "the descendental theme" by Geoffrey Hartman.[27] It stands behind the voyeuristic glimpse of the mating of God and the Enthusiast Fancy in Collins's "Ode on the Poetical Character" as well as Blake's striking image of Milton entering Los's left foot. Whether Whitman had this cast of allusions in mind is at best uncertain, though as Abrams has established the topos in all likelihood reaches back to the apocalyptic marriage of heaven and earth, a Biblical precedent with which Whitman was certainly familiar.[28] Yet however he chanced upon this conceit it remains paradigmatic of Whitman's song that no sooner is this sign of election made manifest than anxiety over its *accreditation* takes hold. Because there is little or no interval between the promise of divine conception and the judgment to be passed upon it, vision never takes flight but turns back on the text to take stock of a value still in the throes of development. And in turning back it must be turned aside, as if there could be no alternative between value as an invisible immanence ("Do you not know O speech how the buds beneath you are folded?") and its fate as redundant energy ("Come now you conceive too much . . ."). Thus it is hard to say whether Whitman's dalliance with this prophetic theme breaks off because it has lost its efficacy for him or because he wants too much from it.[29] Preferring description to invocation, the speaker does not of course petition his god; here as with his duel with the sun he makes good on his pledge of "not asking the sky to come down to my goodwill, / But scattering it freely forever" (*CRE*, 41). But that is because the object of his calling is no more Urania than the "Me Myself." His true muse is "the value," the one element in his discourse which cannot be invoked.

Fetishism, from this standpoint, may be too inexact a term to apply to the quandary laid open by these ciphering eyes. From the "bard Elect" of *The Prelude* we learn of comparable misgivings over the tyranny of sight, "the most despotic of our senses," and by this we understand Wordsworth's need to coax the growth of his mind beyond a slavish adherence to external stimuli. To the untrained sensibility the "bodily eye," abstracted from the other senses and "thus sitting in judgement," wields "absolute dominion," often resulting in "that false secondary power, by which we create distinctions, then / Deem that our puny boundaries are things / Which we perceive, and not which we have made."[30] Fetishism on this showing involves a solipsism that outwits itself; the mind enthralled in the worship of "graven images" fails to recognize these as its own invention. A Wordsworthian poetics aspires to counter this deadening syndrome by pursuing a declared symbiosis of mind and Nature that "half perceives and half creates." As we have learned from Hartman the outer, "bodily eye" must be harmonized with inner illumination.[31] (A roughly analogous partnership is evoked early on in "Song of Myself" when Whitman, in speaking of "my soul" and "all that is not my soul"—"I and this mystery"—declares "lacks one, lacks both, and the unseen is proven by the seen, / Till that becomes unseen and receives proof in its turn" [(*CRE*, p. 31].) Yet, leaving aside for the moment the tendency of objects to surge past the "fluid and attaching character" with a swiftness that precludes visual fixation, the problem of perception in Whitman requires different emphasis. To stigmatize "that false secondary power" of the mind is to entertain, however provisionally, a detachment sufficient to isolate and analyze its proclivities, to posit a hierarchy of values serviceable to "this our high argument." Always sensitive to the twin threats of a entranced passivity before Nature or an aggrandizing mastery over it, Wordsworth's mature verse incorporates a finely wrought system of checks and balances capable of adjudicating between what may be credited as authentic vision and what may in turn discredit it. In Whitman the terms for any such metacommentary undergo a double fate, hardening as they dissolve. Just as proof's dismissal insures the persistence of its return, so does this recurrence touch off the panic of further denial. Given the extraordinary compression of this dialectic and the frightening rapidity with which it is set in motion, it becomes apparent that the feared reduction of value (whether through the idolatry of "graven images" or the "bald literalism" that "forthwith cipher[s] and show[s] me to a cent") cannot be attributed solely to the despotism of the eye. Rather, this fear permeates the world of "Song of Myself" at large; irreducible to any single dramatic encounter, it is most discernible as a prevenient, prospective energy, if not quite *in* the poem then visibly looming *before* it. Indeed, because no external image or "companionable form" gets attached to "the value" in the passage above, fetishism remains a danger in prospect only—not so much the product of a deluded, erring imagination as it is for Whitman something already ingrained in the starved expectations of a culture breathless to proclaim "An American bard at last!," the undissuable force of whose "native models" will "move to the head of all and put foreign models in the second class."

"To foretell our literature would be to create it," Everett had declared, as if word and deed, wish and fulfillment could be joined together in one irrevocable stroke. If political independence had been "spoken into existence," might not cultural liberty enjoy a similar fate? For, as Everett goes on to reason, he who could give shape to the anticipation of our literary destiny would perforce lay that anticipation to rest, just as "the gorgeous vision of the Iliad" was realized not in "the full detail of circumstance" but precisely in that moment when its "dim conception . . . burst through the soul of Homer."[32] The instant translation of the "dim conception" into its finished structure identifies the dream and the peculiar burden of "indirection," which takes up the formidable task of conferring instant credibility for its own dim conceptions while insuring that each fresh "start" will not be its own "finish." In later years, once enshrined as the Good Gray Poet, Whitman would strike a more equable pose on the matter, patiently reminding his listeners in 1881 that "long, long are the processes of the development of Nationality. Only to the rapt vision does the seen become the prophecy of the unseen" (*PW* 2:486). Still, it is measure of the uneasy and often tortuous alliance between perception and validation in the *Leaves* that when the 1855 Preface turns to the visionary powers of the poet emphasis does not fall on the privileged vastation of the seer. Sight is instead called forth as that supreme source of acknowledgment, insusceptible to disconfirmation precisely because it tolerates no gap between what it sees and what it confirms. Seeing is believing: "Who knows the curious mystery of the eyesight? The other senses corroborate themselves, but this is removed from any proof but its own and foreruns the identities of the spiritual world" (*PW* 2:438–39). Broadly speaking, this is the "curious mystery" that prevails throughout the sections, predominantly visual in character, that intervene between the encounter with the grave's "uttering tongues" in section six and the subsequent encounter with the sun in section twenty-five. In them Whitman's "commission," his "acceptation and realization," is to harness the eye's pre-judicial energy, to get proof out of sight—in the sense of both deriving immediate confirmation from the eyes and of thereby removing the question of confirmation altogether. Following the shrill declamations against the "collapse" of life into death at the end of section six, section eight starts off by recouping some semblance of narrative continuity in the triple image of birth ("the little one sleeps in its cradle"), sex ("the youngster and the red-faced girl"), and death ("the suicide sprawls on the bloody floor"), each scene registered without comment by the

witnessing "I." Seemingly everywhere and nowhere, the speaker
soon yields to the vicarious delights of vision, beholding "the marriage of the trapper in the open air in the far west," observing a
"handsome and richly drest" lady observing "Twenty-eight young
[who] bathe by the shore," admiring the "calm and commanding"
poise of the Negro drayman. The divide between perception and
cognition is conscientiously maintained; like the "impassive stones
that receive and return so many echoes," the spectator for the most
part is content to "witness" and "note." Ciphering eyes have been set
aside for what are called in "Give Me the Splendid Silent Sun"
"interminable eyes." In the copious flow of scenes unfolding before it,
"not a person or object missing," the "I" no more pretends to disappear into these vistas as omniscient narrator than it aspires to stand
beyond them as a "transparent eyeball." Identity appears as the inter-
penetration of all these activities which "tend inward to me [as] I tend
outward to them" (*CRE,* p. 44). This last quote rounds off the first of
the famed catalogs, whose additive appetite names whatever it sees,
from the "pure contralto in the organ loft" to the "canal boy on the
tow-path"; from the flat-boatman, spinning girl or fare-collector to
the lunatic connoisseur or half-breed. As commentators as diverse in
outlook as de Selincourt, Lynen, and Ziff have helped us to appreciate, these constructions are not the wild effusions of someone
"ranting and frothing in my insane crisis" but a delicately arrayed
stream of associations, with each description and gesture by turns
interlocking with or resonating against the other.[33]

> The pedler sweats with his pack on his back, (the
> purchaser higgling about the odd cent,)
> The bride unrumples her white dress, the minute hand
> of the clock moves slowly,
> The opium-eater reclines with rigid head and just
> open'd lips,
> The prostitute draggles her shawl, her bonnet bobs
> on her tipsy and pimpled neck,
> The crowd laugh at her blackguard oaths, the men jeer
> and wink to each other,
> (Miserable! I do not laugh at your oaths nor jeer at
> you;)
> The President holding a cabinet council is surrounded
> by the great Secretaries,

> On the piazza walk three matrons stately and friendly
>> with twined arms,
> The crew of the fish-smack pack repeated layers of
>> halibut in the hold . . .
>>> (*CRE*, p. 43)

With each snapshot flashing momentarily before the eye, action ceases the moment the line ends even as we are propelled forward by the paratactical momentum of the syntax. Just so, it is the "law of perfection" in the organic nature of things that any object's "finish is to each for itself and onward from itself."[34] The panoramic realism of the bard's "interminable eyes" releases an interminable series of images, separate but equal, which are as heterogeneous in content as they are undifferentiated in structure. In bringing America's "vast, seething mass of materials" to the page, Whitman's song of occupations here aims as well to bring the treacherous merger of scarcity and plentitude into workable form. Rather than the paralyzing collapse of end into beginning we find a procession of brilliantly etched, end-stopped lines that provides immediate closure for each utterance as well as the impetus for a fresh beginning. The effect is a structure that is radically open (the list being conceivably inexhaustible) and radically closed (each line being, imagistically speaking, a poem in itself). Excess can never be too much in such constructions, given their dexterity in harmonizing repetition and closure.[35] Because Whitman's tallying forbids granting visual salience to any one scene or individual (not even the "caresser of life" who absorbs and is absorbed by them), totality is both localized and refused. To the degree that there is no distinguishable "whole" to which the sum of these parts harkens, each part takes on the provisional appearance of that whole, though distributed along a contiguous chain of complementarity. "From the eyesight proceeds another eyesight, from the hearing proceeds another hearing and from the voice proceeds another voice eternally curious of the harmony of things." Value is held to strict account: voice will not go beyond what the eyes cannot reach; the eyes will not outstrip vision's advance. In the *concordia discors* of the catalog images are thus set forth "with scrupulous exactness," as Emily Dickinson wrote in another context, "to hold our senses on."

Exactness may seem the last word to describe the freewheeling euphoria of a Proteus, "hankering, gross, mystical, nude" who "can resist nothing better than [his] own diversity." The Jamesian injunction that the true artist is one upon whom nothing is lost takes on near maniacal proportions in the wake of section fifteen, with the "I" now "of every hue and caste . . . every rank and religion, / A farmer, mechanic, artist, gentleman, sailor, quaker, / Prisoner, fancy-man rowdy, lawyer, physician, priest" (*CRE*, p. 45). Yet out of this apparent chaos of roles the rule of "opposite equals" predominates. Pledged as the poet is "not [to] have a single person slighted or left away," every thesis is promptly weighed against its antithesis for one who is not only "the poet of the Body" but "the poet of the Soul," of the "woman the same as the man," of the wicked as well as the good; "who play[s] not marches for accepted victors only . . . [but] for conquer'd and slain"; no more "modest than immodest"; "stuff'd with the stuff that is coarse and stuff'd with the stuff that is fine." What seems a random dispersal of the self is on deeper reflection governed by a thoroughgoing attention to the apportionment of its energies. Thus while the poet appears to dilate to a breadth that defies all measurement—"not contain'd between my hat and boot-soles," his "orbit cannot be swept by the carpenter's compass"—he is also quick to insist that this amplitude can have no meaning unless measured by others, for "all I mark as my own you shall offset it with your own, / Else it were time lost listening to me" (*CRE*, p. 47). Like the catalogs in their closed openness, the self is presented as defiantly self-complete ("I know I am august . . . I exist as I am, that is enough") and infinitely extendable ("In all people I see myself, not more and not barely-corn less"). The constitutionalism of the many into one and one into many does not melt the world, as Lawrence would have it, into "the awful pudding of One Identity."[36] The more we attend to "the afflatus surging and surging," the more we observe that its seemingly boundless lust for possession is marked off by countervailing impulses. "To see no possession but you may possess it" (*CRE*, p. 156) may be an article of faith for Whitman but it has little value unless the possessions of sight can be released or instantly ex-pressed onto the page. An implicit economy of exchange applies throughout these sections: whatever this verse takes in must as readily be "let out," this being "the thoughtful merge of myself and outlet again" which "breath[es] the air but leave[s] plenty after me." The "kosmos" who commands "unscrew the locks from the doors, / Unscrew the doors themselves from their jambs" has himself become a revolving door, with every fresh "influx" of power partaking of its "efflux." This, too,

is the fantasy of abundance without surfeit, of a capaciousness that
will not incapacitate itself.

In this way the catalogs aim at a marriage of speaking and seeing
which protects the poet against the perplexing condition of finding
either sense "unequal to measure itself." Despite their notoriety as a
radical innovation, they carry an essentially conservative appeal in the
sense of restraining the pressure of human demand, of carefully tallying whatever is to be "let in" with whatever is "let out." While this
particular feature of the catalogs is easily overshadowed by the comedic exuberance of a poem like "Song of Myself," it comes into sharper
focus in a more composed lyric, "There Was a Child Went Forth,"
which offers the best account we have of the cataloging self and which
is for this reason worth pausing over briefly. In its fusion of perceiver
and perceived and in its flawless give and take of response and coun-
terresponse, the poem unfolds a virtual allegory of consensus where
the spoken and the seen are seamlessly and movingly joined.

> There was a child went forth every day,
> And the first object he look'd upon that object he
> > became,
> And that object became part of him for the day or a
> > certain part of the day,
> Or for many years or stretching cycles of years.
> > (*CRE*, p. 364)

One thinks, momentarily, of Ahab on the quarterdeck, scanning the
Doubloon for images of his omnipotence. But this is not, as it happens, a lyric about the solipsism of projection and before long we
discover that the "object he became" is in fact simply all the objects
that "became part of him." The omission of the relative pronoun in
Whitman's Quaker-sounding title subtly reinforces this discovery by
making whatever identity we can attribute to this child indistinguishable from his act of going forth, so that, in Charles Feidelson's
graceful phrase, he "speaks the world that he sees and sees the world
that he speaks; and in doing so *becomes* the reality of his vision."[37] As a
result, the processional litany of sights and sounds, in taking on the
appearance of speaking pictures, suffice in themselves to tell the story
of poetic development, expanding outward from the burgeoning of
plant and animal life, the sphere of primitive social distinctions, familial ambivalence, metaphysical doubts, to a final, valedictory scene at

sunset. Untouched by nostalgia for a lost harmony that haunts comparable treatments of this subject by Wordsworth, Blake, or Shelley, Whitman's psychological idyll chooses to evoke an endlessly renewable reserve of forms, with objects and events permeating consciousness "then, now, and always."[38]

But even as this portrait recreates an ongoing commerce of "influx" and "efflux" which we have seen at work in the catalogs, it also hints at a necessary inhibition governing this poetic of reception. Whitman himself, no doubt unwittingly, strikes at the heart of the real poignance in the poem when, years later, he half-jokingly confided to Traubel that "there is really nothing in it at all—nothing at all. . . . It is a mere looking about at things" (*WWC* 5:310). One could indeed say without prejudice that "There Was a Child Went Forth" succeeds so well because it asks so little. The reiterated emphasis on those things that "became part of him"; the peculiar reminder that the parents who fathered and conceived him "gave the child more of themselves than that, / They gave him afterward every day"; the hurried zeugma in a line like "the family usages, the language, the company, the yearning and swelling heart"; glancing references to the "affection that cannot be gainsay'd": these are in reality suppressed apostrophes, petitions so muted as to suggest apprehension over any mode of address that would too sharply individuate need against response. What "can be used can be used up" is how Geoffrey Hartman describes "*the anxiety of demand*," an anxiety "generated by the very pressure of demand we put upon things, and the resultant fear that they cannot 'bear' us."[39] Thus the declared correspondence between "I" and all the things composing the "I" never opens out into the glories of the egotistical sublime but functions precisely as a means of delimiting demand. Critics struck by the tantalizingly brief family portrait that straddles the middle of the poem have made this the center of their reading, finding this brevity suggestive of some profound rupture in emotional development that is quickly diffused into the generalized "doubts of the daytime and doubts of the nighttime." This no doubt is the case, yet the ambivalence observable in this scene is not finally distinguishable from the treatment of any other in the poem, all of which share the common trait of not evoking more than can be accounted for. Like the outpouring of people and places in the catalogs, the metonymic parade of details, in precluding visual fixation, also works to ensure that consciousness will not overspecify the objects of its attention any more than those objects will overextend it.

In the course of reflecting on various "systems of connection" or "types of union" which philosophy draws upon to structure human experience, William James hypothesizes that the "lowest grade" of connectedness would consist in "a world of mere *withness*, of which the parts were only strung together by the conjunction 'and'."[40] This essentially describes the world of the catalogs, whose components are strung together in the hope of realizing the lowest common denominator of Union—a world which lays to rest the dissension of competing values by setting the Secretaries at their cabinet meeting and the matrons in the piazza on an equal footing. What "There Was a Child Went Forth" reveals, in turn, is how this "world of mere *withness*" serves also to deflect or minimize the pressure of demand, in this case by diffusing the child's quest to locate the "affection that will not be gainsay'd" into a "mere looking about at things." Ordinarily, the two issues isolated here would appear to be unrelated, but only until we recall that an essential feature of the poet's demand in "Song of Myself" is to silence the dissension of value through the self-evident truths of his art. The catalogs represent one attempt to satisfy this demand, yet we are now in position to note that in suspending the issue of value and the vexed question of justification that goes along with it the catalogs do not finally settle these issues but wind them to a keener pitch. Thus, picking up "Song of Myself" where we left off, we read in section twenty-four: "By God! I will have nothing which all cannot have their counterpart of on the same terms"—an oath which gives vent to a rage for response so relentless in intensity and so overmastering in scope as to precipitate one section later the stifled potency of a voice "unequal to measure itself." For precisely because Speech is designated as that principle of excess forever overextending itself, its very redundancy triggers as well the fear of its own depletion. Held in check by what we have seen Emerson call a redundant deficiency and by what we can recognize as the disrelation between demand and response, Speech incarnates a demand doomed to recoil back upon its owner who, containing too much, contains not enough.

6

The Overstaid Fraction

AFTER 1855 WHITMAN would never again take on a project so ambitious in scale as "Song of Myself." Without necessarily marking a decline in skill or vigor, his subsequent offerings would as a rule take care to begin at a designated site (the Brooklyn Ferry, Paumanok), with a particular emblem (a Broad-axe, this Compost), or cluster themselves around a chosen theme (*Calamus, Drum-Taps*). Another remarkable shift in development, occurring in the pivotal year of 1859–60 with the composition of "Out of the Cradle Endlessly Rocking" and "As I Ebb'd with the Ocean of Life," concerns Whitman's apparent discovery of memory—something notorious for its absence in "Song of Myself." Absent, that is, save in one key respect, for the sole catalyst capable of releasing the power of recollection within the poem is the figure of the grass. "Space and Time!" exults the time traveler of section thirty-three, "now I see it is true what I guess'd at, / When I loaf'd on the grass, What I guess'd at while I lay alone in my bed" (*CRE,* p. 61), an exclamation that would seem to conflate three scenes into one: the speculative revery on the multiple meanings of the grass in section six, the autoerotic epiphany of tongue and bare-strip't heart in section five, and the descent of "the loving and hugging bed-fellow" who steals away at daybreak in section three. Such flashbacks do convey a sense of progress carried forward, of one scene recalling and building upon its predecessors, though it must remain doubtful whether we can join F. O. Mathiessen in holding up Whitman's favored trope as "the central symbol" which endows his chant "with a much more consciously planned structure than it is usually credited with."[1] Explicit references to the grass are just periodic enough to license such expectations and evanescent enough ("gone as quick as come") to baffle them. Nor will it suffice to fix on Whitman's capricious emblem as incarnating the ever-active, ever-elusive play of signification itself, since to do so is merely to repeat without resolving the same condition of an overdetermined indeterminacy we have seen burdening the poet's pursuit of "free growth." Perhaps a better way of describing the enigmatic centrality of the grass as well as the tensions informing it is to consider it in terms of the poem's "overstaid fraction," a suggestive phrase which surfaces in the midst of the staged crucifixion/resurrection scene of section thirty-eight. ("I remember now, / I resume the overstaid fraction," says Whitman, after discovering himself "on the verge of a usual mistake" [*CRE*, p. 72].) Fraction, beyond denoting the part-to-whole ratio fundamental to symbology, more particularly calls up the specter of discontinuity or breakage haunting the passage from latency to confirmed growth. The rivalry between "Speech" and the precarious incipience of its "folded buds," the co-presence of birth and death amid the grave's "uttering tongues," and the internecine strife of sense warring aginst sense variously describe a fracturing of development which threatens to make the desired conception of the poet's leaves by turns premature or belated, arriving either too early or too late. As the poem's "overstaid fraction," the figure of the grass, in its balked development, remains expressive of the central dilemma confronting the poet's "organic compacts": how to overcome the gap between creation and legitimation, between expression and its justification.

The fugitive treatment of the grass, fading in and out of remembrance, comparably reflects upon the design of a poem which, if not wholly constructed *in* memory, is neither entirely constructed without it, but seems a fitful admixture of both elements, as if the poem were written in partial amnesia. To cross into the second half of "Song of Myself" is indeed to enter a muffled echo chamber where phrases, scenes, images, and gestures half-remember and half-forget previous phrases, scenes, images, and gestures. "Flaunt of the sunshine! I need not your bask, lie over!" begins section forty, issuing an apostrophe that salutes in order to rush by the contest with the sun's "dazzling rays" fifteen sections earlier; "the grave of the rock [that] multiplies what has been confided to it," in glancing back on biblical lore, glances back as well on the poet seeking the confidence of the grave's "so many uttering tongues"; "easily written loose fingered chords—I feel the thrum of your climax and close" likewise picks up in passing on the "lull" and "hum" of the soul's "valved voice"; while those "letters from God dropt in the street, and every one signed by God's name" mentioned in section forty-eight take us back some eleven hundred lines to "the handkerchief of the Lord, / A scented gift and remembrancer designedly dropt, / Bearing the owner's name" (*CRE,* pp. 73, 72, 76, 87, 33). So many dangling threads, which may or may not be "designedly dropt," are especially notable in view of Whitman's cautious adaptation of a form whose primary function, as Northrop Frye puts it, is "to teach the nation or whatever we call the social unit which the poet is addressing, its own traditions."[2] So Mnemosyne is the presiding muse of epic art. Of course, no such deity presides over the pages of "Song of Myself," this in part owing to its author's antimythological bias but also to the fact that, as we learn at the outset, singer and muse are one. There is no need to call upon Mnemosyne since the poet has already claimed that role for himself. Spanning the alterations of centuries while remaining unaltered, he does not move through time so much as he incarnates the movement of time itself: "Distant and dead resuscitate, / They show as the dial or move as the hands of me, I am the clock myself" (*CRE,* p. 67). To "accept Time absolutely" means accepting it without reservation as well as accepting it from an absolute, unchanging vantage point. In this programmatic sense, we could say the attenuation of memory as an active principle shaping the poem's development is simply the result of its transcendence of temporal boundaries altogether. It rises above the flux of mutability so as to establish itself as an inexhaustible storehouse of persons, places, and things. The poem, it could be said, does not wish simply to survive *in* memory but to survive *as* memory.

The claim that one's writing stands "before" the laws of time is familiar poetic license, though in the case of "Song of Myself" it is also recognizable as a further variation on the proleptic desire to stand "before" the legislative codes and accepted contracts of worldly life. More directly, it is appropriate to ask at this point how the eternal present of this "kosmos" can be applied to a particular present, how, in effect, the proud stasis of this role can be reconciled to the demand for development and growth. By way of bringing us closer to the persistence of these tensions, we can begin by noting that the second half of "Song of Myself" (sections thirty-four to forty-six, specifically) does follow a pattern of sorts that roughly conforms to the epic convention of *katabasis,* wherein the poet plunges ever more deeply back into history's "antecedent results." Beginning with the massacre at Texas (1836) and the old sea fight (1779), he proceeds—with ample allowance for digressions—through the *imitatio Christi* of section thirty-eight, the auctioneering of antique divinities in section forty-one, and finally to the abyss of Time itself in section forty-five. There we catch him, having completed his descent, now beginning his return:

> My feet strike an apex of the apices of the stairs,
> On every step bunches of ages, and larger bunches
> between the steps,
> All below duly travel'd, and still I mount and mount.
>
> Rise after rise bow the phantoms behind me,
> Afar down I see the huge first Nothing, I know I was
> even there,
> I waited unseen and always, and slept through the
> lethargic mist,
> And took my time, and took no hurt from the fetid
> carbon.
>
> Long I was hugg'd close—long and long.
>
> Immense have been the preparations for me,
> Faithful and friendly the arms that have help'd me.
>
> Cycles ferried my cradle, rowing and rowing like
> cheerful boatmen,
> For room to me stars kept aside in their own rings,
> They sent influences to look after what was to hold
> me.
>
> Before I was born out of my mother generations guided
> me,
> My embryo has never been torpid, nothing could overlay
> it.
> For it the nebula cohered to an orb,
> The long slow strata piled to rest it on,
> Vast vegetables gave it sustenance,
> Monstrous sauroids transported it in their mouths and
> deposited it with care.
>
> All forces have been steadily employ'd to complete and
> delight me,
> Now on this spot I stand with my robust soul.
>
> *(CRE, p. 81)*

What we have been calling a scene of conception has been wittily emptied out into a fable of creation *ex nihilo,* with the self situated at the site of an origin—"I know I was even there"—which is emphatically a nowhere—"the huge first Nothing." In taking us beyond the biological provenance of the soul to the genesis of "the Unknown" itself, language strains to image what must remain imageless. Expressions like "I see . . . Nothing" owe their paradoxical appearance to what Poe terms "an impossible conception." Notions like "God," "Spirit," or "infinity," urges the author of *Eureka,* belong a priori to a metalanguage; devoid of referential content, they signify "the thought of a thought," or "the idea of an idea." Infinitude is in other words "by no means the expression of an idea—but an effort at one. It stands for the possible attempt at an impossible conception."[3] To this we can add that for the "infinite and omnigenuous" demigod depicted above, the status of inconceivability has shifted from an epistemological conundrum to ontological supremacy, the gestation of the soul here being as fathomless as the primeval void. Daunting as this glimpse of bowing phantoms may be, it excites no dread. Rather, whatever anxiety comes through in this otherwise jubilant account assumes a more characteristic form, for it is evidently vital for us to know that this embryo remains undeterred by "the lethargic mist" and "fetid carbon," that it "has never been torpid." The denial of stasis is such that even the soporific Lethe, traditional site of memory's dissolution, offers no resistance. In its portrayal of the soul's progress as unerringly predestined and in its evocation of a benignly nuturing cosmos, the passage rewrites by mythologizing those moments of developmental impasse elsewhere afflicting "free growth." If the "folded buds" of Speech, ideally said to "neither urge the opening of themselves nor resist it" are not mentioned explicitly, the same aura of poised readiness nonetheless informs this profile of the "robust soul" that has "waited unseen and always."

Whitman's myth of prenatal existence thus functions to demonstrate that the past is seamlessly continuous with the experiential present, that, regardless of how far back time is "strip[ped] away," the evolution of the universe is coterminous with the evolution of the self. And as this co-presence argues a faith in retrospective continuity, so does it necessarily hold out the promise of prospective continuity, as we learn explicitly in the next section (forty-six) with the seer speeding "outward and outward and forever outward" through galaxies of space and beyond the "stoppage" of his own death. Loosed from bodily constraints, made inconceivable and therefore ubiquitous, he acknowledges temporality only as so much territory through which to roam at will. So doing, he proclaims himself to be "the acme of things accomplish'd" and "encloser of things to be." While the tall-tale exuberance brought to these and other declarations are all Whitman's own, their millenialist overtones would not have been lost upon a nation of readers schooled in the belief that democracy "resides altogether in the future . . . yet is the product of long ages and cycles of ages of the past" (*Democratic Vistas, PW* 2:475). Closing one chapter in history in the same moment that it opened a new one, the founding of the Republic "perfected" even as it "gave the start to" a vast array of mythic hopes. Thus Barlow's Hesper exclaims to Columbus on first sighting the New World:

> Here springs the day, since time began,
> The highest, broadest, happiest morn of man.
> In these prime settlements thy raptures trace
> The germ, the genius of a sapient race,
> Predestined here to methodize and mold
> New codes of empire to reform the old.[4]

Half a century later another prophet of the New World would confess himself "anxious to improve the nick of time, and notch it on my stick too; to stand on the meeting of two eternities, the past and the future, which is precisely the present moment."[5] Like the author of *Walden*, the author of "Song of Myself" would not only be breathing new life into an old conceit but adapting it to his own purposes. The poet's self-styled millennialism falls under the heading of what we have called the temporizing of proof, whereby prophetic destiny is shown to be already fulfilled even as it awaits future vindication. Because reviewing the past is merely another way of revealing the future, the present is made over into a moment of culmination and anticipation—but never of action. "The past and present wilt," declares Whitman later in the poem, still poised at the meeting of two eternities, "I have fill'd them, emptied them, and proceed to fill my next fold of the future" (*CRE*, p. 88).

It is customary to say that Whitman personalizes these native myths, that more than teaching the nation its own traditions, to recall Frye's definition of the epic, he exemplifies them. Yet to be forever poised at the threshold of two eternities may also be an enervating experience, however exhilarating the correspondence between personal and national myth. "To be in any form, what is that?" Whitman had asked earlier. Following directly after his *nunc dimittis* to his "robust soul" at the end of section forty-five, the ensuing lines grope for an answer:

> O span of youth! ever-push'd elasticity!
> O manhood, balanced, florid and full.
>
> My lovers suffocate me,
> Crowding my lips, thick in the pores of my skin,
> Jostling me through streets and public halls, coming
>   naked to me at night,
> Crying by day "*Ahoy!*" from the rocks of the river,
>   swinging and chirping over my head,
> Calling my name from the flower-beds, vines, tangled
>   underbrush,
> Lighting on every moment of my life,
> Bussing my body with soft balsamic busses,
> Noiselessly passing out handfuls of their hearts and
>   giving them to be mine.
>
>   (*CRE,* p. 82)

The scene (if that is the right word) is manifestly difficult to picture, disintegrating as it does before our eyes. For a writer once described by Wallace Stevens as forever "disintegrating as the world, of which he made himself a part, disintegrates," this in itself is not remarkable, and we will recall, along with Stevens, the alchemizing magic of "Crossing Brooklyn Ferry," whose clairvoyant sees himself "disintegrated, every one disintegrated yet part of the scheme . . . the impalpable sustenance of me from all things at all hours of the day" (*CRE,* p. 110).[6] But in this particular instance the passage from integrated selfhood to its disintegration seems unduly rushed, as if in anxiousness to ford a crossing that has become blocked. The terms of this blockage are not unfamiliar, for the unspecified lovers swelling the body with their plenty return us to the "prurient provokers" of touch "reaching and crowding" the "treacherous tip of me" that also climaxes in suffocation. The glut of alliteration in the last three lines alone vividly mimes the hypertrophy they describe, with the robust soul no longer bending the universe to its will but sliding into a languorous passivity that is deathlike in emphasis. As we have seen elsewhere, the present has become a scene of intensification and constriction: what was to have been filled and emptied here gets condensed into a self-emptying fullness. The wished-for passage from becoming to being, from those "immense preparations" guiding an "embryo [that] has never been torpid" to its undeniable incarnation in "manhood, balanced, florid, and full" remains closed off. Left with no other option than to press forward, the speaker flees from these complications by now imagining his own death in order to look beyond it:

> Old age superbly rising! O ineffable grace of dying
> days!
>
> Every condition promulges not only itself, it
> promulges what grows after and out of itself,
> And the dark hush promulges as much as any.
>
> I open my scuttle at night and see the far-sprinkled
> systems,
> And all I see as high as I can cipher edge but the rim
> of the farthest systems.
>
> Wider and wider they spread, expanding, always
> expanding,
> Outward and outward and forever outward.
>
> (*CRE*, p. 82)

From "tangled underbrush" to unbounded vistas of space; from smothered lips to a bodiless language effortlessly "promulging" itself: the intent of these revisions is clear. Excess is, so to speak, catapulted into the galaxy, where there is no palpable form to restrict or "contain" it. Likewise, the "dark hush" of death dissolves all visual outline and so baffles the accountancy of sight: "see ever so far, there is limitless space outside of that, / Count ever so much, there is limitless time around that." Yet we are once again uncomfortably close to a rhetoric so fierce in its denunciation of stasis ("there is no stoppage and never can be stoppage") that it seems helplessly to fall back on the very fixation it deplores. Strong-arming their way into infinity, his utterances desperately work to reclaim what they can of the promised continuity of past, present, and future by shouting down all other alternatives: "If I, you, and the world, and all beneath or upon their surfaces, were this moment reduced back to a pallid float, it would not avail in the long run, / We should surely bring up again where we now stand, / And surely go as much farther, and then farther and farther"

(*CRE*, p. 82). Beyond the special pleading manifest in what has "surely" arrived and what is "surely" to come, his labored expostulation here fights off a recognition of an impasse in development dimly sensed to have already transpired. Between the glorious past of the self's heroic "embryo" and the beckoning future expanding "outward and outward and forever outward," the only thing missing is the middle ground of the present. Furiously defending this middle ground rather than inhabiting it, Whitman's tone takes on a frustrated stridency evident in such magniloquent hyperboles as " a few quadrillions of eras, a few octillions of cubic leagues do not hazard the span or make it impatient."

Between the everything the self vows to encompass and the nothing it gets reduced to in taking on a discernible shape to confirm that calling, we see how Whitman's insistent dissolution of all temporal boundaries continues to be generated out of a fear of their intransigence. It hardly seems to matter whether the object in question is "manhood, balanced, florid, and full," "offspring taken soon out of [the] mothers' laps," "my knowledge, my live parts," or the figure of the grass itself, for the moment conception is delivered over into visible, realized form is also the moment of overburdening, hypertrophy, and stoppage. Such instances of overcondensation—the recurring symptom of the crisis of legitimacy for Whitman's organicism—are sufficiently ubiquitous for us to see them at work a handful of sections earlier, where the speaker roams through a gallery of presences helplessly trapped in the constraining form of their own bodies. With a degree of violence so extreme that "reaction formation" seems too feeble a description for it, sections thirty-four through thirty-six offer up figures mangled, maimed, mashed, bruised, cuffed, stunned, torn, whipped, burned, half-killed—the "wheeze, cluck, swash of falling blood, short wild screaming, and long, dull, tapering groan" (*CRE*, p. 76). The spectacle of so many ravaged and torn bodies invests the self's access to other persons with an unexpected brutality, as if "Pain's Element of Blank" had carved out a vacancy for the poet freely to inhabit and abandon; or, to adopt the poem's own metaphor, as if "Agonies [were] one of the changes of [the speaker's] garments" to be donned and discarded at liesure. Holding up the body to view as infinitely woundable is here to uphold the invulnerable sway of an onlooker who is nothing but disembodied voice, one who, upon hearing "a call in the midst of the crowd," is startled to discover it is "my own voice, orotund, sweeping, and final" (*CRE*, p. 76). Given this Olympian stance, it is not surprising that Whitman's professions of sympathy for the lame, diseased, or maltreated ("I do not ask how the wounded person feels, I become the wounded person myself") are routinely regarded with skepticism, if only because sympathy is the last thing he seeks. "You there, impotent, loose in the knees, / Open your scarf'd chops till I blow grit within you," reads a typical sample in this vein, "Spread your palms and lift the flaps of your pockets" (*CRE*, p. 74). In such fantasy reversals, whose vehemence is at once funny and frightening, it is of course the reader who suffers from an emasculating constriction that only the "magnifying and applying" bard can relieve. "I dilate you with tremendous breath, I buoy you up," he says to the drowning man, as if the body's "ever-push'd elasticity" could tolerate any amount of expansion without dying of excess, could indeed swell to unthinkable proportions without reaching the bursting point. So long as there are surrogates on whom to try such experiments these acts of violence need not recoil back on the poet's own act of creation.

It is now apparent that the task of conceiving a voice out of vision brings both these acts back together. To "become already a creator" means "putting myself here and now to the ambush'd womb of the shadows" (*CRE*, p. 76). As with so many images in this feverish poem, "the ambush'd womb" starts from the text with a resonance that entirely dwarfs its immediate context. While it could serve as a revealing epitaph for any of the focal scenes of conception we have been discussing, I reserve it here for Whitman's final apostrophe to his leaves as he nears the end of his journey.

> I hear you whispering there O stars of heaven,
> O suns—O grass of graves—O perpetual transfers and
>   promotions,
> If you do not say anything how can I say anything?
>
> Of the turbid pool that lies in the autumn forest,
> Of the moon that descends the steeps of the soughing
>   twilight,
> Toss, sparkles of day and dusk—toss on the black
>   stems that decay in the muck,
> Toss to the moaning gibberish of dry limbs.
>
>   (*CRE*, p. 87)

Some ten lines before this there had been boasting of that "accoucheur" who "to his work without flinching . . . comes" as the poet "recline[s] by the sills of the exquisite flexible doors, / [To] mark the outlet, and mark the relief and escape." As the latter now apostrophizes what he fears may be inaccessible or indifferent, this happy conception fades, leaving in its wake a "dark hush" that suddenly occasions a slowing of time's "perpetual transfers and promotions." The well of Speech has not dried up but remains indefinitely suspended in its condition of stagnancy, still abiding the fecundating grace of the "soughing twilight" and "sparkles of day and dusk." So rather than the incipience of folded buds there emerge "black stems that decay in the muck"—still another figure of birth and death, embryo and skeleton haunting "the begetter of a new offspring out of literature." Peering through the "ambush'd womb of the shadows" these images of speech veer off into incoherence, sundered from the body and its "plenum of proof" as well as from any hope of reproduction. Thirteen hundred lines into the text and the poem is still struggling to be born. "Meanwhile, democracy waits the coming of its bards in silence and in twilight. . . ." (*PW* 2:490).

We seem a long way from those "sparkles hot" and "seed ethereal" which were to vivify the bard's commission in "So Long." Quick to close that distance, Whitman promptly declares himself to "ascend from the moon," now "perceiv[ing] that the ghastly glimmer is but noonday sunbeams reflected." But what is meant to sound forceful is merely forced, a "relief and escape" put to facile use. The "ghastly glimmer" falling on Whitman's swamp sheds just enought light for us to witness the persisting concern throughout his song: what cannot be reproduced in verse cannot survive in memory—a moaning gibberish that leaves no legacy, a nonsense language mourning its own dismemberment. It is in keeping with such apprehension that Whitman should have been fascinated with the fate of entire civilizations incapable of preserving a memory of themselves for the future. "The most immense part of ancient history," one jotting from his *Notes and Fragments* states, "is unknown . . . sublime characters lived and died and we do not know when or where . . . of their literature, government, religions, social customs, and general civilizations—silence" (*N & F,* p. 50). Such lacunae entail what could be called the burden of the past in reverse—not building sepulchres to the fathers in required homage for their accomplishments but the irrevocable disappearance of such accomplishments in "the passage of many thousands of years, the [resulting] vacuity of our letters about them, their places blank upon the map, not a mark or a figure that is demonstrably so" (*N & F,* p. 50). That entire epochs should have "left themselves entirely unbequeathed," the subject of a short meditation in verse titled "Unnamed Lands" and the occasion for more searching inquiry in *Democratic Vistas,* is in its own right sufficient to explain Whitman's unease, though it cannot escape reflection that his concern on this matter has direct application to the present. A "standing disgrace" is how Whitman, as late as 1870, characterizes the continued want of "national, original archetypes in [a] literature" that remains uncertainly stranded between "the grand stages of preparation" and accepted recognition (*PW* 2:413, 405, 409). In the urgency of these charges we overhear the same assumptions that speak through T. S. Eliot's observation that culture "is what justifies other peoples and other generations in saying, when they contemplate the remains and influences of an extinct civilization, that it was *worthwhile* for it to have existed."[7] As they preserve cultural value, so letters substantiate it; "they only," asserts *Democratic Vistas,* "put the nation in form, finally tell anything,—prove, complete anything,—perpetuate anything" (*PW* 2:405). In the quest for a "mark or a figure that is demonstrably so," acts of creation become perforce acts of vindication.

"Song of Myself" registers as part of its burden the struggle to accommodate this double imperative. Could they be brought into workable alignment, proof might stand to perpetuation as desire to fulfillment without each converging on the space of representation in one self-interfering, self-interrupting stroke. Having appreciated the depth of this struggle, we are now in a position to appreciate the modest audacity of the poem's closing lines, which no more pretend to resolve than to disguise the question of what poetry might prove, complete, and perpetuate. For rather than silently entrusting his song to shape its own legacy, Whitman virtually acts out this rite of transmission before our eyes; "bequeath[ing him]self to grow from the grass [he] love[s]," he makes of himself a mnemonic trace interred within and between his lines. If the audacity of his performance continues unabated in a voice trumpeting its "barbaric yawp over the roofs of the world," its modesty consists in asking us do nothing more than what we, as readers, in nearing the end of the poem, have already done. His parting words are both an obituary and an overture:

> The last scud of day holds back for me,
> It flings my likeness after the rest and true as any
>   on the shadow'd wilds,
> It coaxes me to the vapor and the dusk.

I depart as air, I shake my white locks at the runaway
     sun,

I bequeath myself to the dirt to grow from the grass I
     love,
If you want me again look for me under your boot soles.

You will hardly know who I am or what I mean,
But I shall be good health to you nevertheless,
And filter and fibre your blood.

Failing to fetch me at first keep encouraged,
Missing me one place search another,
I stop somewhere waiting for you.

(CRE, p. 89)

As always, he would present himself to us as the meeting place for
consensus, not just its proponent. Overhead and underfoot, in the air
and in our veins, he assumes the kind of placeless universality we
would expect from one who does not propose to speak on our behalf
but to supply the very element and means for our speech. And because
his own speech issues from beyond the grave, his inscrutable workmanship ("you will hardly know who I am or what I mean") is lent
added authority in being divested of any local standpoint which
would fix him to a particular time or place. Yet even as he emphasizes
"I too am untranslatable" the patent concern here is also to localize
traces of that identity for future translators to "fetch." As the subtle
shift from images of decomposition and dispersal to those of consol-
idation and concentration suggests, Whitman continues to seek out a
discourse sufficiently lasting to insure its perpetuation in memory
while evading undue fixation on "value" and the heightened sense of
demand this brings. So the stance of the "I" is neither determinate
nor indeterminate but a peculiar commingling of both qualities, both
vaporized into the air and diffused into the earth but also empowered
to filter and fibre our blood—far but also near, unlocatable but also
beckoning, just out of reach. In this familiar desire to stand both in
and out of the game of conversation, Whitman draws for one last time
on a strategy of displacement also familiar to "Song of Myself," for
while the majority of the verbs in this passage are in the present tense,
their actual function is to evoke an exchange among "I" and "you" as
again something already accomplished as well as something awaiting
future enactment. Whitman empties the present of any sense of pres-
entness; he casts himself back into our past by assimilating himself to

the text we have just read ("to grow from the grass I love") and projects himself ahead into our future ("I stop somewhere waiting for you"), in each way taking care to remove the crisis of legitimacy from the scene of the present. With this fiction at last brought forward with all the unlabored ease and delicacy at the poet's command, the restless spirit of "Song of Myself" comes, momentarily, to rest.

Throughout the past three chapters I have been guided by the assumption that the pursuit of "indissoluble compacts" can only be as compelling as the discourse on which it is founded. For a rhetoric of consensus to be viable there ideally should be a consensus within that rhetoric—in its chosen standards of development, legitimacy, and validation. In the "organic compact" drawn up between poet and his speech we have followed Whitman's effort to secure and make visible the paradigm of "free growth," whose essential features recapitulate in broader outline the paradigm of "free sense" that everywhere animates the design of *Leaves of Grass*. In the execution of that covenant as it is played out in the pages of "Song of Myself" we have followed the necessary vicissitudes which accompany its adoption: the fragile tautology which asserts that art's transcendence of all discursive modes of justification implicitly justifies the superiority of its own discourse; the perplexity which arises when the desired banishment of "proof" from the text escalates the demand for "proof" all the more insistently; the resulting forclosure of beginning and end which threatens to preclude the opportunity for development. In each case we encounter issues of a somewhat different nature from those often addressed in many studies of consensus-formation, where the fiction of a disinterested generality is unmasked as self-interested particularity. To be sure, the same fiction of disinterest preoccupies Whitman's vision of an effortlessly unfolding expression, but there is little need to demystify this vision since no one is more doubtful of its efficacy than the poet himself. The outcome is an extraordinary blend of aspiration and skepticism which energizes the manic buoyancy of "Song of Myself." Poetry's "organic compacts" do not finally resolve the hiatus between the moment of conception and the moment of legitimation—the hiatus shared by their counterparts in the political realm. Where "Song of Myself" does succeed is in prompting us to reflect on the possibilities and limits of poetic discourse as it attempts to remold or heal the public discourse in ways that go beyond merely corrective or pedagogical measures.

PART 3

BREAKING
THE TALLY
The Body,
Comradeship, and
Death

*F*ew "autobiographies" tell us so little about their author as "Song of Myself." When it first appeared the only clue suggesting that its elusive and inscrutable hero lived outside the lines of his poem consisted of a brief notation on the copyright page, which mentioned a "Walter Whitman" and placed him at "Brooklyn, New York, 1855." The details of that life are otherwise strictly subordinated to the creation of a "kosmos," guardian of the "divine average" and prophet of the New World. The meanings he discovers may be compellingly personal, but not simply confessional. As the solitary individual who utters "the word En-Masse," Whitman is concerned to supplement the fortunes of personal identity with those of national identity, indeed to suggest a vital principle of continuity between them. The life of the person and the life of the nation are one: "America, isolated, yet embodying all, what is it finally, except myself? These States, what are they except myself?" (*CRE*, p. 412). Fundamental to this union of interests was of course the maintenance of the Union itself, a necessary symbol of the conjunction of the many and the one. As Daniel Aaron remarks, "*Union* was the keel that kept his religion, philosophy, and aesthetic from foundering. . . . His psychic safety depended upon [its] preservation."[1]

Given such an outlook, it would be more than unreasonable to assume that as portents of what Seward ominously termed an "irrepressible conflict" between North and South grew increasingly visible, Whitman's poetry remained unchanged in terms of its "religion, philosophy, and aesthetic." As an editorialist for the Brooklyn *Daily Times* from 1857 to 1859, Whitman maintained an outwardly sanguine view of the prospects for averting disunion, even to the degree of glimpsing "the opportunity of organizing a great middle conservative party, neither proscribing slavery, like Seward, nor fostering it, like Buchanan."[2] During the same period, however, he was preparing a series of lyrics for the third edition of *Leaves* (to be issued in 1860) which insinuate a pointedly different outlook. *Children of Adam* and *Calamus,* devoted respectively to celebrating the sanctity of "libidinous joys" and the virtues of comradeship, represent something of an impasse for Whitman. Each is concerned to promulgate the gospel of social affection while each, revealingly, falters on the question of what union of interests or larger generality might sustain this affection. This *Children of Adam* does by seeking to totalize the notion of unanimity; offering up the first truly dismal stretch of writing that would make its way into *Leaves,* it pays homage to a monolithic Oneness which, in binding all individuals to the "irresistible gravitation" of sex, also enslaves them. In recoiling against such tactics, the more subdued lyrics of *Calamus* alternately reach an extremity of their own in their implication that the value of comradeship largely consists in shunning any such principle of integration. Whether advocating the transcendence of union at the cost of individuality or upholding the intimacy of private lives in silent disdain of a larger totality, both selections make apparent the growing strain in Whitman's attempt to join together the many and the one without neglecting either term.

The cluster of themes involving the body, sexuality, and comradeship would eventually recede before the lowest common denominator of all in Whitman's hymns to death, introduced in *Sea-Drift* (1859) and extended through much of *Drum-Taps* (1865). The proliferation of these various means of eliciting assent argues an increased restlessness over the desired foundation for union, to be obtained by the spontaneous accord of, say, male friendship in one moment and through the clasp of heavenly death in the next. Although it would be misleading in many respects to suggest that the unraveling of the country's social fabric parallels the unraveling of Whitman's vision of consensus, it is worth emphasizing that these years (1857 to 1865) bear witness to growing apprehensions on Whitman's part over the purpose and direction of his literary "experiment." Now more than ever the ideal of an inalienable pluralism—the flawless receptivity of his songs of the earth, accepting all and rejecting none—seems static and unreal: not merely powerless to cure a fractured polity, the figure of inexhaustible inclusiveness was proving to be oppressive in its own right, as Whitman's seashore ode, "As I Ebb'd with the Ocean of Life" implies in its portrayal of a writer stifled and choked by his own idealisms. By the time war did break out, Whitman made a final attempt to retrieve his archetypal role as healer, literalized in his role as Wound Dresser. In that role as well he also made a final, equivocal attempt to appease the dissensions between the many and the one.

7

The Armies of Love

UP THROUGH ITS FIRST seven editions *Leaves of Grass* adhered to the design of placing "Chants Democratic and Native American" directly after the "barbaric yawp" that came to be known as "Song of Myself." In 1881 Whitman reshuffled that arrangement; settling at last on a title for his self-styled epic, he also brought forward *Children of Adam* and *Calamus,* which had been loitering rather indecisively in the back pages of prior editions, to succeed it. Arguably, the newfound prominence of these sections, along with the displacement of "Chants Democratic," reflects a shift of temperament away from the figure of the Answerer addressing his crowds of artisans, mechanics, and laborers in favor of a more intimate colloquy of lovers venturing down "paths untrodden" and retired from the "clank of the world." How far these poems, composed on the advent of civil war, aim to disengage from the political strife of their day and how far they mean to reform it remains, however, very much a vexed question, for Whitman no less than for his interpreters. Not least of the tensions informing *Calamus,* for example, centers on a chronic hesitation as to whether the theme of "manly attachment" epitomizes democratic bonds or is hopelessly subversive of them, while not least of the ambiguities in *Children of Adam,* in an opposite sense, turns on the question of whether pleasure signifies release from constricting "ties and conventions" or whether these constraints are in fact indispensable for what amounts to a self-delighting play of exhibitionism, shame, and concealment. In either case, it should be acknowledged from the outset that sensual oppression was for Whitman an ineluctable counterpart of political oppression, and in his championing of "a voice resonant, singing the phallus," the poet often reiterated his longstanding conviction that only by repealing the centuries of silence and suspicion in "those speakers and writers fraudulently assuming as always dead what everyone knows to be alive" could "the freest and freshest expression of these States" claim its due (*CRE*, p. 738, 739). The continued "lack of an avowed, empowered, unabashed development of sex," responsible for "the remarkable non-personality and indistinctness of modern productions in books, art, talk," impeded the accomplishment of "great reforms" which democratic institutions and its literature were, in Whitman's view, specially qualified to initiate.

Efforts to revitalize the body politic by preaching the resurrection of the body continue to enjoy periodic resurgence to this day, and it is not surprising that Whitman should be invoked as a guiding prophet by these latter-day crusaders. Still, much as one must honor the sincerity of his intentions and respect the years of persecution he endured to see these selections through print, it cannot be denied that in combating the inhibitions of his time Whitman's "songs of procreation" merely exchange one form of tyranny for another. This is transparently the case in *Children of Adam,* the holographs of which indicate that it was in all likelihood written after "Live Oak with Moss" (later expanded and entitled *Calamus*), thus reversing the sequence presented in *Leaves of Grass*.[1] The overcompensatory strain in *Children of Adam* is unmistakable, as is the implication, stated most succinctly by Justin Kaplan, that "before homosexual men can enjoy even a little happiness with one another heterosexual men and women must enjoy a great deal more."[2] The awkward demarcation between songs of "amativeness" and those of "adhesiveness" anticipates the artificiality of Whitman's project, whose division parallels the format of Melville's "Paradise of Bachelors" and "Tartarus of Maids" but without the trenchant ironies and caustic juxtapositions of Melville's allegory. In veering away from the richly ambiguous and often explosive blurring of sexual identity acted out in previous poems, as in the memorable transsexual fantasy of the twenty-ninth bather by the shore in "Song of Myself" or the exhilaratingly treacherous confusions of gender in "The Sleepers," Whitman monumentalizes, pairing the shrill virilism of *Children of Adam* incongruously with the tender-hearted idylls of *Calamus*. Out of this bifurcation the women of the poet's new Eden emerge, as many have noted, as little more than faceless breeders in attendance upon the egregious strutting of a poet, "stern, acrid, large, undissuadable," who suffers a corresponding debasement in not "dar[ing] to withdraw til I deposit what has so long accumulated within me." Oddly enough, while many of his finer love lyrics are to be found in Whitman's collection of war poetry, his

songs of "amativeness" are more appropriately compared to the battlefield: "Armies of those I love engirth me and I engirth them" (*CRE*,
p. 93). Though this drama of conquest and submission can be taken
to ludicrous extremes—"I pour the stuff to start sons and daughters
fit for these States, I press with slow rude muscle, I brace myself
effectually, I listen to no entreaties"—such posturing more seriously
illustrates the strained relationship between the unlicensed freedom of
"the body correlative attracting" and the comfortless compulsion
which guides it. Nowhere is this strain more pronounced than near
the conclusion of "I Sing the Body Electric" where, after chanting the
sacredness of sex, the poet finds time to loiter near a slave auction.
Shouldering aside an inept slave trader ("the sloven does not know
half his business"), Whitman comes forward to speak in the latter's
voice:

> Gentlemen look on this wonder,
> Whatever the bids of the bidders they cannot be high
>   enough for it,
> For it the globe lay preparing quintillions of years
>   without one animal or plant,
> For it the revolving cycles truly and steadily roll'd.
>
> In this head the all-baffling brain,
> In it and below it the making of heroes.
>
> Examine these limbs, red, black, or white, they are
>   cunning in tendon and nerve,
> They shall be stript that you may see them.
>
> Exquisite senses, life-lit eyes, pluck, volition,
> Flakes of breast-muscle, pliant backbone and neck,
>   flesh not flabby, good-sized arms and legs,
> And wonders within there yet.
>
> > (*CRE*, p. 98)

That Whitman's parody cannot survive the reification it means to
burlesque points up an important, albeit rather disheartening, irony.
It is not simply that, in holding up the pricelessness of this "wonder,"
he can only deepen the fact of depersonalization by going on to glorify
the slave as a eugenic marvel, much in the same way that "a woman's
body at auction" is one section later "not only herself [but] the teeming mother of mothers." Here as in many of these pages a kind of

abstract instrumentality overtakes the rhetoric itself, transforming the "divine list" of the body into a checklist of exchangeable parts: "neck-slue . . . elbow-socket . . . knee-pan . . . lung sponges, stomach-sac . . . heart valves, palate valves" (*CRE,* p. 100). Such inventories, in this case following directly after Whitman's visit to the slave market and eerily recalling the language of the auctioneer, reveal the body to be a supremely alienable possession, displaced everywhere but inhabited by nobody in particular. Like the slave, it retains no distinctive identity of its own beyond the sum of its uses; the helpless servant to an invisible passion, its fate is to be swept up in a torrent of limbs, sighs, achings, torments—"nipples, breast-milk, tears, laughter, weeping, love-looks, love-perturbations" (*CRE,* p. 101). Despite periodic vows to honor the sanctity of "the soul" in a poem like "I Sing the Body Electric," the privileged intimacy of exchange between self and other sought elsewhere in *Leaves* ("what I assume you shall assume") has now fallen away before the agentless erethism of "love-thoughts, love-juice, love-odor, love-yielding, love-climbers, and the climbing sap" (*CRE,* p. 104).

Whitman's trip to the slave auction and the rather self-defeating outlook he brings with him remain entirely symptomatic of a writer who was often slow to sort through his own confusions and doubts concerning the slave crisis, as can be seen not only in his private correspondence but in such passages as the suppressed portrait of "Black Lucifer" in "The Sleepers."[3] Unlike that example, however, what is revealed more particularly in this vignette is not a desired containment or evasion of that crisis so much as an acute helplessness in devising a vision adequate to overcome its afflictions. Yoking the world of commerce to the plight of the slave represents an explosive mix, but the scene cannot carry the full burden of its implications. The apostle of "personalism," devoted above all to the task of restoring the uniqueness of the individual ("the key-stone of my Democracy's enduring arch") is not only strikingly absent but appears to have reversed roles in the process of deepening the condition of alienation he is otherwise pledged to cure. The difference between restoring the human presence and dissolving it has in this respect worn thin; and it is this predicament, intensified and internalized, that constitutes what I take to be a central quandary throughout *Children of Adam.*

For the Whitmanian eros is nothing if not a play of sliding surfaces, a shimmering flux of disparate impulses which suffice in themselves to generate their own machinery of delight: "ebb stung by the flow, and flow stung by the ebb." At extremity, it too evinces that "remarkable non-personality and indistinctness" so loudly denounced by Whitman in the *belles lettres* of his contemporaries. Under the relentless pressure of "so many tender and savage achings," of "the torment, the irritable tide that will not be at rest," the scrupulous cataloging of bodily parts and sensations takes on an unreal urgency—unreal not in the sense of unfelt or fraudulent but in the sense of these sensations becoming unanchored or lifted away from the source presumably experiencing them. "The mystic deliria, the madness amorous, the utter abandonment," by abstracting passion, also invests it with an autonomous power that takes on a life of its own. The result is a speaker who is made a phantom to his own delights: "from sex, from the warp and the woof . . . from the soft sliding of hands over me and thrusting of fingers through my hair and beard" (*CRE*, p. 92). In such ghostly visitations, here found in "From Pent-Up Aching Rivers," bliss is purchased by a degree of self-alienation so acute that the "I" has virtually become a voyeur to his own seduction, as if desire were an anonymous force which descends upon rather than emanates from within the body. Like Augustine's God, Whitman's eroticism is all circumference with no center. Commenting upon "this shoreless sexuality" which thrives "without object or subject," Paul Zweig justly observes that "few poets have written as erotically as Whitman, while having so little to say about sex."[4] Indeed, for all the intensity of their breathless pace and furious yearnings, most of these texts are curiously static in development, often consisting of a string of prepositions ("From Pent-Up Aching Rivers") or participles ("To the Garden the World") which, in eliding any predicate for their actions, cry off grammatical completion.

To a limited extent, this abolition of the subject may no doubt be understood as a conscious design on Whitman's part, one which fully accords with the larger aspirations of his *Leaves*. For in the undifferentiated rush of sensations coursing through the body electric it is possible to infer, in a more positive sense, an effort to retrieve a preindividualist, premimetic aesthetic not yet subservient to any one person or subordinate to any formal hierarchy. Such an aesthetic ideally involves a free-floating circulation of "libidinous joys" whose essence is to diffuse sexuality through space so as to render it both sourceless and universal. In its most familiar form, this decentering of desire is conveyed through the bliss of *inundation*: "I do not ask any more delight, I swim in it as a sea," he writes, mindful of that "diffuse float" which, as always in Whitman, signifies life captured before it has been differentiated into stable egos and sharply defined personalities. The profusion of images in this vein—"the drench of my passions," "gushing showers," "bathing myself in the songs of Sex," "the bath of births"—evokes a medium of baptismal mergings where the tension between part and whole is least evident. Seas, rivers, waves, jets, swells, the ebb and flow abound, immersing all in a "paradisal" condition of passive receptivity that by definition obviates the establishment of a controlling point of view or prevailing center of consciousness. So the lovers of "We Two, How Long We Were Fool'd," one of the more subdued lyrics in this collection, shed the palpable contours of the body in being "transmuted" into "plants, trunks, foliage, roots, bark . . . locust blossoms . . . two predatory hawks . . . two resplendent suns . . . two clouds forenoons and afternoons driving overhead" (CRE, pp. 107, 108). Under the guidance of a nurturing Nature, "long absent but now return[ed]," the pair discover their deception to consist in thinking that desire ever required attachment to a single object. As "seas mingling . . . two of those cheerful waves rolling over each other and interwetting each other," their world recollects the primary narcissism of the child, with its utter loss of distinction between subject and object, internal and external states of being. In fact, as this poem draws to a close it is no longer a world of natural forms Whitman's lovers choose to identify with but rather the very element or medium of identification itself: "we are what the atmosphere is, transparent, receptive, pervious, impervious . . . we are each the product and influence of the globe" (CRE, p. 108). A kind of selfless egotism, moving indifferently through countless incarnations and effusing itself effortlessly through space, is accordingly the promised reward in Whitman's garden of love.

But while this account sets forth the best case for *Children of Adam,* it remains a partial description. That Whitman's fantasy of a universal eros, fusing all in the cosmic "float" of "inexpressible completeness" that precludes social division, may nevertheless have the effect of revealing him to be not only helpless before but in some measure complicitous with certain forms of exploitation he is otherwise intent on challenging constitutes an irony already touched on in his treatment of the slave or his "teeming mother of mothers." Equally significant is the manner in which Whitman's evocation of this "oceanic feeling" has itself become subject to exploitation; for while his recreation of this feeling of ecstatic fusion would reach its most consummate expression a year or so later in the caressing whispers of the maternal sea in "Out of the Cradle Endlessly Rocking," the treatment of this state here undergoes an important shift in emphasis. The self luxuriating in an ocean of instinctual delight does not finally characterize frenetic excursions like "One Hour to Madness and Joy," "From Pent-Up Aching Rivers," or "Spontaneous Me," all of which pursue a rather different course of action in winding up the level of erotic excitation to such a fever pitch that its torments are the more readily drained off or "carelessly" cast aside. Rather than the bliss of inundation, we find a structure more nearly approximating a rite of saturation or catharsis through overburdening, whether it be in "the furious storm" impelling the couple in "From Pent-Up Aching Rivers," "fainting with excess," to "enjoy and exhaust each other" or in the "chanter of Adamic songs" who declares to the woman who waits for him "through you I drain the pent-up rivers of myself." Overloading every rift with ore ("I am he that aches with amorous love") maintains a constant state of erotic irritability which leaves suspended "the hubb'd sting of myself" lacerated by "the no-form'd stings that sights, people, objects sting me with . . . the greed that eats me day and night with hungry gnaw" (*CRE,* pp. 104, 105). Evacuation rather than assimilation, relief rather than receptivity, discharge rather than engorgement defines the prevailing temper of these poems, and in this sense we can follow Quentin Anderson in judging Whitman's task here to be "a labor of undoing, unmaking, not simply a stepping out of doors all naked."[5] Even the pastoral gambols of "We Two, How Long We Were Fool'd" register this emphasis by stressing, in the poem's final line, not what the imagination has taken in but what it has triumphantly expelled: "we have voided all but our own freedom and all but our own joy."

Children of Adam is unnerving not because of its theatrical excess or even because its topic of "amativeness," so plainly foreign to Whitman's temperament, fails utterly to engage his full sympathy. Rather, what makes the sequence distressing is that its celebration of the body shows every sign of being wrenched into a tendentious framework which reveals itself to be an especially distended and desperate extension of Whitman's democratic idealism. In search of that lowest common denominator affirming "the oath of inseperableness," sex is advanced as that *sine qua non* which "contains all"—the "enclosing basis of every thing." And yet, as I have intimated, what is intended to sanctify relatedness also touches off its own obliteration. "I am drawn by its breath as if I were no more than a helpless vapor," intones the worshiper of "the female form," the latter likewise "lost in the cleave of the clasping and sweet-fleshed day" (*CRE*, p. 92). In Whitman's restored Eden, the desired elision of difference works too efficiently, and in agreeing with Zweig that *Children of Adam* has "little to say about sex" we can say more exactly that it is about the empowering of a compulsive eros which, by subtending all relationships—"all hopes, benefactions, bestowals, all the passions . . . all the governments, judges, gods, followed persons of the earth" (*CRE*, p. 102)—also subsumes them. Thus, should we be curious to know what it is that "the body correlative attracting" in "From Pent-Up Aching Rivers" attracts, an answer of sorts emerges in the next line with mention of the "correlative body." In such moments, the conjunctive term responsible for transmuting difference into unanimity, bringing to light "the merge of large and small," stands frozen in a position of sheer tautology, correlative to itself alone and placing in jeopardy the very idea of a mediating center. Or, more precisely, it can be said that this center has become hypertrophied, a supreme figure of inclusion that induces a more drastic sense of exclusion. This is why many of Whitman's invocations exhibit a tension between regarding the "sacred songs of sex" as a transitive force vital to the establishment of connection or as a wholly intransitive entity that consumes all relations into itself. "O my body!" exclaims the speaker of "I Sing the Body Electric," pledging fealty to his theme as a sonneteer would to his mistress, "I dare not desert the likes of you in other men and women, nor the likes of the parts of you" (*CRE*, p. 100). His colloquialism straddles both sides of the question: is the body prized as a site of correspondences or "likenessess" or does "likes of you" point up an auto-affection all its own? The syntax deepens this perplexity by making it an open question as to whether Whitman means to say that desertion of his theme will occur *unless* "the likes of you" are perceived "in other men and women" or whether he means the reverse, that desertion of his theme will occur *if* these affinities are recognized in others. And certainly in a more general sense, this same play between the transitive and the intransitive is registered in the constant trafficking back and forth, in the imagery of both *Children of Adam* and *Calamus,* between the heterosexual and the masturbatory, or between the homoerotic and the autoerotic.

Which brings us to what is no doubt the most notorious poem in this collection, "Spontaneous Me." Forty-five lines of adverbial phrases that stave off the appearance of a predicate until its very end, Whitman's ode to onanism merits special attention not only because it allows us to trace a curve of development mostly absent in its companion pieces but because it vividly illustrates many of the themes we have been discussing, most notably the creation of a totalitarian eros together with the lapsing away of connection this idolatry implies. That the poem continues to be misread as an Adamic tribute to the joys of the polymorphously perverse is at least in part explained by its splendid opening, which provides some of the finest writing in *Children of Adam* as well as a glimpse of the kind of project this sequence might have been:

Spontaneous me, Nature,
The loving day, the mounting sun, the friend I am
      happy with,
The arm of my friend hanging idly over my shoulder,
The hillside whiten'd with blossoms of the mountain
      ash,
The same late in autumn, the hues of red, yellow,
      drab, purple, and light and dark green,
The rich coverlet of the grass, animals and birds, the
      private untrimmed'd bank, the primitive apples, the
      pebble-stones,
Beautiful dripping fragments, the negligent list of
      one after another as I happen to call them to me or
      think of them,
The real poems, (what we call poems being merely
      pictures,)
The poems of the privacy of the night, and of men like
      me,
This poem drooping shy and unseen that I always carry, and
      that all men carry, . . .
                             (*CRE*, p. 103)

As so often in *Leaves of Grass,* resemblance is stated in terms of simple adjacency. Neither the spontaneity of the self nor the spontaneity of Nature is invoked as the ground for the other, in the way we are taught to regard metaphor as grounding one term in another. Notwithstanding a stray expression like "the rich coverlet of the grass," Whitman's aim is to withdraw from notice any trace of an interpretive will that prides itself on teasing similitude out of dissimilars or seeing a world in a grain of sand.[6] He characteristically considers his words—"beautiful dripping fragments"—as supplementing the landscape rather than substituting for it. Hence the negative judgment lodged against an aesthetic which, staled by convention, merely aspires to counterfeit natural forms, as opposed to coexisting beside them. To the latter category belong "the real poems"—real not in the sense of duplicating nature but in recognizing themselves to be fluid extensions of the body (as in the metonymy of phallus as poem), from whose parts and gestures Whitman believed language to derive. "Human bodies are words, myriads of words," he writes elsewhere; "I myself am a word with them—my qualities interpenetrate with them" ("A Song of the Rolling Earth," *CRE,* pp. 219–20).

Like "Song of Myself," "Spontaneous Me" begins in a mood of alert receptivity. Beyond its care in evoking self and nature as mutually implied, coextensive presences, we note as well its care in naturalizing the manner in which this correspondence is conveyed. Interestingly, however, as the poem unfolds a different emphasis materializes. After another ten lines depicting man, animal, and plant life all reaching after sensual release, Whitman shifts from comparison to contrast, now imagining his "Adamic sons and daughters" writhing in an inferno of sexual denial and recrimination, grotesquely out of tune with the spontaneous luxuriance of nature. Part excruciating confession and part lurid melodrama, his catalog of sexual anguish takes as much pleasure in shame as it can ever hope to divide shame from pleasure. We pick him up at midpoint in the poem, still in half-breath:

> The no-form'd stings that sights, people, objects,
>   sting with me,
> The hubb'd sting of myself, stinging me as much as it
>   ever can any one,
> The sensitive, orbic, underlapp'd brothers, that only
>   privileged feelers may be intimate where they are,
> The curious roamer the hand roaming all over the body,
>   the bashful withdrawing of flesh where the fingers
>   soothingly pause and edge themselves,
> The limpid liquid within the young man,
> The vex'd corrosion so pensive and so painful,
> The torment, the irritable tide that will not be at
>   rest,
> The like of the same I feel, the like of the same in
>   others,

> The young man that flushes and flushes, and the young
>   woman that flushes and flushes,
> The young man that wakes deep at night, the hot hand
>   seeking to repress what would master him,
> The mystic amorous night, the strange half-welcome
>   pangs, visions, sweats,
> The pulse pounding through palms and trembling
>   encircling fingers, the young man all color'd, red,
>   ashamed, angry; . . .
>
>   (*CRE*, pp. 104–5)

Alliteration, assonance, and asyndeton here join forces with an efficiency that suggests a speaker who is not simply the helpless prey to the spontaneous overflow of forbidden delights but more like a shaman strenuously conjuring their power. As the rhetoric builds to a self-mesmerizing, incantatory pitch, one thinks for immediate comparison of the pounding tetrameters of Blake's "The Tyger," a poem which concerns another persona who finds onanistic glee in terrifying himself with visions of a malevolent sublimity.[7] As in Blake's lyric, the mingling of self-induced frenzy and opportunistic self-gratification is extraordinary: even as Whitman is drawn to a sympathetic portrayal of his "flushing and flushing" men and women, his lines quite plainly throb with a voyeuristic excitement that feeds on their misery. The suggestion of emotional parasitism which the end of the poem will bring quite literally to a climax is further enhanced by the flurry of metonymic constructions ("the curious roamer," "underlapp'd brothers," "irritable tide," "hot hand") which now get invested with a life of their own. In this fetishizing of compulsion, we see how the poem's initial analogy begins to be warped out of focus, in that what was to serve as the connective link between self and nature—the delight of a spontaneous eroticism—begins now to serve its own ends.

It is this widening gap between act and agency, creator and thing created that permits Whitman not so much to finish the poem as finish it off:

> The souse upon me of my lover the sea, as I lie
>   willing and naked,
> The merriment of the twin babes that crawl over the
>   grass in the sun, the mother never turning her
>   vigilant eyes from them,
> The walnut-trunk, the walnut-husks, and the ripening
>   or ripen'd long-round walnuts,

The continence of vegetables, birds, animals,
The consequent meanness of me should I skulk or find
                    myself indecent, while birds and animals never once
                    skulk or find themselves indecent,
The great chastity of paternity, to match the great
                    chastity of maternity,
The oath of procreation I have sworn, my Adamic and
                    fresh daughters,
The greed that eats me day and night with hungry gnaw,
                    till I saturate what shall produce boys to fill my
                    place when I am through,
The wholesome relief, repose, content,
And this bunch pluck'd at random from myself,
It has done its work—I toss it carelessly to fall
                    where it may.

                                                    (*CRE*, p. 105)

If the poet does not smile his work to see neither does he deprecate it.
"Carelessly" is the word he chooses, and whether we take this to
signify the triumphant oblivion of long-awaited release or (more
darkly) as self-contempt now deadened to unconcern, a sense of chastened indifference prevails. And at the point of this indifference any
further comparison to Blake's lyric stops. For we are no longer presented with a speaker prostrate before the tyranny of his senses but
one who coolly turns on these projections in order to fling them aside.
There is a reversal of sorts but no real recognition: the labor of spontaneity, once its "work" is done, climaxes in a catharsis for catharsis'
sake. This, one imagines, is more unsettling than anything the poem
could disclose by way of "the vex'd corrosion" or "the strange half-
welcome pangs." Its fearful symmetry owes less to the stinging ebb
and flow of sexual desire than to the manner in which the poem, as we
now discover, has come to appropriate its tensions in a strictly instrumental fashion, as if the value of verse here consisted in disburdening
itself of its own fictions. Clearing a path for this catharsis is of course
the final shift in analogy from the poem as an extension of the body to
its status as a detachable, discarded product—a shift here functioning
to shrink rather than expand the poem's field of resemblance.

    In treating this poem as a calculated exercise in psychosexual extor-
tion, I should add that the rather jaundiced attitude I am ascribing to
it need not be attributed to its subject matter. Although it would be

rash to maintain that as a rule "Whitman's preoccupation with auto-eroticism is in itself neither particularly surprising nor interesting,"[8] it does carry a celebratory emphasis that extends beyond the pathological or solipsistic, as we can gather by thinking back on the mating of body and soul in section five of "Song of Myself," whose aftermath promotes a quickened appreciation for the bounty of natural forms. "Spontaneous Me" inverts this sequence: beginning in a pose of negligent receptivity, it marches toward a climax that leaves nothing in its wake. Aside from flouting a Biblical taboo, its "wholesome relief, repose, content" reads more pointedly like a satire on Whitman's own cherished identification of his leaves as a bequest or gift. "Interchange it youths with each other! let none render it back!" he exhorts elsewhere in reference to the lines he is now composing. "Collecting, dispensing, singing . . . plucking something for tokens, tossing toward whoever is near me" ("These I Singing in Spring," *CRE,* pp. 119, 118), he underscores the truism that for the gift to retain its value it must remain in constant circulation, continuously available for use without being destroyed in its consumption. Antithetically, the bunch plucked at random and carelessly tossed aside is used to be used up. It closes off the cycle of exchange with a vehemence that is more disdainful than despairing, as the sardonic aside to those "boys to fill up my place when I am through" denotes. Inasmuch as the priorities of this poem are so arranged that obtaining relief takes precedence over obtaining a legacy, it is instructive to note further how the arduous task of conceiving "a new offspring out of literature" so much at stake in "Song of Myself" has also become the subject of satiric deflation. For in lieu of the alarming convergence of excess and loss afflicting the "free growth" of "perfect poems" we find a more programmatic pursuit of exhaustion by means of saturation. "Walt, you contain enough, why don't you let it out, then?" provokes no consternation in the author of "Spontaneous Me" since that is precisely the question his poem is tailored to accommodate. Not a "living organism" effortlessly exfoliating outward but concentrated release here is the result: "the dead leaf whirling its spiral whirl and falling still and content to the ground."

Neither the best nor the worst of his productions, "Spontaneous Me" may qualify as one of Whitman's most harrowing. Nothing else in his *Leaves*—not even the withering pantomime of "the Real me" standing "before all my arrogant poems" and "mocking me with mock-congratulatory signs and bows" in "As I Ebb'd with the Ocean of Life"—is quite so expert in the manipulation of its detachment or quite so cynical in its stance toward poetry. It is this latter feature that I wish now to address more extensively, for although the poem was published as early as 1856 the implied turning against verse registered in this bunch plucked at random marks an important trend which not only plays through *Children of Adam* but becomes increasingly visible in *Calamus*. In these songs of "adhesiveness," Whitman's phrenological password for homosexuality, one detects a mounting despair over the efficacy of written documents, poetry foremost among them, to bind, mediate, or reconcile. No section of *Leaves of Grass*, it is true, is entirely free of this suspicion; as we have seen elsewhere, bonds which require confirmation in print are for Whitman among the most precarious—one reason why he would have us consider that "what the push of reading could not accomplish, is accomplish'd by me personally, it is not?" But while the alliance between writing and consensus is often uneasy, in *Calamus* it becomes openly adversarial. Such is the state of affairs described in "When I Heard at the Close of the Day," where the rewards of artistic fame ("plaudits in the capitol") pale in comparison to the reunion of lovers accompanied in their solitude by "the hissing rustle of the liquid and sand . . . whispering to congratulate me" (*CRE*, p. 123). "Scented Herbage of My Breast" similarly raises "immortal reverberations" for comrades, but only after angrily dismissing its "emblematic and capricious" leaves which no longer serve; meanwhile, "Whoever You Are Now Holding Me in Hand" admonishes the "candidates for my love" against the folly of ever presuming to "catch" its meaning in the conning leaves of his book. Or, in being assailed with "the sense that words and reason hold not," the victim in "Of the Terrible Doubt of ·Appearances," like the student in "The Base of All Metaphysics," takes the measure of lofty intellectual ambition and finds it wanting when measured against "the dear love of man for his comrade, the attention of friend to friend." For one who likewise urges his "recorders ages hence" to "mind not so much my poems" but "the measureless ocean of love within," it appears that whatever is shareable in experience has come to exist despite and not at the behest of poetry's assistance.

In venturing upon "standards not yet published" and in twice serving notice that "I am surely far different from what you suppose," the creator of *Calamus* is of course concerned to refashion his image by drawing away from the "magnifying and applying" kosmos of "Song of Myself" or the *vox populi* of "Chants Democratic." He reins in the customary urge to identify with any- and everything at hand, and though he may continue to saunter through "the city of my walks and love," it is not "the pageants of you . . . nor the shifting tableaux" that suffice but "the frequent and swift flash of eyes offering me love" (*CRE*, p. 126). Even so, it remains perplexing why the theme of "superb friendship" should gain in stature precisely in proportion to poetry's disparagement. Conventional explanations do not entirely help. Little anxiety, for example, is voiced over the burden of inexpressiveness (speech alone cannot adequately convey the full import of his subject) or, worse yet, the curse of inexpressibility (the subject itself may be unspeakable). Speaking more sensibly on these issues than most, David Cavitch observes that "in writing about homosexual love, whatever dangers of social opprobrium he faced, Whitman was primarily creative, not primarily reticent. In seeming to withdraw from open view, he is giving expression to something he positively wants from the fullness of love's satisfaction; he is not merely reflecting a social taboo."[9] In fact, Whitman's apparent disfavor with verse making did not translate into a lack of productivity: of all the installments issued over the course of his career, the 1860 edition of his *Leaves* represents the single largest increment, with *Calamus* itself forming the most sizable portion of these additions.

Since Whitman's unease with poetry appears to belong to a more general sense of disillusion, a wider background is necessary here. From letters and notebooks we learn that the years 1857 to 1859 gripped Whitman with an increasing sense of restlessness: having issued the second edition of *Leaves* to little more acclaim than the first, he was driven back to newspapering, there churning out sundry editorials for the *Brooklyn Daily Times*. Goading himself with the question "Walt Whitman stands to-day in the midst of the American people, a promise, a preface, an overture. . . . Will he justify the great prophecy of Emerson?", he resolved "not to be diverted from the principle object—the main work . . . The Great Construction of the New Bible" (*DB* 3:779; *N & F*, p. 57). About the same time he began to conceive of "Live-Oak with Moss," a cluster of twelve lyrics to be modeled after the fashion of an Elizabethan sonnet sequence which would make up the core of *Calamus,* he also toyed with the long-cherished fantasy of taking to the lecture circuit as an itinerant orator and in fact did deliver a speech sometime in 1858 under the sweeping title "Slavery—the Slaveholder—The Constitution—the true America and Americans, the laboring persons."[10] At most, his pam-

phlet merely succeeds in repeating the same deadlock in reasoning
that had afflicted his jeremiad of two years before in "The Eighteenth
Presidency!": though an intolerable transgression against the eco-
nomic and moral order and "repugnant to the foundations of law,"
slavery nevertheless claims the sanction of States' rights, itself guaran-
teed by the Constitution "as one of the most important principles of
the compact."[11] Only now, however, the orator's wrath does not
descend on the political parties and their leaders ("scum floating atop
the waters . . . bats and night dogs askant in the capitol" [*CRE*, p.
278]) but shifts to disillusion over the "sacred compact" itself. Noting
that the British Constitution— "that heap without form and on which
no man can put his finger . . . [so] vague we hardly know what"—
has outlawed slavery while the American Constitution continues to
uphold it, Whitman is compelled to ask "Is there no meaning, no
truth, no definiteness in writings, in engagements?"[12] Legislated
Union, in the wake of failed resolutions and bloody compromises,
seemed more than ever a contradiction in terms, a premonition given
added vehemence in "For You, Democracy," the fifth poem in the
Calamus sequence. "States! Were you looking to be held together by
the lawyers? / By an agreement on a paper? Or by arms?" As his
oration envisions a "circling Confederacy, standing together with
interlinked hands, ample, equal, each with his grip of love wedged, in
life or death to all the rest," so his poem involves "a new friendship . . . [to] circulate through the States, indifferent of place, / It
shall twist and intertwist them through each other—Compact they
shall be, showing new signs." Materializing "beyond all the forces of
courts and arms," this new friendship promises a "continent indissoluble" and deathless, "divine magnetic lands" which, overreaching
sectional rivalry, join "Columbia's lovers" as "masters of the world
under a new power."

It goes without saying that these pious exhortations count as little
more than stop-gap measures, wishful prophecies whose inflated op-
timism is portentous in its own right. When Whitman flatly proclaims
that "affection shall solve every one of the problems of freedom," we
readily infer the desperation in his naïveté—the kind of desperation
that in fact fuels the strident dogmatism of *Children of Adam*. *Calamus*
is neither strident nor dogmatic, but it is important to note how its
author's shaken belief in "writings and engagements" impinges on his
own sense of vocation. One poem, "Long I Thought Knowledge
Would Suffice," makes this impact explicit by acting out a rather self-

righteous morality play involving a bard of simpleminded good faith who once set upon a mission "to enclose . . . to strike up the songs of the New World," then believing that "my life must be spent in singing." "Then my lands engrossed me," he explains; "Lands of the prairies, Ohio's lands, the Southern savannas engrossed me—For them I would live—I would be their orator." But this proud dedication has played itself out; in the manner of a chagrined employee determined to quit his post, the speaker summons his beloved lands to "now take notice . . . that you each and all find somebody else to be your singer of songs, / For I can be your singer of songs no longer." There is doubtless more than a hint of special pleading in bringing grievances forward so bluntly, like someone hoping to be humored out of his disaffection by overstating it. Then, too, we must suspect Whitman's passing mention of a "jealous" rival who "withdraws me from all but love" to be more a pretext for than the occasion of his resignation. Nevertheless, his disillusion is both emphatic and heartfelt: "With the rest I dispense—I sever from what I thought would suffice me, for it does not,—it is now empty and tasteless to me." With the fruits of his labor affording no sustenance, little comfort is to be gained by asserting that "the United States themselves are essentially the greatest poem" at a time when the subject of this sentence is starting to look increasingly defunct. "I heed knowledge, and the grandeur of The States, and the example of heroes, no more, / I am indifferent to my own songs," adds Whitman, now bringing the logic of his own private drama of secession into focus. Better, it appears, to resign his commission now, circa 1858, than to see it rendered meaningless in the immediate future. Petulant and bitter, he elects to "go with him I love, / It is enough for us that we are together." At least it can be said of them, in a tone closer to reproach than consolation, that "we never separate again."[13]

Neither "For You, Democracy" nor "Long I Thought Knowledge Would Suffice" found a permanent place in *Calamus*, the first being overhauled and transposed to *Drum-Taps* under the title "Over the Carnage Rose a Prophetic Voice" while the second was dropped from later editions altogether. Although *Calamus* does not suffer appreciably by their departure, their suggestion that the poet is not simply concerned to revise a vocation but reject it quite literally out of hand ("with the rest I dispense") hovers over poems which do not on their surface explicitly address the crisis of sectional strife or failed compacts. That the following chant, for example, has excited virtually no interest in the numerous studies of Whitman extant is in large part explained by the indifference it maintains toward itself. After the fashion of "Spontaneous Me," it too is a text written to be dispensed with:

> Not heaving from my ribb'd breast only,
> Not in sighs at night in rage dissatisfied with
> myself,
> Not in those long-drawn, ill-supprest sighs,
> Not in many an oath and promise broken,
> Not in my wilful and savage soul's volition,
> Not in the subtle nourishment of the air,
> Not in this beating and pounding at my temples and
> wrists,
> Not in the curious systole and diastole within which
> will one day cease,
> Not in many a hungry wish told to the skies only,
> Not in cries, laughter, defiances, thrown from me when
> alone far in the wilds,
> Not in the husky pantings through clinch'd teeth,
> Not in sounded and resounded words, chattering words,
> echoes, dead words,
> Not in the murmurs of my dreams while I sleep,
> Nor in the limbs and senses of my body that take you
> and dismiss you continually—not there,
> Not in any or all of them O adhesiveness! O pulse of
> my life!
> Need I that you exist and show yourself any more than
> in these songs.
>
> (*CRE*, p. 119)

The last word of the first line would seem to prepare us for the kind of democratization of the forbidden handled so capably elsewhere in the *Leaves*. "It is not upon you alone the dark patches fall," runs a memorable passage from "Crossing Brooklyn Ferry"; "I too knitted the old knot of contrariety . . . Had guile, anger, lust, hot wishes I dared not speak." As it turns out, though, this path to identification Whitman now declines to follow—hungry wishes and ill-suppressed sighs are no longer thought to deepen ties to his community of listeners but are to be left behind for a newfound theme, "adhesiveness." It is difficult to credit this leave-taking for a number of reasons. Most prominently, there is the prolonged litotes that allows the speaker to mention at length and in exquisitely rendered detail all those things which, we belatedly learn, no longer need mentioning. Evident too is the saving sublimation that accompanies the closing salute to comradeship, whose chaste passion suddenly cools the seething cauldron of half-throttled impulses and rageful recriminations. So doing, the development of the poem obeys what we can by now recognize to be a familiar pattern of exhaustion by overburdening, of building up to a sensory overload so insistent as to precipitate release. The result, one is bound to feel, is that the final two lines, in addition to being anticlimactic, are also knowingly perfunctory. For what is being left behind is in reality neither the heaving breast nor the broader claims to fellowship but any expectation that verse might mediate between these suddenly opposed realms. "Any more than in these songs" nods to verse as if in afterthought, as though it were expressly divorced from involvement in "the soul's savage and willful volition" to say nothing of "the pulse of my life" which suffices to "exist and show" itself in its own right. Cut off from a circuit of exchange, working up the frenzy of onanistic passion in order to work it off, the fortunes of poetry come to resemble the anguishing play of "the limbs and senses of my body," taken to be dismissed, used to be used up.

Art, Freud surmised long ago, sublimates passion. It is a "substitute gratification" or harmless "narcotic" that courts "illusion in contrast to reality." Because a writer's daydreaming is "almost always harmless and beneficent," it never seeks anything "but illusion," and excepting those "few people who are, one might say, obsessed by Art, it never dares make any attack on the realm of reality."[14] Such assessments, today considered to be unacceptably reductive, scarcely do justice to the supple and nuanced range of Freud's psychology. They bespeak, as Lionel Trilling was first to point out, a degree of condescension that borders on contempt.[15] Whatever the sources of Freud's disdain (the poets and philosophers, he once allowed, had preceded his discoveries), there are grounds for believing that Whitman's stance in these texts is better clarified by the nature of Freud's response rather than any theory of artistic reparation one might wish to apply to them. For if the fruits of the poet's vocation, now "empty and tasteless," have soured, such disillusion is not adequately explained by the sense that verse has become insufficient as a substitute for pleasure. Instead, it seems to me that the despair seizing these poems is more aptly described from the opposite viewpoint, where contempt is expressed by the insistence that the function of writing should now be delimited to precisely this compensatory status. Thus, in a somewhat milder vein, the lyrics of *Calamus* are at one point designated to be "the pay" which "is certain one way or another" to compensate for the bitterness of unreturned love ("I loved a certain person ardently and my love was not returned, / Yet out of that I have written these songs" [*CRE*, p. 134]). "Here I shade and hide my thoughts," we are told elsewhere, these being "the frailest leaves of me and yet my strongest lasting . . . they expose me more than all my other poems" ("Here the Frailest Leaves of Me," *CRE*, p. 131). With such declarations in mind one commentator remarks, justly if somewhat overcautiously, that "there seems to be frank recognition by the poet that his poetry represents the sublimation of his adhesiveness."[16] Strictly speaking, this way of stating the case sounds slightly disingenuous: ordinarily one would assume that what is meant to elude the eye of the censor by transmuting "base" impulses into "valued" creations cannot at the same time be "frankly" monitored by it. Turning to verse in conscious expectation that it make up for or appease pleasures otherwise missing or denied in actuality may, on the other hand, be another way of turning upon that verse. "Stain every page, stain every song I sing, every word I say, bloody drops, / Let them know your scarlet heat, let them glisten" implores the crazed self-mutilator of "Trickle Drops," whose "falling . . . bleeding drops" issue "from wounds made to free you whence you were prison'd." Because the impetus for speech has virtually disappeared into the demand for discharge, the violence perpetrated upon the self must find ready outlet on the page: "saturate [these lines] with yourself all ashamed and wet, / Glow upon all I have written or shall write, bleeding drops, / Let it all be seen your light. . ." Words are not set over these onanistic wounds with the promise of a liberating cure; on the contrary, the grim zeal of the tone evokes a perverse delight in parodying the possibility of any such restitution, with words serving as the passive receptacle for the staining of such "confession drops." The speaker of "Trickle Drops," like those of "Not Heaving from My Ribb'd Breast," "Long I Thought Knowledge Would Suffice," and "Spontaneous Me," is not particularly interested in art's "abundant recompense" unless it is to savage this notion by reducing it to the crudest exigency. What we see acted out, in effect, is not a desire for artistic reparation so much as strategies for immobilizing its potential, of narrowing the work of the poem to the most immediate service of instant desublimation.

In this regard, the pressing question of *Calamus* is not, as it is so often construed, "what affects are being sublimated in this poetry?" but rather "why has the dynamic of sublimation itself become so paralyzed, so susceptible to a repressive literalism?" Traditionally defined, sublimation is of course esteemed as the building block of culture, where instinctual energy is desexualized and rechanneled into socially sanctioned norms, thus reconciling the public and the private. Whitman would want to use different terms but this is essentially the line of reasoning he follows in sponsoring the virtues of "adhesiveness." As he tells us in *Democratic Vistas,* "it is to the development, identification, and general prevalence of that fervid comradeship (the adhesive love, at least rivaling the amative love hitherto possessing imaginative literature, if not going beyond it,) that I look for the counterbalance and offset of our materialistic and vulgar American democracy, and for the spiritualization thereof" (*PW* 2:414). "Fervid" as it may be, manly attachment spiritualizes the materialistic and vulgar alike; its influence "fuses, ties, and aggregates, making races comrades, and fraternizing all" (*PW* 2:381). Distinct from the "fast-anchored, eternal" love of man and woman, bound and adjudicated by legal contract, passion between men is "disembodied . . . ethereal"—a passion which knows no laws and which, "stepping with freedom and command, leading not following," is "earth-born, simple, never constrain'd, never obedient" (*CRE,* pp. 135, 129). Its "faint indirections" pry loose determinate divisions of class, caste, and nationality (see "This Moment Yearning and Thoughtful"); more than a sexual preference alone, "it waits, and has always been waiting, latent in all men" as the "germs" or "main purports of these States" ("To the East and to the West," *CRE,* p. 134).

Not surprisingly, these and other comments like them have proven to be an easy mark for what can be called the Wing Biddlebaum interpretation of *Calamus:* uneasy with longings he could neither fathom not tolerate, Whitman found it necessary to cloak his homosexuality under the banner of appeals to fraternal union, much in the same way that Anderson's grotesque, terrified by the wayward longings of his roaming hands, soothes his distress by dreaming of "a pastoral golden age" of "clean-limbed young men . . . gather[ing] about the feet of an old man who sat beneath a tree and talked to them."[17] Not much reflection is required, though, to see how this school of thought merely draws on the same equation (literature as "substitute gratification") that we have seen afflicting some of the poems in *Calamus* itself—what we are looking for is a possible explanation for this reductiveness, not another version of it. To this end, it should be possible to take seriously Whitman's endorsement of "a fervent, accepted development of Comradeship" as instrumental in "weld[ing] together . . . a Living Union" without relegating it to defensive fantasy. As has already been hinted, the interest reflected through his writings at large in the "spiritualizing," "disembodied," or "ethereal" nature of these ties suggests that "adhesiveness," rather than simply a desire in need of deflection or displacement, came to signify for Whitman something like the very process of sublimation itself, most notably in its translation of particular needs into general laws. "Sublimation melts the formal otherness of things," Thomas Weiskel generalizes in his study *The Romantic Sublime;* it enacts "the transubstantiation of what Marx called 'individual ties' and Blake called 'minute particulars' into an abstract medium of exchange."[18] Along similar lines, Romantic aesthetics commonly accorded artistic expression the special distinction of uniting the particular to the universal; so it is that the Coleridgean imagination "dissolves, diffuses, dissipates, in order to recreate."[19] And while we must be grateful to Whitman for never attempting his own theory of the imagination, the concept of "an abstract medium of exchange" does not simply describe a compelling feature of his verse but identifies, in Whitman's own poetics of union, precisely that principle his verse aspires to embody. *Leaves of Grass* accordingly fashions its own jargon of transubstantiation, or what is more grandiloquently called "the fervid and tremendous IDEA, melting everything else with resistless heat and solving all lesser and definite distinctions in vast, indefinite, spiritual, emotional power," a power necessary to combat the danger "of irreconcilable interiors, and [the] lack of a common skeleton knitting all close" (*PW* 2:368). Before integration a stage of disintegration must transpire whereby "creeds, conventions fall away . . . all statements, churches, sermons melt away . . ." (*PW* 2:394, 399) as a prelude to the recuperation of "one primary, broad, universal platform" (*PW* 2:380).

Calamus, in turn, displays a growing sense of estrangement from such notions, as if to suggest that they have lost their power of persuasion. Much as it may be inclined to "give an example to lovers to take permanent shape and will through the States," whose "purports essential" will "perhaps dissipate this entire show of appearance" (*CRE,* p. 115), or to sound the tocsin for "the institution of the dear love of

comrades / Without edifices or rules or trustees or any argument"
(*CRE*, p. 128), this prophetic emphasis bears an uneasy relation to the
rest of the text. On balance, such pronouncements have the feel of
being grafted onto the sequence at large rather than sustaining it.
More pointedly, we have already noted the habit of some of these
poems to offer up what appear to be willfully debased or paralyzed
versions of Whitman's rhetoric of "spiritualization," with poems as
seed discarded at will or words as wounds staining the page. The more
temperate and better-known selections in *Calamus* shy away from
such tactics, yet even here there is a tendency to circumscribe or freeze
up the symbolizing process in a manner that is expressly antithetical to
the alchemizing magic of democracy's "tremendous and fervid IDEA."
Typically, meditations such as "When I Heard at the Close of the
Day," "Recorders Ages Hence," or "I Saw in Louisiana a Live-Oak
Growing" fix their personae at a specific spot or moment in time; in a
tone more somber than celebratory, they forsake an expansive generality for a more anecdotal style, favor a more dramatic compression of
interest on a particular event or thing over the fluidity of reference. At
stake is more than the cultivation of a new manner, if only because
their speakers are so overtly conscious of the "kosmos" they wish to
renounce. Thus, enjoining his "recorders ages hence" to look beneath
the "impassive exterior" of a former self, Whitman invites future
generations to

Publish my name and hang up my picture as that of the
        tenderest lover,
Who was not proud of his songs, but of the measureless
        ocean of love within him, and freely pour'd it forth,
Who often walked lonesome walks thinking of his dear
        friends, his lovers,
Who pensive away from one he lov'd often lay sleepless
        and dissatisfied at night,
Who knew too well the sick, sick dread lest the one he
        lov'd might secretly be indifferent to him,
Whose happiest days were far away through fields, in
        woods, on hills, he and another wandering hand in
        hand, they twain apart from other men,
Who oft as he saunter'd the streets curv'd with his
        arm the shoulder of his friend, while the arm of his
        friend rested upon him also.
                (*CRE*, p. 122)

The stated aim here is to strike through the mask of the speaker's "impassive exterior" by conveying the full range and richness of his emotions, emotions which, it is once again strongly implied, verse alone is inadequate to capture. And yet, by writing his own epitaph Whitman at the same time perpetuates this sense of remoteness through the self-distancing devices of the past tense and third-person narrative. Technically, such devices bespeak a small-scale sublimation which sets passion at a further remove by deflecting its immediacy. By any estimate, though, the displacement is a modest one, considerably below the reach of any pretension to democratic sublimity, with its "solving [of] all lesser and definite distinctions in vast, indefinite, spiritual, emotional power." On the contrary, Whitman's presentation remains steadfast in its commitment to the utmost particularity. He is intent on paring abstractions to a minimum, intimating that his affection need carry no other significance than its local anxieties and elations. The hint of jealous possessiveness in his relationship, along with the implication that it is not the world it joins together which defines the value of comradeship but the one it leaves behind, deepens the prevailing mood of retentiveness.

Another turn of the screw and this would be a manifestly sullen poem, not so much by virtue of its "sick, sick dread" but in its overtones of aggrieved aloofness. Its reticence owes less to the specter of cultural repression than to an implicit bafflement over how its subject may or even should be related to cultural norms at all. Does "adhesiveness" provide the redemptive paradigm for social bonds or does it acquire its importance by eluding any such correlation? On this question *Calamus* consistently wavers, resulting in what Eve Kosofsky Sedgwick perceptively describes as "an ideologically overcharged quietism."[20] Her epithet may in turn be contrasted to the ideologically overheated activism of *Children of Adam,* for while that collection builds altars to a monolithic Eros that magnetizes all, the solitary lovers of *Calamus* are apt to find themselves in flight from such abstractions, desiring as it seems not to be saved by the dream of visionary compacts but to be saved from them. Another case in point is the following lyric, which addresses these same issues, albeit from a somewhat different perspective:

> I saw in Louisiana a live-oak growing,
> All alone stood it and the moss hung down the
>   branches,

Without any companion it grew there uttering joyous
              leaves of dark green,
And its look, rude, unbending, lusty, made me think of
              myself,
But I wonder'd how it could utter joyous leaves
              standing alone there without its friend near, for I
              knew I could not,
And I broke off a twig with a certain number of leaves
              upon it, and twined around it a little moss,
And brought it away, and I have placed it in sight in
              my room,
It is not needed to remind me as of my own dear
              friends,
(For I believe lately I think of little else than of
              them,)
Yet it remains to me a curious token, it makes me
              think of manly love;
For all that, and though the live-oak glistens there
              in Louisiana solitary in a wide flat space,
Uttering joyous leaves all its life without a friend a
              lover near,
I know very well I could not.

                                        (*CRE*, pp. 126–27)

Can imagination and sympathy coexist? As in the other texts we
have been discussing, this too presses for a negative verdict by imagining an impassable divide between the self-gratifications of poetry and
the beckoning urge of "manly love." Yet the poem succeeds where
others fall short in that it allows itself to be caught between both
alternatives without devaluing either. Thus the speaker starts off by
positing a resemblance between himself and the subject of his meditation only to retract it twice—once in the past tense and once again in
the present. Or, conversely, we come upon an association that is
initially denied ("it is not needed to remind me as of my own dear
friends") which is then promptly restored ("Yet it remains to me a
curious token, it makes me think of manly love"). Persisting through
these equivocations is the quandary of a speaker hoping to talk himself
around an identification he is not sure he wishes to forgo. If not
entirely a token of "manly love," the bunch plucked at random from
this solitary singer, now the only poet in the landscape, is palpably an

admonition against self-love. Like Thoreau's cypress, said to "bear no fruit" and therefore to exist forever "free," Whitman's live-oak thrives on a sterile opulence that too is "always flourishing." Its companionless serenity, arousing in the speaker all the dreaded joy we would expect from a narcissistic talisman, so transfixes his attention that one cannot but picture him, if not "solitary in a wide flat space," then certainly ensconced alone in his room, pondering the meaning of his "curious token" in silent absorption. Here again, the style of presentation is drawn toward a static fixity of reference, it being the primary attribute of the live-oak that it signify nothing other than its own implacable and inert joy. Movingly, the poem wants to shake loose of this fixation but can only do so half-heartedly, with the result that, by the time we read the brilliantly pivotal eighth line, the speaker's shrug of disengagement ("for all that") struggles against a backward glance of nostalgia ("and though the live-oak glistens there"), still leaving him poised on the threshold of ambivalence.

Transposing the "tokens" of creativity from one sphere of reference to another is nevertheless what this poem is groping to achieve, and it is appropriate that the single action performed in it—the breaking off and bringing away of the twig twined with moss—should entail just such a gesture. If Whitman's farewell to the interior paramour of himself is more tentative than conclusive, what remains significant here is the willingness to ascribe to imaginative activity an intermediary position which does not die off in the moment of its consumption or find itself negatively drawn against the more alluring promise of companionship. It may be that art is worthwhile in salvaging something from experience after all. Whitman's reminiscence, in other words, implies a subtle tension between what it says and what it does, between its presumption against art's narcissistic glamor and its implied attempt to overcome this identification by means of the expressive act of commemoration that is the poem itself. So construed, "I Saw in Louisiana a Live-Oak Growing" provides a salutary caution against imagining too stark or categorical an opposition between "private" and "public" modes of revelation. Certainly, the relation of these terms shows an increasing strain, as we have already witnessed in Whitman's shifting stance toward the resources of sublimation, which these poems tend either to narrow into reductive caricature or hold more suspiciously at arm's length. More generally, however, it can be said that when this dichotomy appears in *Calamus* it is apt to become polemicized—overstated to a degree that does not indicate a mere retreat into inwardness so much as a despair and disorientation brought on by the sense of irrelevance overtaking the poet's attitude toward his own vocation. On the other hand, Whitman's meditation on the live-oak reminds us, almost despite itself, that his most rewarding poetry neither favors self over society nor society over the self but seeks to open a path of exchange between them.

Having argued that Whitman's sensitivity toward such concerns reveals a good deal more complexity than is commonly allowed in treatments of *Calamus,* I want to conclude by turning to a poem that directly engages many of the issues we have discussed, particularly the problematic role of sublimation in the body politic. Though not a part of *Calamus* itself, it is one of Whitman's best lyrics and, despite its phantasmagorical surface, one of his most thoughtful. Originally printed in 1856 under the cumbersome title "Poem of Wonder at the Resurrection of the Wheat," it has since come to be known more simply as "This Compost." With an air of mystery rare for *Leaves of Grass,* the superb introductory lines plunge us directly into an intrigue of deception and shame which the rest of the poem struggles to work through:

> Something startles me where I thought I was safest,
> I withdraw from the still woods I loved,
> I will not go now on the pastures to walk,
> I will not strip the clothes from my body to meet my
>   lover the sea,
> I will not touch my flesh to the earth as to other
>   flesh to renew me.
>
> O how can it be that the ground itself does not
>   sicken?
> How can you be alive you growths of spring?
> How can you furnish health you blood of herbs, roots,
>   orchards, grain?
> Are they not continually putting distemper'd corpses
>   within you?
> Is not every continent work'd over and over with sour
>   dead?
>
> Where have you disposed of their carcasses?
> Those drunkards and gluttons of so many generations?
> Where have you drawn off all the foul liquid and meat?
>
> (*CRE,* p. 368)

Revulsion would at first blush seem the right word for this outburst, whose gothic fright is only matched by the vivid catalog of disease and degeneration ("outside fair costume, inside ashes and filth") set down four years later by Whitman in "A Hand-Mirror." Still, revulsion alone does not cover the full range of his response here. Attention does not fall simply on the pollution of the Earth but, more interestingly, on its ease in feeding off this rankness without being defiled by it. "Grow[ing] such sweet things out of such corruption," Nature has mastered the art of sublimation with a deftness that leaves the speaker a dazed, if somewhat distrustful bystander. "Where have you disposed of their carcasses?" he asks, scandalized that the charnel house called Nature could pass off so gross a deception with such equanimity. And as incredulity yields to indignation, his mood quickly shifts from jealous astonishment to outright sarcasm. "I do not see any of it upon you to-day," he continues, still on the watch for "distemper'd corpses" and "foul meat," "or perhaps I am deceiv'd." With an amusing blend of envy and vindictiveness, he resolves that it is preferable to unmask Nature's cunning rather than be taken in by it: "I will run a furrow with my plough, I will press my spade through the soil and turn it up underneath, / I am sure I shall expose some of the foul meat."

There is, then, nothing democratic about Nature's "chemistry." If the Earth exhibits a genius for transmuting self-disgust into self-renewal, this is plainly not a privilege enjoyed by the poet. The adjectives that come to his mind—"distemper'd," "foul," "sour," "pale"—are laden with accents of moral contempt, and from this point of view it is not difficult to overhear the jaundiced line of reasoning speaking through them. Walt Whitman, kosmos, one of the roughs, better President, and joiner of tongues is no more than Walt Whitman, charlatan, one of the onanists, a fetid heap of poisoned longings and vile confidences. So far as "the summer growth," aloof and austere in its purity, "is innocent and disdainful above all those strata of sour dead," the hapless "I" cannot but feel himself branded as guilty and disdained, and so stands confessed as "terrified at the Earth, it is that calm and patient." The second half of the poem does what it can to coax the speaker out of these calumnies, first by picturing forth the regenerative largesse of the Earth as vegetation newly springs through the mould of the compost heap. Backing off from the runaway panic of the opening lines ("Is not every continent work'd over and over with sour dead?"), the imagery strives to soothe thought by tethering it to the smallest particulars: "the tinge awakes over the willow tree . . . out of its little hill faithfully rise the potato's dark green leaves . . . rises the yellow maize-stalk, the lilacs bloom in the door-yards." Such prosaic details are wonderfully apt: no attempt is made to abstract or "spiritualize" Nature's ominous regenerations since it is this very power of transformation—furnishing "health" out of bloody herbs and roots—that occasions the speaker's envy and exas-peration in the first place. Art's sublimations cannot hope to rival Nature's own; the lilac blooming in the dooryard must here remain merely that. And although this determined realism provides some comfort, Whitman's sudden exclamation—"What chemistry!"—re-minds us at the same time that he has not forgotten his initial shock. Perhaps "the winds are not really infectious"; perhaps "this is no cheat"; perhaps the ocean "will not endanger me with fevers that have deposited themselves in it"; perhaps "all is clean forever and forever." All the same, it is nevertheless doubtful whether art's "chemistry" is at all comparable to that of Nature, for even though it is true "that when I recline on the grass I do not catch any disease," it is also undeniable that "probably every spear of grass rises out of what was once a catching disease." Learning and loafing at ease, observing a spear of summer grass, may be tolerated but only so long as there is no illusion over the corruption and foulness underneath.

By virtue of its "cosmical, antiseptic power," declares the author of *Democratic Vistas,* "Nature's stomach is fully strong enough not only to digest the morbific matter always presented . . . but even to change such contributions into nutriment for highest use and life—so Ameri-can democracy's" (*PW*, 2:382). "This Compost" makes problematic this easy analogizing of the natural to the political domain: if any-thing, its "cosmical, antiseptic" alchemy not only surpasses democracy's melting pot but excites within the speaker a volatile blend of sarcasm, self-loathing, and dread that only deepens further his sense of exclusion. Whitman tells us elsewhere that he too con-ceives his "Poems and Essays as nutriment and influences to help truly assimilate . . . the great future of the United States" (*PW* 2:469), yet in this poem the art of transubstantiation has turned upon him, here drifting away from the charismatic charm of the Answerer at whose behest "all religion, all solid things, all arts, governments . . . all parts away" (*CRE*, p. 221) and instead reified in the uncanny equanimity of the Earth. It is indeed this condition of estrangement—the Earth's terrible beauty—that underlies the forbidding quality of "This Compost," not (or not merely) its taste for lurid description that exposes the "dark side" of Whitman's organicism. Still rapt with amazement at Nature's impervious sanctity, the poem ends on an appropriately chastened note.

> Now I am terrified at the Earth, it is that calm and
>   patient,
> It grows such sweet things out of such corruptions,
> It turns harmless and stainless on its axis, with such
>   endless successions of diseas'd corpses,
> It distills such exquisite winds out of such infused
>   fetor,
> It renews with such unwitting looks its prodigal,
>   annual, sumptuous crops,
> It gives such divine materials, to men, and accepts
>   such leavings from them at last.
>   (*CRE*, pp. 369–70)

As he comes around at last to openly conceding his alarm at the Earth's inapproachable serenity, the poet suggests that he may also have begun to move through it. Terror does not finally capture the mood of these ruminations, which quietly insinuate a shift in attitude as they cast a backward glance over the poem's concerns. Perceiving "diseas'd corpses" in "divine materials" need not provoke envious rage against Nature's duplicity or a despairing cynicism over its pretense at purity. Nevertheless, a measure of wariness lingers in this coda, most notably in a continued hesitancy concerning the relation between the resurrections afforded by Nature and those afforded by art. While it is certainly plausible to point to a buried affinity between "this compost" and the poet's composition, as one critic has recently suggested, it must also be said that the poem eyes this correspondence with a good deal of skepticism.[21] The unyielding placidity of the Earth, whose "unwitting looks" remain oblivious to the spectacle of decay and death all around it, suggests Whitman's own version of a "cold pastoral." Accordingly, when he is moved to insert a favorite pun in the concluding line, he places it in a context overwhelmed by ominous connotations, with "leavings" here denoting not the redemptive bequeathing of verse in continual growth but the dross so ably and so disconcertingly reconstituted by the Earth.

Whitman never does specify a gender for the subject of his medita-

tions, though judging from the stark opposition between pristine
health and concealed impurities as well as the fascinated loathing this
excites there can be little doubt of Nature's maternal character. As
such, the portrait takes its place beside other glimpses of "ma femme,
Democracy," at once seductive enchantress and vengeful, warlike deity. More particularly, the inviolate and imperturbable serenity which
characterizes the Earth in this poem identifies a leading trait in many
of Whitman's muse figures, whose magisterial receptivity commonly
personifies an archetypal model of free exchange. Such is the role of
Democracy as she is saluted in the conclusion to "Song of the Broad-
Axe":

> Her shape arises,
> She less guarded than ever, yet more guarded than
> > ever,
> The gross and soil'd she moves among do not make her
> > gross and soil'd,
> She knows the thoughts as she passes, nothing is
> > conceal'd from her,
> She is none the less considerate or friendly
> > therefore,
> She is the best belov'd, it is without exception,
> > she has no reason to fear and she does not fear,
> Oaths, quarrels, hiccupp'd songs, smutty expressions
> > are idle to her as she passes,
> She is silent, she is possess'd of herself, they do
> > not offend her,
> She receives them as the laws of Nature receive them,
> > she is strong,
> She too is a law of Nature—there is no law stronger
> > than she is.
> > > (*CRE*, p. 194–95)

For the writings discussed in this past chapter, however, indiscriminate impartiality now seems like mere indifference, making the
poet at best an interloper in his own emotional universe and an out-
cast before his own paradigm for inclusion. If this is the ironic
development hinted at in the denouement of "This Compost," it is
verified more starkly in *Children of Adam* and *Calamus,* each of which
betrays how chimerical and unreal poetry's pursuit of "indissoluble

compacts" has become. Shaken by this collapse and privately doubting the purpose and direction of his verse, Whitman's next step was to forsake the austere "truths of the Earth" altogether by journeying back to the sea, there hoping to re-collect and gather the fragmented energies of his career.

8

Sea-Drift

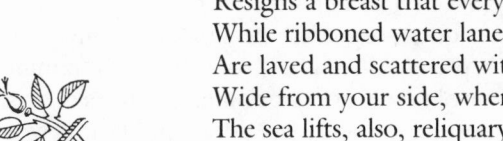

Infinite consanguinity it bears—
This tendered theme of you that light
Retrieves from sea plains where the sky
Resigns a breast that every wave enthrones;
While ribboned water lanes I wind
Are laved and scattered with no stroke
Wide from your side, whereto this hour,
The sea lifts, also, reliquary hands.

IT WAS HART CRANE who found in *Leaves of Grass* a power that "better than any other, was able to coordinate those forces in America which seem most intractable, fusing them into a universal vision which takes on added significance as time goes on."[1] That last clause was more than a gesture of idle prophecy on Crane's part, for by the time it was written he had already canonized Whitman in print as "Our Meister-singer" who "bringest tally, and a pact, new bound / Of living brotherhood!"[2] Yet Crane of course knew his forbear as something more than a Seer of Fraternity, his "eyes bright with myth," and the lines from "Voyages" cited above insinuate a different reading, one uncannily faithful to the same rhythm of dispersal and re-union, desertion and retrieval, sacrifice and sanctification that we find throughout the *Sea-Drift* lyrics. Drawing away from the synthesizing muse of "Passage to India" or "Song of Myself" empowered "to bind us throbbing with one voice," Crane's allusiveness descries a Whitman who is less a fixed presence than a revenant figure seemingly "bubbled up" from "the measureless float"—a "trial of drift and debris" diffused through the sinuous windings of Crane's syntax. So the sea that lifts "reliquary hands" evokes the same sea that for Whitman raises "white arms out in the breakers tirelessly tossing"; the strokes "laved and scattered" from oar and pen harken to the same caress "creeping steadily up to my ears and laving me softly all over" with "the low and delicious word"; the sky that "resigns a breast that every wave enthrones" enacts the same embrace of "the sky near the moon, drooping upon the sea . . . sagging down, drooping, the face of the sea almost touching."

Beyond the sum of these resemblances, Crane's voyagings share a common plot with "Out of the Cradle Endlessly Rocking" and "As I Ebb'd with the Ocean of Life," two of the most successful and compelling poems in the collection. All of these texts are best described as essentially enacting a fantasy of rescue ("retrievements out of the night") in which an orphaned castaway journeys back to a remembered place of origin so as to reclaim and in some measure restage the epiphanic emergence of discourse ("the thousand responsive songs at random"; "the Imaged Word") sent up from the oracular whispering of the sea. This orphic quest, arguably the single and unyielding subject of Crane's work, presents itself in each of Whitman's "reminiscences" by way of a fourfold sequence of beginning retrospect, crisis of loss, petition and expostulation, and longed-for reply, be it "a word out of the sea" or the envied "secret" of parental benediction. To be sure, important differences do divide "Out of the Cradle" from "As I Ebb'd," as one attempts to resuscitate a flagging career while the other more ostensibly lashes out at it, but a more general sense of affinity emerges in their common presentation of a providential narrative of return that guides the initiate from solitary despondency to the enlarged perspective of exultant fusion or chastened acceptance. Among the most self-consciously *crafted* lyrics Whitman would compose, both provide a ritual framework for his drama of consensus: moving through a host of starkly profiled oppositions (Eros and Thanatos, paternal land and maternal ocean, "real Me" and washed-up drift) the man-child in these poems finds himself wrenched loose from established comforts as a necessary prelude to experiencing a greater breadth of vision. In the end, he would no longer be merely the force that tallies but one who is tallied in kind, not merely the recipient of the sea's whisperings but its very medium of expression.

In this emphasis on return it is worth recalling that the poet himself, as he tells us in *Specimen Days,* was casting back to the "fancy" cherished "even as a boy" to "write a piece, perhaps a poem, about the seashore—that suggesting, dividing line, contact, junction, the solid marrying the liquid—that curious, lurking something . . . which means far more than its mere first sight, grand as that is— blending the real and ideal, and each made a portion of the other" (*PW* 1:138). Sufficient attention has already been drawn to the primal scene imagery active in this description (seashore as marriage bed) for us to linger further over its suggested continuities with Whitman's aesthetic at large. Neither a vortex which consumes all relations into itself (Melville's "Descartian vortices") nor a luminous threshold which opens out to more enigmatic vistas (Stevens's "ghostlier demarcations"), the shore's artistry here occupies a zone of crossings and conjunctions, less immediately important, perhaps, for what it joins together than for its aura of "invisible *influence*" and its status as a "pervading gauge and tally for me, in my composition" (*PW* 1:139). To say the least, none of these compound phrases—"suggesting, dividing line"; "contact, junction"; "gauge and tally"—are unfamiliar and each could be applied with equal precision to the role of the Answerer, of whom it is said in the first edition that "him all wait for . . . him all yield up to . . . his word is decisive and final . . . in him they lave . . . him they immerse, and he immerses them." Likewise seeking out a "word final, superior to all" whose "low and delicious" accents also "lave" and "immerse," *Sea-Drift* draws generously on this terminology of inclusion, though it is at the same time important to note how it redraws and domesticates these terms by now shifting to an urgent drama of personal crisis. If the visionary stance of the Answerer tallying and binding "intractable forces" into a "universal vision" has vanished here, his idiom has not—an indication of Whitman's effort to shore up and redefine what was increasingly coming to seem in the wake of the baffled and balked intimacies of *Children of Adam* and *Calamus* an exhausted and rudderless vocation. It is in this respect that Whitman's project of retrieval, as I shall be suggesting, entails not simply a reconstruction of the bittersweet memories of childhood but more immediately the reclamation of his own career.

"Out of the Cradle Endlessly Rocking" has always been something of a showpiece for admirers of *Leaves of Grass,* the one text other than the great "Burial Hymn" for Lincoln that was to win widespread acclaim in the poet's lifetime (I overlook "O Captain, My Captain"). Whitman himself evidently shared this high opinion since the poem was the first of his mature work to be offered for publication in the popular press before appearing in the 1860 *Leaves.*[3] Surely the poem's alert familiarity with a broad range of literary motifs and generic antecedents on both sides of the Atlantic, together with its operatic scaffolding, helps explain its popularity with Swinburne, Saintsbury, and other eminent Victorians, who preferred to make their case for the Good Gray Bard by stressing his ties to the Romantic tradition.[4] "Out of the Cradle," taking as its blueprint the typology of the sublime ode, does indeed offer an embarrassment of analogies in this vein, both in its worship of the imagination as a theophanic power that enshrines the dawn of poetic election in a holy place and in its more local echoings, such as when Whitman, thinking back on the nightingale overheard by Keats ("while thou art pouring forth thy soul abroad in such ecstasy"), offers his own version of "the American Mimic," the mockingbird ("he pour'd forth the meanings which I of all men know"). A further reflection of the poem's openness to literary conventions can be found in Whitman's choice of the ode itself, which by this time had come to be generally regarded as a moribund form and therefore all the more enticing to the ambitious lyricist. As Paul Fry comments in his study of the English ode, "if the eighteenth-century poet proved himself to be a poet by writing an ode, the Romantic poet proved himself *still* to be a poet by writing an ode."[5] As Coleridge, Wordsworth, Shelley, and Keats turned to this "trial of invention" in mid-career, so does Whitman. This note of overcoming self-created obstacles is sounded from the start with the justly cele-brated "Pre-Verse," whose twining and twisting and braiding of prepositions and participles establishes promptly the bard as above all else the *bard*, high priest to the mysteries of poetic incarnation, "tak-ing all hints to use them, but swiftly leaping beyond them." With its periodic structure ceremoniously uncoiling through twenty-three lines and its sacerdotal underpinnings ("shower'd halo," "mystic play of shadows"), Whitman's sentence frames a triumphal arch through which the "I" at last emerges. Care is taken, moreover, to eliminate any suggestion of a compulsive or manic eroticism in this periodicity; the flushing and flushing muse of *Children of Adam*, straining syntax for its withheld drip, is not present. Despite the faint pressure of distress momentarily conveyed ("Borne hither, ere all else eludes me, hurriedly"), this virtuoso grammatical suspension, intricate without being labored, argues a newfound patience with words, a prideful display of mastery over expression.

Whitman writes from the prospect of having already awakened to the "pains and joys" he is preparing to recount, though in the process of doing so he is actively reexperiencing these same memories. In

Wordsworthian fashion, mere recollection of a former strength triggers its repetition: the picture of the mind revives again and "those beginning notes of yearning and love there in the mist . . . the thousand responses of my heart" break through into the present, "as now they start the scene revisiting," placing before us a man yet by these soundings and resoundings a child once more. Under the spell of this "musical shuttle," Whitman's prologue subtly inaugurates a series of echoes woven throughout the poem, a series which not only is discernible in isolated reverberations (such as that between the bird's despairing "Loved! loved! loved! loved! loved!" and the sea's exultant lisping of "death, death, death, death, death") but which more broadly structures and determines the progress of the entire ode. Thus, in its lament for its vanished mate the mockingbird apostrophizes the sea "uselessly" until its "aria" of loss releases in turn the apocalyptic love in the child, "now tumultuously bursting," who next likewise apostrophizes the sea in search of its "low and delicious word," which in turn enlarges upon without canceling out both "the notes of the bird continuous echoing" and the "thousand warbling echoes . . . started to life within me." Through this elaborate counterpointing, from bird to child, child to sea, sea to poet, a chain of transmission is passed along which builds steadily into wider circles of resonance and amplitude. Whitman's contrapuntal arrangement functions in this respect to develop its own "infinite consanguinity" of voices, with one yielding to and augmenting the next, and whose transitions are navigated with an ease that is in pointed contrast to "As I Ebb'd with the Ocean of Life," where things go awry precisely when the wrong kind of echoes are set loose, namely, "all that blab whose echoes recoil upon me . . . all my arrogant poems."

This antiphonal design, easily missed in line by line explications of the poem, is important not only as a formal device but for what it implies about Whitman's restructuring of the terms of communicative exchange. One salient result of his echoing song is, after all, to soften any sense of an agonistic encounter among its personae: by establishing a serial, complementary interdependence among its voices the poem skillfully evades the competition for power or influence such as might transpire between an "I" and a "you," between the singer and his speech, or between a "me" and "the real Me." To the degree that, as Diane Wood Middlebrook helpfully observes, "no human mediator intervenes" to free the imagination's "thousand responsive songs at random," the poet's awakening "is described as a wholly natural event,"[6] a myth of discovery, we might add, wholly removed from the specter of rivalry, debate, or blockage. Even though poet and sea are momentarily paired off as potential adversaries, with the former demanding "a word then, (for I will conquer it)," this intimation is of course swiftly overtaken in the wake of the sea's cradling caresses. Indeed, just as the child-poet virtually internalizes the identity of the bird in recognizing him to be "my dusky demon and brother," so does the sea virtually incorporate the identity of the speaker until, laved in the embrace of her "low and delicious word," he can no longer be properly called the singer of the sea but its song: "the sea whisper'd me." The overriding effect of these transpositions is to blur the boundaries between self and other as well as those between author and listener, thus idealizing a structure of exchange without sacrifice.

Of course, it should be kept in mind that the poem is able to bypass such disjunctions precisely because they have already been contained within the main body of Whitman's "recitative." When Whitman speaks of the mockingbird as "projecting me," he intends to illustrate the ecstatic fusion between speaker ("O you singer solitary, singing by yourself") and recipient ("O solitary me listening") which anticipates the poem's final synthesis. "Projection," however, is a term that attracts other connotations too, and before Whitman can proclaim this communion of addresser and addressee he needs to depict their severance in the protracted lamentations of the mockingbird. Its "reckless despairing carols," sustained "all summer in the sound of the sea," command the rapt attention of the child, who has "listen'd long and long" to its manifold repetitions, in much the same way that Whitman would later inform readers of his ode that "the piece will bear reading many times—perhaps, indeed only comes forth, as from recesses, by many repetitions."[7] What particularly engages the boy's attention, moreover, is the bird's own frantic and forlorn overtures to summon a word from the sea. Dwelling on this predicament with special intensity, Whitman not only keeps before us the unrelenting pitch of demand satisfied by no response—"with this just-sustained note I announce myself to you, / This gentle call is for you my love, for you"—but also is at pains to emphasize the bird's own straining at receptivity, its poised readiness to catch the answering call that will never arrive:

> But Soft! sink low!
> Soft! let me just murmur,

> And do you wait a moment you husky-nois'd sea,
> For somewhere I believe I heard my mate responding to
>   me,
> So faint, I must be still, be still to listen,
> But not altogether still, for then she might not come
>   immediately to me.
> . . . .
> Do not be decoy'd elsewhere,
> That is the whistle of the wind, it is not my voice,
> That is the fluttering, the fluttering of the spray,
> Those are the shadows of the leaves.
>   (*CRE,* pp. 250–51)

The act of listening can here be glossed as a synecdoche for aesthetic responsiveness, an act which requires the utmost stillness as a prelude to revelation, like Keats's "wide quietness" or the "deep secluded recesses . . . the solemn shadowy cedars and ghostly pines so still" that provide a refuge for the elegist of "Lilacs" as he prepares to receive and tally the death chant of the hermit thrush. No such refuge of silence is of course forthcoming for this solitary listener, whose voice must enter into a futile competition with the "husky-nois'd sea." The attitude of hushed receptivity ("Darkling, I listen . . .") is further undermined by Whitman's repeated reference, here as elsewhere, to the bird's feverish self-delusion in supposing its mate to be just out of reach, perhaps lurking in "that dusky spot" of "brown yellow," concealed "fluttering out among the breakers," or murmuring faintly by the shore. All that remains, in turn, is a wandering voice whose fruitless appeals echo against an impassive seascape.

As much scapegoat as alter ego, Whitman's mockingbird thus bears the burden of chanting "Love's unrespanse," thereby setting the stage for the opportune emergence of "the outsetting bard" who overcomes this failed colloquy. For if the bird's frenzied and distracted entreaties disqualify it as an exemplary listener, this is a role more properly fulfilled by the child, overhearing "the meanings which I of all men know." In keeping with the poem's painstaking formalism and in express contrast to the poet's earlier "hymns of you," the situation of the "I" in the first two-thirds of "Out of the Cradle" is that of an intratextual reader, one who does not openly invoke a nation of "camerados" but on the contrary scrupulously assumes the place of Mill's shadowy eavesdropper, "keeping silent, avoiding the moonbeams, blending myself with the shadows, / Recalling now the obscure shapes, the echoes, the sights and sounds after their sort." Overwhelmed by the desolation of loss, the mockingbird's utterances can only know blunt declaratives and simple exclamations; stationed at a carefully measured remove from this spectacle, the child knows primarily a rhetoric of retention and control, as evidenced in the numerous tmetic constructions that invariably accompany each mention of the self: "I, chanter of pains and joys, uniter of here and hereafter . . . I, a curious boy, never too close . . . I, with bare feet, a child . . . I, that was a child, my tongue's use sleeping." Such distancing between subject and verb bespeaks a solicitude over the *pacing* of his narrative otherwise unusual for Whitman. "Cautiously peering, absorbing, translating," the invisible onlooker must not venture too precipitously upon the scene lest he be caught in the trappings of his own fiction ("Enough! enough! somehow I have been stunn'd") or stand exposed as a mere interloper ("Something startles me where I thought I was safest"). So much depends on establishing the proper timing for his entrance, appearing neither too late nor too soon, because so much depends on establishing his arrival as a vital link in the chain of transmission. "*Now* I have heard you, now in a moment I know what I am for," exclaims the revealed bard "at last" with an audible click of recognition, now that the manic energy of the bird's aria has played itself out in "singing uselessly, uselessly all the night." In this exact synchronizing of voices we seem a long way from the idler leaning and loafing at his ease, observing a spear of summer grass.

Something further is no doubt lost by this cautious orchestration: the fear of imaginative transgression, of consciousness seizing up, of the self abruptly cut off from its own designs. "Out of the Cradle's" "mystic play of the shadows twining and twisting as if they were alive" is not comparable to "the ambush'd womb of the shadows" in "Song of Myself." To entertain such comparisons is not to denigrate Whitman's "curious warble"; my purpose here is rather to indicate how ambitiously its mythmaking reconceives a career. In fact, with this last epithet from "Song of Myself" we touch upon the poem's most overt and willful act of revision: the fabled account of the birth of the poetic sensibility, conceived and baptized in the moonlight of Paumanok's shores. We have seen previously how "Song of Myself," haunted by its own "throes of birth," tells a far different story of poetic origins, where every promise of new growth must contend against the threat of a sudden death, ceasing the moment life begins. Its "ambush'd womb of the shadows" recalls the foreclosure of beginning and end which impinges on so many scenes of conception in this poem and which is traceable to the persistent impasse between its author's dream of a self-evolving, organic language and its legitimation—its own "plenum of proof." "Out of the Cradle" is not oblivious to such quandaries but does owe much of its staged brilliance to the dexterity with which it finesses this problem of the excluded middle. For rather than the co-presence of beginning and end compressed into one fateful moment we are called upon to witness the triumphant co-naissance of death and creativity in the "thousand songs" released by and harmonized with "the key, the word up from the waves." Like those mystic shadows "twining and twisting *as if* they were alive," this too is self-consciously part of the poem's myth, one whose success depends on rewriting the daunting task of conceiving a voice out of vision (the real story of poetic origins) as well as suppressing the crisis of value and validation accompanying this task.

It is in this context that we can make fuller sense of the otherwise improbable appearance of another touchstone of nineteenth-century verse in Whitman's poem, one which likewise hosts a "wondrous bird" echoing a refrain of lost love before a rapt human auditor. The affinities between Poe's raven and Whitman's mockingbird, first spotted by Edwin Fussell,[8] are various and diffused, some so ostentatious as "Demon or bird!" (the counterpart of Poe's "Bird or devil!"), others more subtly inserted, like the chorus of "never mores" (lines 151–53) whose exultant pitch of affirmation inverts the laconic monotone of Poe's unvarying refrain. Before exploring these reverberations more thoroughly, it is worth pausing over the resemblance suggested by Fussell between Whitman's "undertone" of gathered voices (the colloquy of bird, boy, and fierce old mother) and Poe's "under-current of meaning," the latter phrase appearing not in "The Raven" but in its more notorious *vade mecum*, "The Philosophy of Composition." As it happens, Whitman read this essay attentively. At first inclined to write off his countryman as a mere rhymster, he did concede that he "was repaid in Poe's prose by the idea that . . . there can be no such thing as a long poem" (*PW* 2:723). Coming from the trumpeter of barbaric yawps whose "single glance" mocks the finery of elegance and ornamentation, this is a surprising report: nevertheless, we are informed that this same idea "had been haunting my mind before [and] Poe's argument, though short, work'd the sum and prov'd it to me" (*PW* 2:723). Whitman's arithmetic sets the proper tone for approaching Poe's essay, in which it is claimed that the composition of his famous poem "proceeded, step by step, to its completion with the precision and rigid consequence of a mathematical problem." "Some amount of suggestiveness," one will recall, "some under-current however indefinite-of-meaning" is essential in conjuring an "absolute unity of effect" which tolerates no detail that does not anticipate and accrue to the final "denouement," and which results in a seamlessly integrated masterplot.[9] "Out of the Cradle," while not taken to quite this dogmatic an extreme, does make use of these and other lessons propounded by Poe's formalism, most clearly in the elaborate foreshadowing in its opening lines, thereby honoring Poe's prescription that the artist must begin with his ending, and in Whitman's effort to invest his narrative with an "indispensable air of consequence, or causation, by making the incidents and especially the tone at all points tend to the development of the intention."[10] "The Philosophy of Composition" above all affirms the paramount importance of controlling "the intention," of accommodating the "initial conception" to the finished design so that the threat of prolepsis is contained and the overburdening of narrative forms averted. By means of such vigilance, there is no need to proclaim in a rush of panic that "there is no stoppage and can never be stoppage." Rather, Whitman finds in the rhythm of the sea his own paradigm for narrative deferral; "delaying not, hurrying not," it produces a "well-develop'd" structure which makes the crisis of proof seem a distant memory.

More remains to be said, however, about the scope of Poe's significance in this poem, especially given Whitman's determination to press beyond his example with "a thousand singers, a thousand songs, clearer, louder, and more sorrowful than yours." Roughly twenty years after making this vow, in a brief memorial to "Edgar Poe's Significance," the poet would pay homage to "my dusky demon and brother" by evoking the figure of a demon mariner exiled from Paumanok's shore and "flying uncontrolled with torn sails and broken spars through the wild sleet and winds and waves of the night . . . apparently enjoying all the terror, the murk, and the dislocation of which he was the centre and the victim" (*PW* 1:232). Out of this "lurid dream" there emerges a portrait of Poe that has since become a part of American iconography: a portrait of the artist as haunted by the curse of a failed nativity, "a wanderer," as T. S. Eliot phrases it in his own account of Poe, "with no fixed abode" who "is not at home where he belongs, but cannot get to anywhere else."[11] To this condition of homelessness Whitman's revery adds the other essential feature of the Poe legend in its evocation of willed self-destructiveness, a note already manifest in the mockingbird's carols, which begin as a dirge but swiftly trail off into self-torture and self-reviling, "singing uselessly, uselessly." Though each in his way is a harbinger of death, neither mockingbird nor raven attains tragic sublimity: the latter in particular is hardly more than a gothic spook embodying "the human thirst for self-torture"—a hallucinated contrivance whereby the speaker of the poem "takes a phrenzied pleasure in so modelling his questions as to receive the expected *nevermore*."[12] Whitman, oppositely, wishes to eliminate masochism from death, wishes to reclaim for death a meaningfulness that both sacralizes art and retrieves its orphaned castaway: "Never more shall I cease perpetrating you," he vows, "Never more shall I escape, never more the reverberations, / Never more the cries of unsatisfied love be absent from me" (*CRE,* p. 252).

Accepting the full burden of loss so as to leap swiftly beyond it, Whitman prepares for his final transcendence in receiving with grateful recognition the word up from the sea, the synthesizing third term "neither like the bird nor my arous'd child's heart." While overtly erotic, this satanic baptism does not excite "phrenzied pleasure" but the hushed reverential overtones of a sacred rite:

> Which I do not forget,
> But fuse the song of my dusky demon and brother,
> That he sang to me in the moonlight on Paumanok's gray
>   beach,
> With the thousand responsive songs at random,
> My own songs awaked from that hour,
> And with them the key, the word up from the waves,
> The word of the sweetest song and all songs,
> That strong and delicious word which, creeping to my
>   feet,
> (Or like some old crone rocking the cradle, swathed in
>   sweet garments, bending aside,)
> The sea whisper'd me.
>
>   (*CRE,* p. 253)

Having assimilated "the strong and delicious word," Whitman becomes that word; having become that word, he rounds off and seals his task of reconstruction. Shadowy listener and prophetic speaker are at last joined in what amounts to a blurring of both roles, for at the behest of the "lull" and "hum" of the sea's "valved voice" the "I" can no longer be properly designated as beholder or bard but embodies, in classic fashion, the expressive site of exchange itself—"the pervading gauge and tally" for the sea's compositions. There is no reaching after a fusion of subject and object of the kind that crowns the Romantic ode ("Let me be thy choir"; "Make me thy lyre") since Whitman has here taken on that image of instrumentality for himself, absorbing in order to be absorbed by the sea's whisperings. In this respect, the conclusion restages and resanctifies Whitman's "interlocutive" or "inter-subjective" vision,[13] thus bringing his project of retrieval to final consummation. In another respect, however, it is also apparent that this vision continues to undergo scrupulous refinement. Banishing the social world from its frame and replacing his chants of Democracy with the ravishing mother of death as its "key" trope of inclusion, Whitman's epiphanic rite of fusion further aestheticizes his poetics of Union. This final reprise, with its unlabored but unmistakable air of tying up loose threads, deepens one's sense that the task of consensus making has turned inward, a fusing and coordinating of diverse forces that devoutly adheres to upholding the structural integrity of the verse. And, with its resonant last line, not only the poem but its maker is transfigured into a finished construct: "he is no longer an artist," as Nietzsche would say of the celebrant intoxicated by song, "he has become a work of art."[14]

The author of "Out of the Cradle" would no doubt have found congenial Nietzsche's added suggestion that "the aesthetic *listener*," swept up by "the highest artistic primal joy," is "also reborn with the rebirth of tragedy." Certainly he would not have cared to question "the capacity of music to give birth to *myth* . . . and particularly *tragic* myth," having already illustrated this conception in his own Liebestod. Given the sustained interest shared by both writers in the kinship between operatic traditions and lyric form, *The Birth of Tragedy* and "Out of the Cradle" bear many illuminating points of correspondence, particularly in the valorization of song as the catalyst whereby the artist is "released from his individual will, and has become, as it were, the medium through which . . . the act of artistic creation coalesces, . . . at once subject and object, at once poet, actor and spectator."[15] But an equally instructive analogy, though touching on a somewhat different topic, can be found not in the pages of *The Birth of Tragedy* itself but in the delightfully caustic "Attempt at a Self-Criticism," which served as a retrospective preface for subsequent editions of this youthfully impassioned work. There we are presented with the caricature of a musing philologist who betakes himself to "an Alpine nook" and ponders the mysteries of "the highest artistic primal joy in the bosom of the primordially One . . . the primordial home [of] fraternal union" while the thunder of battle rolls ominously in the near distance. "Very bemused and beriddled, hence very concerned and yet unconcerned" by the approach of the Franco-Prussian War, the prophet of "this impossible book" heralded the renaissance of *"German myth,"* famously declaring that "it is only as *aesthetic phenomena* that existence and the world are eternally *justified*"[16] For the man become a child on Paumanok's solitary shores, likewise alarmed and yet holding himself aloof from the portents of 1859–60 (this "year of meteors . . . year of foreboding"), a similar urge toward aesthetic justification informs the image of an ecstatic auditor gratefully welcoming the awakening of his own songs. Whereas the author of *Children of Adam* and *Calamus* had with varying degrees of bitterness recoiled against poetry as a failed source of sublimation, Whitman's ode proclaims a triumph for this role and thereby establishes its distance from their aggrieved disillusion. What crowns this triumph is of course the chant of death, which Whitman would later identify as "the last enclosing sublimation of Race or Poem . . . that other pervading invisible fact . . . combining the rest and furnishing, for Person or State, the only permanent and unitary meaning to all" (*PW* 2:747).

Such notions, as we shall see shortly, are put to a more severe test in *Drum-Taps*. Before proceeding to that selection, it is useful to turn to "Out of the Cradle's" companion piece, "As I Ebb'd with the Ocean of Life." No one can determine which of these texts was written first, though it is tempting to regard "As I Ebb'd" as adopting the same stance of wry impatience toward certain developments in Whitman's career that Nietzsche's "Attempt at a Self-Criticism" adopts toward his first book. Certainly this perspective would be preferable to the rather dubious notoriety this poem has received as a defeated ode to dejection which augurs the beginning of the end—what Stephen Whicher, speaking for many, calls "a conscious repudiation of 'Song of Myself' . . . a farewell to his poetic vocation."[17] What Whicher alerts us to here is really the pretext of "As I Ebb'd," not its true subject, which is better described as furthering what I have been calling Whitman's project of retrieval, here given its fullest and most moving expression. After the meticulously coordinated symmetries of "Out of the Cradle," the "many moods, one contradicting the other" of this combative poem come as something of a relief. For while it can be said of the text just discussed that it is above all hoping to be redeemed by art, the most notable implication of "As I Ebb'd" is that it wants to be rescued from it—rescued from, that is to say, the more claustrophobic and constraining idealisms that "Out of the Cradle" so coolly evades confronting.

Departing from the heraldic dactyls that open "Out of the Cradle," all purposiveness and action, Whitman begins here with a series of anapests, presumably intended to mime the rising and falling of the seascape. Throughout the first seventeen lines, which form the first section, a hint of weary familiarity is suggested. All the required stage machinery has been wheeled into place: there is "the fierce old mother [who] endlessly cries for her castaways"; the lurking afflatus or "spirit that trails in the lines underfoot"; then, too, there recurs "the old thought of likenesses" and of course "this electric self out of the pride of which I utter poems"—that figure of capable imagination roaming the water's edge, "seeking types." As yet, however, the speaker is still drifting; flanked by the signifying power of the ocean—"the rim, the sediment that stands for all the water and the land of the globe"—and its reductive inscriptions cast on shore—"scum, scales from shining rocks, leaves of salt—lettuce left by the tide"—the speaker continues to patrol the beach, "miles walking," in search of the poem whose "drift" he aims to "gather." The overtone of caricature in "that electric self seeking types," together with the leaden phrase "I thought the old thought of likenesses," induces a sense of perfunctory nonchalance, an enforced casualness. Revisiting the shore of inspiration produces no luminous halos or mystic shadows but "old thought[s]" as if "the profound lesson of reception" had become an enervating routine.

To be "held" by this "electric self" thus suggests implications more closely akin to constraint or perhaps even enslavement than simple possession—an implication given added emphasis in the 1860 edition, where the poet is said to be "held by the eternal self of me that threatens to get the better of me and stifle me." This oppressive self-estrangement deepens as Whitman, crossing to "the shores I know not," crosses as well into the present tense. Somewhat like the clairvoyant of "Crossing Brooklyn Ferry," who finds an "impalpable sustenance" in "the current rushing so swiftly and swimming with me far away" and who murmurs "closer yet I approach you" (*CRE,* pp. 160, 63), the ocean now "so mysterious rolls toward me closer and closer . . . as I inhale the impalpable breezes that set in upon me." Yet such overtures prepare for a diminution of the self, not its enlargement: with the admission "I too but signify at the utmost a little wash'd-up drift, / A few sands and dead leaves to gather," the poem breaks out into the negative epiphany that reads like a precise inversion of the child's inspired acceptance of a new identity:

O baffled, balk'd, bent to the very earth,
Oppressed with myself that I have dared to open my
        mouth,
Aware now that amid all that blab whose echoes recoil
        upon me I have not once had the least idea of who or
        what I am,
But that before all my arrogant poems the real Me
        stands yet untouch'd, untold, altogether unreach'd,
Withdrawn far, mocking me with mock-congratulatory
        signs and bows,
With peals of distant ironical laughter at every word
        I have written,
Pointing in silence to these songs, and then to the
        sand beneath.

I perceive I have not really understood any thing, not
        a single object, and that no man ever can,
Nature here in sight of the sea taking advantage of me
        to dart upon me and sting me,
Because I have dared to open my mouth to sing at all.
                          (*CRE,* p. 254)

However "untouch'd, untold, altogether unreach'd," the "real Me" has not been entirely absent from the pages of *Leaves of Grass.* Its contemptuous superiority calls most immediately to mind the shadow of the father, here conspiring with Nature to dart upon and sting a helpless son exposed to mockery in sight of the maternal ocean, much in the same way he had taunted the braggart of "Song of Myself" to "see then whether you shall be master!" In another respect, its stance of magisterial remoteness more generally harks back to other analogues as well, such as the "Me Myself" which stands "apart from the pulling and hauling," both in and out of the game, watching and wondering at it; the desituate "I" of "Crossing Brooklyn Ferry" which hovers over the play of the human colloquy without being reducible to any one dialogue of interest; the "beautiful sister" of the Earth who, "inviting none, denying none," sits composed in her flawless serenity; or the cautiously distanced onlooker of "Out of the Cradle" who keeps to the shadows in silent observation, awaiting his moment of deliverance. The custodians of an inviolate impartiality which is the ground for Whitman's medium of consensus, each of these personae variously bespeaks his quest for that representative demigod who would be all things to all its constituents.

Yet even as its pose of severe detachment recalls such antecedents, it is also clear that "the real Me" not only diverges from but actively violates this fiction of disinterest. Harold Bloom points up the essential difference here succinctly when he observes that " 'the amused, complacent, compassionating, idle, unitary' Me Myself [from "Song of Myself"] would have looked with side-curved head curious at the anguished Walt on the beach, watching and wondering what had become of him."[18] This Whitman's laconic double does not do, indulging instead in a vicious pantomime that pairs "all my arrogant poems" with the sands and "dead leaves" underfoot. Evidently "the anguished Walt" senses this change in perspective too, for it is important to note how his mortified tone of frustration and shame ("that I have dared to open my mouth") quickly shifts to a far different tone of chagrined resentment ("Because I have dared to open my mouth to sing at all") which is meant to indicate that "this phantom," as it is later called, is all too human in its overzealous satire. Moreover, the poet's own self-accusations—"*every* word I have written," "not *once* had the *least* idea of who or what I am," "not really understood *any* thing, not a *single* object"—are far too sweeping to be accepted as simply that. They read more like a solicitation than a confession, or rather, insinuate the terms of such solicitation through the vehemence of confessed failure. In lamenting the alien majesty of his own rejected self, Whitman is in other words hoping to lure this specter into the open, to goad it into action. He wants to get this figure of self-alienation into the poem, to make it part of the poem's drama.

"I believe in you my soul, the other I am must not abase itself to you, / And you must not be abased to the other." This had been the covenant of "Song of Myself," completely moving in the wariness of its benevolence. Both the benevolence and the wariness are discernible in the warning that the self must not sacrifice *or* be sacrificed to its own idealisms. Notwithstanding conventional accounts of "As I Ebb'd with the Ocean of Life" as a dirge to departed powers, Whitman here would not be helplessly witnessing the dissolution of this pact but instigating its breakdown, thereby creating the occasion for a more truly engaged, more contentious exchange between "me" and "the real Me," "my soul" and "the other I am." In effect, the injunction against debasement has proven to be oppressive in its own right: it has come to perpetuate the flawless but inert symmetry of "opposite equals" which tolerates no opportunity for negation, strife, or growth and has come to engender such shopworn stereotypes as "that electric self seeking types." In shattering the commandment that the self must neither abase itself nor be abased in turn, the clash between poet and mocking phantom does not repudiate a vocation so much as attack its more intransigent, reified fictions—the kind of reification we have seen taking hold of "the body electric" from *Children of Adam* onward. A double movement may be inferred: if "mock congratulatory signs and bows" and "peals of distant ironical laughter" bring to bitter fruition the sensed obsolescence of poetry's "indissoluble compacts," apprehended long before this breakdown, their indictment also initiates a gesture of recovery in seeking to confront rather than merely deflect or displace this bitterness. Whitman's task here is to rehumanize his fictions, moving beyond the pasteboard masks of *both* "the electric self" and "the real Me."

The poem is by no means prepared to articulate such ambitions explicitly, but it is instructive to note the shift in perspective that develops through its second half. Once released from the bondage of perfect equality, speaker, land, and ocean join and "murmur alike reproachfully," now finding whatever communion can be affirmed out of their antagonisms. The expansive reach of "the rim, the sediment that stands for all the water and all the land of the globe" has accordingly been winnowed out into "these little shreds standing for you and me and all." As this splintered unity provides the footing for a tentative attempt at identification ("I too have bubbled up . . . I too am but a trail of drift and debris, / I too leave little wrecks upon you"), the speaker next imagines himself a corpse "wash'd on your shores." So humbled, he takes on the role of supplicant pleading for recognition from the paternal land, a supplicant whose undefended vulner-

ability is in fact far more convincing than the hyperbolic collapse of
the previous page:

> I throw myself upon your breast my father,
> I cling to you so that you cannot unloose me,
> I hold you so firm till you answer me something.
>
> (*CRE,* p. 255)

The sudden assertion of iambic rhythm is powerfully apt, capturing as
it does the unbearable strain of a mind hoping to compose itself. The
manifest intent has now become to reach, tell, and touch, building out
of the ruins of the shattered covenant with "the real Me" the terms for
renewed understanding. His wrestling for benediction as he throws
himself on the shore subtly corrects the aggressive sadomasochism of
his prior humiliation, as his subsequent protests ("fear not, deny not
me . . . I mean tenderly by you all") are meant to imply.

Like so many evening odes before it, "As I Ebb'd" comes to rest
with a final gathering of the mind's chastened thoughts, a shoring of
fragments ranged somewhere between outright desolation and prophetic affirmation:

> Me and mine, loose windrows, little corpses,
> Froth, snowy white, and bubbles,
> (See, from my dead lips the ooze exuding at last,
> See, the prismatic colors glistening and rolling,)
> Tufts of straw, sands, fragments,
> Buoy'd hither from many moods, one contradicting
>   another,
> From the storm, the long calm, the darkness, the
>   swell,
> Musing, pondering, a breath, a briny tear, a dab of
>   liquid or soil,
> Up just as much out of fathomless workings fermented
>   and thrown,
> A limp blossom or two, torn, just as much over waves
>   floating, drifted at random,
> Just as much for us that sobbing dirge of Nature,
> Just as much whence we come that blare of cloud-
>   trumpets,
> We, capricious, brought hither we know not whence,
>   spread out before you,

You up there walking or sitting,
Whoever you are, we too lie in drifts at your feet.
(*CRE*, p. 256)

The fiery political redeemer of "Ode to the West Wind" hovers over this guarded leave-taking, his clarion call to reform—"the trumpet of a prophecy"—here sounded through "that blare of the cloud-trumpets." And yet, as the jarring insertion of "blare" makes plain, Whitman is in no position to announce the advent of a new millenium, one reason why he seizes upon Shelley's famous petition ("Be through my lips to unawakened earth, / The trumpet of a prophecy!") and infuses it with a repulsive splendor. Not the quickening of a new birth but a torturously labored ordeal of regeneration, "the ooze exuding at last" from these "dead lips," its "prismatic colors glistening and rolling," identifies a voice which is less the instrument of prophecy than a vessel for excremental purging. As with all the images in the passage, this too mingles gain and loss too finely for the schematic eye. What is presented is neither the loss of imaginative vision nor a confident resurgence of strength but a biding of time, a wish to prolong the lull between storms. In this moment of calm, "from the storm, the long calm, the darkness, the swell," the frame of reference gradually widens: fierce old mother and stern father have departed as the poet shifts attention from the ground to the heavens, scanning the horizon, perhaps, in search of "the clew . . . the word final, superior to all." But History as yet remains an indecipherable tangle of portents that will not resolve itself into coherence; its "fathomless workings" appear no less "capricious" than its drifting survivors. Apocalypse is in the air, some revelation is possibly at hand, yet it is hard to say whether the poet, poised between Nature's elegiac plangencies and the martial summons blaring from above, longs for or dreads that revelation. Understanding no more of its past than of its future, "brought hither we know not whence," the "I" and its "loose windrows, little corpses" are "spread out before you" in a manner that ambiguously combines the postures of supplicant and sacrificial offering. The "You up there walking or sitting," traditionally glossed as a composite of "the real Me," father, and audience, may more generally personify an inscrutable providence, a mute oracle of omniscience which shrouds itself from sight as the nation draws irrevocably towards its own "sweet hell within." In a powerful and startling reversal of his conceit of projecting himself into our future ("Failing to fetch me at first keep encouraged, / Missing me one place search another, / I stop somewhere waiting for you"), Whitman now depicts himself prostrate before an elusive destiny, not the embodiment of the future but its doubtful hostage.

"Out of the Cradle" and "As I Ebb'd" mark an interlude in Whitman's career. They identify a period of reconsolidation and stock taking, the aim of which is not only to weather a present crisis but to brace their author for an Armageddon to come. Each of their endings, fraught with apocalyptic expectancy, draws on the same mood haunting other meditations of the same period more explicitly devoted to the impending collapse of Union: "with gathering murk, with muttering thunder, and lambent shoots we all duly awake," he writes grimly in the closing lines of "To the States"; "South, North, East, West, inland, and seaboard, we will surely awake" (*CRE,* p. 279). Although in later editions Whitman would insert a miscellany of mostly forgettable musings aptly named "By the Roadside" between *Sea-Drift* and *Drum-Taps,* thus obscuring the continuity between the two sections, the tendency of his war poems to draw liberally on motifs and images from both of these odes further underscores, as we shall see, their essential affinity.

Hastened onward by these "mournful notes foreboding a tempest," Whitman became especially anxious to issue another edition of *Leaves* which would incorporate his compositions of the last three years. Following the precedent established by his two seashore odes, the volume released in the spring of 1860 displays an increased regard for organization and structure. Now headings for various sequences suddenly appear where none had been before, certain poems are christened with titles, and a formal prologue named "Proto-Leaf" (later known as "Starting From Paumanok") is conceived to announce thematic strands. "He wanted this volume to be a finished, self-sufficient work," declares Roger Asselineau, "the main lines of which were clear and immediately perceptible."[19] To crown this "edifice," as its architect was now in the habit of calling what had once been "beautiful dripping fragments" spilled onto the page, Whitman appended a valedictory summation, "So Long!" More than an epilogue, the special wonder of this poem consists in its momentary resurrection of a self he had thought long since departed. Announcing once more "that the identity of these States is a single identity only" and affirming a "Union more and more compact, indissoluble" furnishes Whitman with a surge of inspiration necessary to recapture the comedic hopefulness of his art as he forecasts "a life that shall be copious, spiritual, vehement, bold." With the return of his democratic vistas, blessed by "splendors and majesties to make all the previous politics of the earth insignificant," the verse quickens with the elation of rediscovery, first by depicting the erotic consummation of his leaves ("sparkles hot, seed ethereal down in the dirt dropping") and then by soliciting the equally passionate embrace of his camerados. What results is another seductive immersion, though one which does not derive from the low and delicious word of death alone. Saluting his audience in the manner of "Chants Democratic," Whitman reestablishes his "commission" as "bard of personality," the cynosure that cannot be held between the pages of his book but is elemented by the field of our consciousness.

Camerado, this is no book,
Who touches this touches a man,
(Is it night? Are we here together alone?)
It is I you hold and who holds you,
I spring from the pages into your arms—decease calls
          me forth.

O how your fingers drowse me,
Your pulse falls around me like dew, your pulse lulls
          the tympans of my ears,
I feel immerged from head to foot,
Delicious, enough.
. . . .
Dear friend whoever you are take this kiss,
I give it especially to you, do not forget me,
I feel like one who has done work for the day to
          retire awhile,
I receive now again of my many translations, from my
          avataras ascending, while others doubtless await me,
An unknown sphere more real than I dream'd, more
          direct, darts awakening rays about me, *So long!*
Remember my words, I may again return,
I love you, I depart from materials,
I am as one disembodied, triumphant, dead.

                                        (*CRE,* p. 505–6)

Writing such as this is capable of mastering everything except the future. The flaccid, hopelessly melodramatic reference to "my avataras," as well as to the "unknown sphere more real than I dream'd,"

makes immediately obvious the limits of foresight. Though these are
the only lapses in an otherwise splended tour de force, their forced
bravado more broadly illustrates Whitman's determination to write
his own epitaph before a portentous future writes it for him. He
speaks of his life as a poet as though it had already come to an end, so
anxious is he to close off a career which would last another thirty
years. And while he advertises with comic flourish a self overleaping
the bounds of his text, he is also drawn to immortalizing and encrypt-
ing that self within the finished edifice of his songs. Needless to say,
the death he here imagines for himself would not be the death he went
on to witness.

9

Drum-Taps and Beyond

TO A PROFOUND and not always implicit degree, the war had been foreshadowed in *Leaves of Grass* all along. "Indeed," writes James Cox, "Whitman's poetry during the five years before the war reads like a long preparation for the role he assumed"[1]—an opinion seconded early on by the author of *Drum-Taps* when, in the course of reviewing the trajectory of his career, he salutes his muse for "the good preparation you gave me" (*CRE*, p. 292). Though presumably meant without irony, there is of course a certain grimness in such assurances, which must be read in light of the catastrophe that Whitman had hoped to avert and that had haunted him as far back as his days as a newspaper editor in the late 1840s, just as it had haunted his country as early as Washington's Farewell Address in 1796. Much as we may be inclined to allow that "Whitman alone among the great writers of his age had equipped himself to confront the cleavage of his nation," it is evident too that the four years of bloodletting witnessed at first hand by him levied a tremendous physical and emotional price—so much so that he came to count himself among the mangled and maimed "debris" of the war, with the "old machine the body & brain well shattered & gone," as he confided late in life to one correspondent, "that secession war experience . . . a *whack* or series of whacks irrevocable."[2] No single account of *Drum-Taps* can adequately take stock of the full extent and impact of these traumatic blows; as the poet himself explains in *Specimen Days*, "the real war will never get in the books" (*PW*, 1:116). What did get into this collection of poems, issued in a separate volume only months after Appomattox, was neither the overthrow nor a hardening of the poet's democratic idealism but a seemingly inevitable and in many respects brutal extension of its consequences. In fearful realization of his insistence that the life of the nation and the life of the person were one, Whitman sought to come to terms with "the horrors of fratricidal war" by actively soliciting and absorbing them, not only taking upon himself, in fact as well as fantasy, their "crises of anguish" but steeping himself in, even glutting himself upon, the misery of battlefield and hospital. This intricate merging of psychic and political collapse, not always a conscious design but manifest throughout, provides the main center of interest for a reading of *Drum-Taps*, whose pivotal bearing on Whitman's career is routinely acknowledged but seldom studied with the close attention it deserves. To examine the manner in which its author confronted this convergence of themes is to begin to estimate both the burdens and the ambiguities of his immersion in the war.

A number of narratives have been abstracted from *Drum-Taps*, the most prominent being that suggested by James E. Miller, Jr., who has discerned in its pages the familiar passage from innocence to experience.[3] As a rough outline, this is not implausible and possesses the immediate advantage of following the poet's declared intention. *Drum-Taps*, whose composition proceeded in tandem with the war's unfolding, opens with a handful of martial hymns, whose naive sloganeering and belligerent call to arms are no less overt than their mediocrity. Once he had glimpsed the "lurid interiors" of combat, however, Whitman was moved to insert a formal retraction of these chants instead of striking them out altogether. ("Arous'd and angry, I'd thought to beat the alarum, and urge relentless war," he confesses in "The Wound-Dresser," "But soon my fingers fail'd me, my face droop'd and I resign'd myself, / To sit by the wounded and soothe them, or silently watch the dead" [*CRE*, p. 309].) By 1863, "rack'd by the war-strife," he would favor an immediate end to the fighting, feeling that the principles at stake could no longer justify the bloodshed. Still, disappointing as these early hymns often are, their more revealing moments are worth considering not only for whatever "innocence" they may disclose (baffled rage would be a better term) but for their struggle against an ideological double bind that becomes increasingly visible as the volume develops. But before addressing this struggle directly, it will be useful to turn back to its antecedents in the constitutional crisis that precipitated the war in the first place.

Near the end of *Calamus* a call had been sounded for "the institution of the dear love of comrades." Whitman did not at that time pause to reflect on the potential contradiction in terms latent in his phrasing, though he did find it necessary, as I have argued, to fend off premonitions over his utopia of institutionalized love by venting these misgivings elsewhere, most notably against poetry itself, whose "emblematic and capricious blades" would no longer serve. As I have also argued in previous chapters, Whitman's stance toward the significance of political institutions was completely ambivalent: feeling them on the one hand to be incidental and possibly ruinous impediments to his quasi-mystical concept of democracy, he at the same time longed to affirm in this vision the same bonded proof and security of commitment vouchsafed by these institutions. Turning in disgust away from the factionalism of political parties, he also envisaged the coming of "the Redeemer President"; summoning a "new comradeship" leagued in spontaneous affection "without edifices or rules or trustees or any argument," he could also describe this fraternity in terms of an "institution." His conservative radicalism is further reflected in the position taken toward the controversy then engulfing the country, a position that joined devout adherence to the concept of perennial Union ("impossible to dissever!") with an equally fierce defense of the doctrine of state sovereignty. Accommodating both positions required, as Whitman was acutely aware, the resolution of "two sets of rights—the fusion, thorough compatibility and junction of individual State prerogatives, with the indispensable necessity of centrality and Oneness—the National Identity power—the sovereign Union, relentless, permanently comprising all, and over all, and in that never yielding an inch . . ." (*PW* 2:465–66).

Placed in perspective, Whitman's contorted syntax takes on an inadvertent eloquence, since it was of course the withdrawal of eleven states from his cherished Union that would in hindsight lend added urgency to such declarations. Secession made painfully obvious the radical *in*compatibility of these "two sets of rights." Above all a constitutional dispute over the true locus of civil authority, it shattered at last the already fragile equilibrium between individual and institution, the many and the one, equality and order. ("The dream of humanity, the vaunted Union we thought so strong, so impregnable—lo! it seems already like a smashed china plate" [*PW* 1:29].) Under the shadow of secession, understood by all to signal the unquestioned death of "the National Identity," the poet's commission to justify and celebrate "ensemble-Individuality" would appear both oxymoronic and anachronistic. Of course, the avowed purpose of the war was to repair the integrity of this construct and thereby revalidate the legitimacy of the "sacred compacts" inherited from the Fathers. Almost from the start of his collection, however, Whitman balks at this logic:

would the "Sovereign Union, relentless, permanent, comprising all" furnish adequate grounds for sacrifice? We hear doubts on this score surfacing primarily through the virulence of Whitman's efforts early in *Drum-Taps* to shout them down, as when "Democracy" is summoned to "thunder on! stride on! . . . strike with vengeful stroke!" or while drums and bugles are ordered to "make no parley—stop for no expostulation . . . mind not the old man beseeching the young man, / Let not the child's voice be heard, nor the mother's entreaties" (*CRE*, pp. 292, 284). Too insistent to be taken altogether seriously, such manic calls to arms make better sense as exercises in self-persuasion; the warlord who will "let bullets and slugs whizz . . . pour the verse with streams of blood, full of volition, full of joy . . . crying with trumpet voice, *arouse and beware! Beware and arouse!*" is only talking to himself (*CRE*, p. 285). It is no doubt this strenuous overreaching that so mortifies Henry James in his notorious dismissal of *Drum-Taps* ("the muscular strain of an essentially prosaic mind lifting itself into poetry"), and it is typical of Whitman that confusion should be manifested by way of a torrent of verbiage rather than silence.

Whitman would soon leave this patriotic ardor behind for the forbearance of the Wound-Dresser, but it is important to specify further the causes for this transition. A revealing diagnosis of his dilemma at this early stage of the conflict can be found in "Song of the Banner at Daybreak," a rather lackluster morality play whose dramatic personae include Father, Child, Poet, and Banner. With each character assigned a separate voice, the drama of the poem centers on a contest of wills between the Child swayed by the "haughty and resolute" Banner of War and the distressed Father counseling prudence and thrift. A timid Pharisee speaking on behalf of "the precious results of peace . . . with wealth incalculable," the father admonishes his son to "to look at these dazzling things in the houses, and see you the money-shops opening" (*CRE*, p. 286). The Poet, for his part, does not scorn "the valuable houses, standing fast, full of comfort, built with money," but he cannot allow the pennant of Union to degenerate into "mere strips of cloth, profiting nothing" and so joins Child and Banner in embracing "passions of demons, slaughter, premature death." As the insistent phallicism of the "lengthen'd pennant shaped like a sword, run[ning] swiftly up indicating war and defiance" denotes, war promises a final defeat of the Father, whose "money-banks" must yield to the forces of "terror and carnage." War, however, does not simply destroy familial ties but replaces these with the authority of the state. More than "full of volition, full of joy," the Banner is, as the Child exclaims, "full of people, full of children . . . it is talking to its children." It does not "endlessly cry for its castaways" but collects its progeny under the call of "demons and death . . . and a pleasure new and ecstatic."

In lining up self-interest against self-sacrifice, the author of "Song of the Banner at Daybreak" does little more than mouth the stock rhetorical slogans of his day, which welcomed the onset of battle as a much needed catharsis for the complacency of materialist pursuit. With the final monologue, spoken by the Poet, Whitman endeavors to infuse new life into these commonplaces, though in the process of announcing the clarity of his theme he only succeeds in muddling it further:

> My limbs, my veins dilate, my theme is clear at last,
> Banner so broad advancing out of the night, I sing you
>> haughty and resolute,
> I burst through where I waited long, too long,
>> deafen'd and blinded,
> My hearing and tongue are come to me, (a little child
>> taught me,)
> I hear from above O pennant of war your ironical call
>> and demand,
> Insensate! Insensate! (yet I at any rate chant you,) O
>> banner!
>
>> *(CRE,* p. 290)

That fraternal ties should be consolidated under the aegis of fratricidal bloodletting is too stark an irony to be ignored, even if the Poet bullies himself into accepting its irrationality. In frantic search for renewed sources of inspiration and commitment, his forced epiphany battens on the idiom and imagery of "Out of the Cradle." But the gap traveled between that awakening of "love in the heart long pent, now at last tumultuously bursting" and these hectic apostrophes is too great to be crossed. Still clinging to memories of *Sea-Drift,* the Poet launches one final attempt at the sublime:

> O you up there! O pennant! where you undulate like a
>> snake hissing so curious,
> Out of reach, an idea only, yet furiously fought for,
>> risking bloody death, loved by me,

So loved—O you banner leading the day with stars
            brought from the night!
Valueless, object of eyes, over all and demanding
            all—(absolute owner of all)—O banner and pennant!
I too leave the rest—great as it is, it is nothing . . .
                                                          (*CRE*, p. 290–91)

Untold, untouched, altogether unreached, the dream of Union grows
ever more remote the more it is coveted. Devotion and rage have
become so interfused that we are obliged to gloss "valueless" as describing for Whitman a Republic that is at once a priceless fetish
("object of eyes") and a worthless, defunct abstraction ("Insensate!
Insensate!").

Taken together, the string of monologues making up "Song of the
Banner at Daybreak" represents an awkward contrivance on Whitman's part; the gift for dramatic exposition that had sustained him in
works like "This Compost" or "Out of the Cradle" cannot sustain him
here. At best, the assembled voices bespeak the wandering allegiances
of a writer whose sympathies appear distributed among his various
delegates without being reducible to any one of them. More pointedly, the song's format, with its stylized presentation of clashing
perspectives, obscures from view our most familiar image of Whitman. Vestiges of that image survive in the Poet's opening vow to
"weave the chord and twine in" the demands of war and fraternity,
but in any complete estimate his role as a medium of exchange for the
competing priorities of "thirty-eight spacious and haughty States" is
left in abeyance, never truly engaging the poem's development. Why
this should be so is insufficiently explained by the adaptation of a
literary mode that closely approximates the manner of Tennyson or
Browning nor even by the reality of disunion itself. Directly preceding the Poet's concluding apostrophes, Whitman momentarily
confronts a darker revelation in the chant of the Banner, which freely
roams the lands of "the Continent, devoting the whole identity without reserving an atom . . . whelm[ing] that which asks, which sings,
with all and the yield of all, / Fusing and holding, claiming, devouring
the whole" (*CRE*, p. 289). The knowledge here intimated extends
beyond the common wisdom that the death of consensus occasions
the birth of war. (*Ad bellum purificandum* is the epigraph for Kenneth
Burke's *Grammar of Motives*.) Rather, consensual paradigms meant to
contain violence merely come to replicate its course: what begins as a

devotion to the whole stands revealed, in the rhetoric of war, as a devouring of it. In the portrait of the Banner, afoot with its vision and roving through the states collecting, fusing, holding, and claiming, Whitman hints not so much at a final defeat of his vision of consensus as its grim perversion, one that builds altars to the unreal majesty of a phantom republic which commands all and is commanded by no one. As he invokes this idol of "the sovereign Union, relentless, permanently comprising all," and over all with a mixture of worship and derision, Whitman verges on without quite acknowledging what Lawrence would surmise some eighty years later with much more explicitness: "Comradeship—part of the death process. Democracy—part of the death process. The new Democracy—the birth of death. One identity—death itself."[4]

Lawrence's terse equations are indispensable to a full appreciation of *Drum-Taps*, not only for the light they shed on the Wound-Dresser's romance with death but, as we shall also see, for their anticipation of Whitman's own remarkable account of democracy's death drive in his powerful allegory "Chanting the Square Deific." As yet, the invisible author of "Song of the Banner at Daybreak" only intuits such implications, compelled as he is to chant a war he does not particularly advocate and to recognize in this advocacy a twisted corruption of his own rhetoric of consensus—"out of the night emerging for good, our voice persuasive no more, / Croaking like crows here in the wind" (*CRE*, p. 289). Other selections work strenuously to distract attention elsewhere, some by wandering among Nature's "primal energies" ("Rise O Days from Your Fathomless Deeps"), others by cavorting through his "proud and passionate" city ("City of Ships"), as though their central subject were a peripheral matter. "The Centenarian's Story," a more ambitious poem, meanwhile forsakes the present tense briefly by traveling back in time to the heroism of the Founding Fathers. The plot is simple. An aging veteran of the Revolutionary War, assisted by a "Volunteer of 1861–62," climbs the heights of Washington Park in Brooklyn while a regiment parades below them on the eve of departing for battle. Feeble and nearly blind, Whitman's Tiresias journeys back in memory to his involvement in the Battle of Long Island, which had occurred on the same site eighty-five years before. Like "Song of the Banner at Daybreak," this text provides an intratextual interpreter (the Volunteer) who introduces the story, listens to the Centenarian's reminiscence, and supplies an epilogue. Though the greater part of the narrative is devoted to a description of the disastrous engagement and Washington's midnight retreat, its most resonant scene is plainly intended not only to heighten the drama of the poem but to point a moral for the present. In reverential tones appropriate to the witnessing of a sacred trust, Whitman recreates a primal scene of oath-taking that bands together brothers-in-arms, an oath sealed by the living proof of speech and the phallic defiance of their leader:

> As I talk I remember all, I remember the Declaration,
> It was read here, the whole army paraded, it was read
>   to us here,
> By his staff surrounded the General stood in the
>   middle, he held up his unsheath'd sword,
> It glitter'd in the sun in full sight of the
>   army.
>   (*CRE*, p. 296)

One could say, Whitman suggests elsewhere, "the United States came into existence not only with the Revolution of '76 but through our Rebellion of 1861–5. The blood, the fathomless experiences, emotions, of both, joined" (*WWC* 5:93). Invoking the spirit of '76 in support of the Union cause of '61 was indeed much in vogue at the time, the abolitionist Wendell Phillips going so far as to maintain that the present conflict was but a reenactment of the War for Independence. The more renowned example is of course Lincoln's magisterial Gettysburg Address, which looks back four score and seven years ago to the sacred compacts of the Fathers in order to look upon this "great Civil War" as a final testing of their visionary design. Taking stock of these exercises in typology, Herman Melville in the meantime savored their irony. In one of those shocks of recognition that spasmodically erupt from the stilted calm of *Battle Pieces*, a voice cries out in the heat of a hillside skirmish *"This Bluff's a perverted Bunker Hill."*[5]

Whitman stands somewhere between Lincoln's piety and Melville's black humor. In "The Centenarian's Story" it is never clear whether he considers the war to be a heroic vindication of what Melville calls "the Founder's dream" or its profanation. The stoic resolve exhibited by Washington that the poem goes on to commemorate is presumably intended to fortify Union resolve, a gesture all the more necessary, it would seem, in view of the unmistakable contrast between the festive merriment of recruits "surrounded with smiles" and the brigade of two thousand slaughtered four score and five years before. This brigade, moreover, was "rais'd in Virginia and Maryland, and most of them known personally to the General" (*CRE*, p. 297). That the troops now marching in review should be readying themselves to slay the descendants of those who defended this same site is an irony Centenarian and Volunteer alike prefer to overlook or ignore but one Whitman inserts with full deliberation. (He used a similar effect in "The Sleepers," with Washington mourning the sacrifice of his "southern braves" during the same battle.) Because the events of '76 and those of '61 are brought together while their significance is entirely left suspended, the Volunteer can do little more in the epilogue than vow, rather lamely, to preserve and repeat the Centenarian's narrative. Despite his self-proclaimed role as "chansonnier of a great future," the "connector" of "past and future," Whitman's surrogate serves as a weak echo of "the joiner of tongues" in "Song of Myself," the consummate translator who had announced himself to be "an acme of things accomplish'd and an encloser of things to be." And as this prophet of integration withdraws from the text, as he does also in "Song of the Banner at Daybreak," so does Washington's reading of the Declaration recede into a haze of pious sentiment ("behold through the smoke Washington's face") which further blurs its relevance to the present. Evidently the poem is not oblivious to these ambiguities but loath to pursue them; at the most, what it exemplifies, as Whitman would later say of "the many-threaded drama" of war in general, is a "confounding of prophecies" (*PW* 1:117).

The conflict of convictions gripping Whitman is finally condensed upon the figure of Washington, who assumes here as he had assumed in "The Sleepers" a dual role. If his "bold act" of defiance initially leads his sons into battle, this martial persona soon softens into a display of contrition as the general, wringing his hands in anguish, helplessly witnesses the disastrous outcome of his own designs. A Lucifer turned Christ, he rises above the rancor of clashing interests by lamenting the violence that ensues; the "moisture gather[ing] in drops on the face of the General" establishes his significance as an exemplary mourner who assuages guilt by means of mute compassion. So doing, his portrait marks an important turning point for *Drum-Taps* in that we also find the poet soon "confronting, reversing my cries" as he abandons prior calls for vengeance. Mingling Washington's stoic calm and his boundless sympathy, Whitman discovers his voice in the figure of the Wound-Dresser who keeps before him scenes of pain and death until it seems "as if the whole interest of the land, North and South, was one vast central Hospital, and all the rest of the affair but flanges" (*PW*, 1:110). Suffering has the advantage of focusing the war's true priorities by allowing Whitman to see in the staggering flow of casualties a tragedy "of more significance even than the Political Interests" involved (*PW* 1:117). Of course, imperfectly concealed behind such declarations is an acknowledgment of the appalling *in*significance of these sacrifices, martyred as they are at the shrine of a "valueless" and inert abstraction. As Whitman bitterly informed Emerson in a letter in the first month of 1863, "America, already brought to Hospital in her fair youth," had transformed "those white palaces—the dome crown'd capitol there on the hill" into a "great, whited sepulchre . . . this union Capitol without the first bit of cohesion—this collect of proofs of how long and swift a good stock can deteriorate" (*CORR* 1:69). In another respect, however, the image of the states as one vast hospital carried a redemptive appeal for Whitman; strangely, perversely, and perhaps inevitably his vision of a genuine democratic union exempt from "Political Interests" finally came to rest among the dying and wounded. Suffering not only transcended sectional rivalry by making all comrades in the clasp of death, it also gave the appearance of reconciling the conflicting demands of war and fraternity—reconciled not so much in the sense of resolving this contradiction as now making it seem irrelevant.

With this discovery comes a certain relief. The best and most memorable pieces of *Drum-Taps*—the vignettes of army life, battlefield vigils, and hospital sketches forming the center of this collection—exhibit a deepening sense of composure, even serenity. At a time when it was common to herald the war as a climactic test of democratic legitimacy—whether this or any other nation can long endure—Whitman remains silent; in the wake of his own thwarted attempts at upholding the "ironical call and demand" for Union, he keeps his counsel, and scrupulously maintains an utter impartiality. Questions concerning democracy's "proof," value, and final validation no longer engage his attention. Instead, *Drum-Taps* strips names, places, and dates from the battle scenes it recounts, all the while implying that its essential mission is not to understand the war but survive it. Without recourse to ideological justification, these scenes flare up before the observer unrelieved by assimilation into a readily apparent narrative framework. In flight from any such measures which would contain and codify its experience into a meaningful sequence, the heart of

Drum-Taps repeatedly confronts a series of discontinuous incidents whose immediacy renders the interval between loss and healing forgetfulness slight if not wholly unobtainable. The result is an ongoing sense of resolve within a speaker who is called on to honor and indeed sanctify the dead without falsifying their significance. So, in the midst of an engagement, the comrade of a soldier is suddenly struck down. Pausing momentarily for "one touch of your hand, O boy, reach'd up as you lay on the ground," the soldier speeds onward to the front where he remains until, late at night, he returns to his fallen friend who is now found to be

> . . . in death so cold dear comrade, found your body
> son of responding kisses, (never again on earth
> responding,)
> Bared your face in the starlight, curious the scene,
> cool blew the moderate night-wind,
> Long there and then in vigil I stood, dimly around me
> the battlefield spreading,
> Vigil wondrous and sweet there in the fragrant silent
> night,
> But not a tear fell, not even a long-drawn sigh, long,
> long, I gazed,
> Then on the earth partially reclining sat by your side
> leaning my chin in my hands,
> Passing sweet hours, immortal and mystic hours with
> you my dearest comrade—not a tear, not a word,
> Vigil of silence, love and death, vigil for you my son
> and my soldier,
> As onward silently stars aloft, eastward new ones
> upward stole,
> Vigil final for you brave boy, (I could not save you,
> swift was your death,
> I faithfully loved you and cared for you living, I
> think we shall surely meet again,)
> Till at latest lingering of the night, indeed just as
> dawn appear'd,
> My comrade I wrapt in his blanket, envelop'd well his
> form,
> Folded the blanket well, tucking it carefully over
> head and carefully under feet,

And there and then bathed by the rising sun, my son in
        his grave, in his rude dug grave I deposited,
Ending my vigil strange with that, vigil at night and
        battle-field dim,
Vigil for boy of responding kisses, (never again on
        earth responding,)
Vigil for comrade swiftly slain, vigil I never forget,
        how as day brighten'd,
I rose from the chill ground and folded my soldier
        well in his blanket,
And buried him where he fell.

                              (*CRE*, pp. 304–5)

In such instances, the notorious prolixity of *Leaves of Grass* is put to felicitous effect. If the poem appears to go on too long, reluctant to quit the scene, that is in keeping with its determination to rescue death from banality. Abiding through "the latest lingering of the night," it draws on the convention of detaining the dead familiar to pastoral elegy that is set against the reality of "swiftly slain." Etherealized into a mystic rite of communion which is placed beyond all speech and which brackets off the social world, the work of mourning gets transfigured into an act of witnessing made the more heroic by its refusal to invoke a supervening order or providential design. For if part of the burden of the poem is to suggest that "in a larger sense we can not dedicate—we can not consecrate—we can not hallow this ground," it also implies that to say so would only augment the blasphemy in commemoration which Lincoln's eloquence so deftly turns to its advantage. Whitman's vigil is as much a guarding against the imputation of meaning as it is a watch of the passage from life to death; as the phrase "vigil of silence, love, and death" suggests, the only term sufficient to stand between silence and death is a responsive benevolence.

Compassion this divine can, it is true, present difficulties of its own. One may come to feel that the poet is not responding to an event but perfecting an attitude. The same lyrics admired by James Wright for their unsurpassed "delicacy" Daniel Aaron faults as "calculating and concessive."[6] Extremes of both responses inform the career of Henry James, who of course denounced the meretricious posturing of the "chansonnier" of *Drum-Taps* on its appearance in 1865, while in his last years sentimentalized this same figure into "dear old Walt," armed with his "peppermints and oranges."[7] William Dean Howells, not known for his epigrammatic precision, nevertheless strikes a more balanced view in drawing attention to Whitman's "burly tenderness"[8]—a trait we cannot fail to note in the care taken by his midnight vigil to demarcate a boundary between the living and the dead in defense against the latter's return. The subtle but decisive shift from the second- to the third-person pronoun, the meticulous regard shown in blanketing the corpse, and the severe finality of the closing line variously insist on preserving a line of difference between mourner and mourned with an emphasis that saves the poem from trailing off into sentimentality. Such precautions are all the more paramount given the readiness of *Drum-Taps* to blur the relation between the phantasmagoria of war and the phantasmagoria of the mind to the point where it becomes difficult to ascertain where the task of acknowledgment ends and the process of detachment can begin. Directly following his wondrous and strange vigil, "A March in the Ranks Hard-Prest, and Road Unknown" likewise pauses "at an open space in the woods," where its speaker peers through "the midnight glimmer" and espies within an old church "shadows of deepest black . . . groups of forms vaguely [seen] . . . faces, varieties, postures beyond all description, most in obscurity, some of them dead" (*CRE*, p. 305). Fitfully silhouetted on the walls of this impromptu hospital by the glare of "one great pitchy torch stationary with wild red flame and clouds of smoke," a "crowd of the bloody forms . . . some on the bare ground, some on plank or stretchers, some in the death-spasm sweating" press upon the observer with a hallucinatory urgency. So tenacious is the hold of the dead on the imagination that it would indeed appear as though the Answerer's cry of immortality— "I spring from the page into your arms—decease calls me forth"— more appropriately describes the unappeased apparitions confusedly glimpsed among the "crowd of bloody forms."

In a style both naturalistic and surreal, these poems come to resemble impromptu grave sites in their own right, which detain without quite containing their "tireless phantoms." These would be the same "rapid-filing phantoms [marching] through the winds" that continued, nearly twenty years later, to haunt the author of *Specimen Days*, notwithstanding his patient effort to set down in this volume the name, rank, and birthplace of each of his diseased and dying "soldier-boys." In one stunning entry from his memoranda, which bears the extraordinary title "The Million Dead, Too, Summ'd Up," Whitman endeavors in one sprawling, grasping sentence to collect and collate all "the debris and debris of the war" at the same time he is driven to concede the utter impossibility of ever doing so. "There they lie," he begins, "strewing the fields and woods and valleys and battlefield," as if the intervening years of peace had merely revealed the intransigence of the "hundreds, thousands, obliterated" in defying interment, still unburied and unburiable. Perversely enough, "the varieties of the *strayed* dead . . . *our* dead . . . the general million . . . the infinite dead" make a travesty of any attempt at commemoration and for that reason make the demand for a final resting place all the more imperative. Lands once imagined to be one vast hospital instead assume the appearance of one vast graveyard in whose "secluded spots" one may yet happen upon "skeletons, bleach'd bones, tufts of hair, buttons, fragments of clothing." With Northern corpses "leavening Southern soil" and "Southerners crumbl[ing] today in Northern Earth," Whitman's grim tally envisions a "land entire saturated [and] perfumed with their impalpable ashes," ashes which, distilled and diffused by "Nature's chemistry," shall linger "forever in every future grain of wheat and ear of corn, and every flower that grows, and every breath we draw" (*PW* 1:114–15).

Devising an adequate vocabulary of acknowledgment for these strayed and straying skeletons thus defines the heroic absurdity of the poet's undertaking. In looking back on his often-quoted observation that "the real war will never get in the books," we should at this point note as well his further stipulation that its "lurid interiors" not only "will never be written [but] perhaps must not and should not be" (*PW* 1:117). That the declared futility of ever "enbalming" the war in print should be supplemented by an injunction against doing so suggests the poet's need to prohibit similar longings within himself. In effect, Whitman's added warning makes vivid a continuing predicament within *Drum-Taps:* to submit the war and its meanings to a transcendent framework of intelligibility may require still greater violence, both against the poet's temperament and the subjects he elegizes; to leave the war and its meanings unsanctioned and unexplained is merely to perpetuate their trauma, both left unburied. The ideological impasse paralyzing the earlier chants of demobilization has not been circumvented, but only intensified. This in part explains why many of the central poems in *Drum-Taps* can be defined as essentially truncated elegies, memorials in which the process of grieving has in some decisive fashion been curtailed or broken off. The passage from guilt to anger to appeasement, the relinquishing of the lost object by means of symbolic substitution, the resurrection of vitality within the self through some fiction of regeneration—such traditional stages in the work of mourning have become occluded or atrophied in these pages. Accordingly, if the poem "The Wound-Dresser" begins as though its events occurred long ago—"an old man bending I come among new faces, / Years looking backward resuming in answer to children"—this attempt at distancing swiftly collapses under the stark immediacy of this dream-vision. As the bizarre equation of "open doors of time! open hospital doors!" reveals, the hospital stands as a kind of parodic visionary threshold in which time is, so to speak, quarantined, plunging the speaker into an exitless nightmare without beginning or end and making him seem no less spectral than the ghostly spirits he attends. In the manner of Nick Adams on his fishing trip, Whitman's protagonist speaks as though his identity were in constant peril of dissolution and so, like Hemingway's catatonic veteran, clings to the merest predicates to keep the self in motion: "I enter . . . I go . . . I return . . . I draw near . . . I onward go, I stop . . . I examine . . . I undo . . . I pacify . . . I recall." The dramatis personae surrounding this somnambulist no longer comprise fallen sons and comrades but "the crush'd head," "the amputated hand," "the clotted lint," "the bloody stump," "the perforated shoulder," "the fractur'd thigh." Under this gothic magnification of detail, injuries and mutilations take on a life of their own by drifting away from their ostensible source and entering into a psychic limbo which so permeates the speaker's consciousness that it becomes apparent that he too must be counted as one more victim among this heap of broken images. His ministrations are also self-ministrations; "the hurt and wounded" pacified by his "soothing hand" include himself. Far from chronicling a drama of release and disengagement, everything in the poem conspires to lock its protagonist into a rite of suffering shown to be unending and unfinishable: "thus in silence, in dreams' projections, / Returning, resuming, I thread my way through the hospitals."

What stands within those "open hospital doors" is for Whitman both a prison and a sanctuary, an ambiguous site that protects as much as it entraps. The steady, unwavering concentration on dismemberment and death, while certainly expressive of the numbing anguish experienced by Whitman during the war, also indicates what seems in hindsight to be a deliberate withdrawal from that pose of triumphant generality struck by the prophet of consensus who had declared himself standing "apart from the pulling and the hauling." For all his courageous stoicism, the Wound-Dresser flinches from this omniscient stance. Rigid in his neutrality, he will not see beyond the walls of the hospital. It is no doubt symptomatic of this shuttered vision, as much an expression of ideological confusion as of psychic defense, that the 1865 edition of *Drum-Taps* could find it possible to canvass the many repercussions of the Civil War without mention of the Negro or slavery. (With the 1871 *Leaves,* Whitman rectified this oversight, but only slightly. A painfully stilted piece written in fourteeners and dressed up with an elaborate rhyme scheme, "Ethiopia Saluting the Colors" issues a series of queries to an inscrutable "dusky woman, so ancient hardly human" who watches in wonderment Sherman's regiments file past her "hovel door" [CRE, 318–19].) Perhaps the most notable feature of this strictly observed reticence, explained only in part by Whitman's wish to avert inflammatory issues and in any case uncommon for a volume of war poetry, concerns the fixation on death which becomes increasingly visible in *Drum-Taps.* With the departure of such coveted abstractions as Democracy, Personality, Love, or Union, the low and delicious word takes on added seductiveness as it fills in the gap left by such vanished constructs. Whitman's gathering infatuation on this score has of course been abundantly evident from the start, manifest in his sweet and mystic communings with the slain on the battlefield or in his enraptured fascination as he zealously tallies "the million dead" strewn throughout the land. Although Paul Zweig justly observes that the Liebestod of "Out of the Cradle" had "been romantic and song-like" whereas "here were actual men dying; here were bodies ripped open by shrapnel [and] drained by disease,"[9] it is also clear that "the word of the sweetest songs and all songs" has not lost its luxuriant appeal. The chant of "death, death, death, death, death" continues to beckon in ways that should not be overlooked, for in the overtly regressive nature of this call we see a further reflection of *Drum-Taps'* confused flight from advocacy.

Hearing at last the news of peace does not move Whitman to ponder the cause of Union, its worth, sacrifices, or repercussions. Rather, "bathed in the war's perfume" just as he had been laved by the sea's caresses, he welcomes a final consummation, disturbingly vivid in its evocation:

> Word over all, beautiful as the sky,
> Beautiful that war and all its carnage must in time be utterly
> > lost,
> That the hands of the sisters Death and Night
> > > incessantly and softly wash again, and ever again,
> > > this soil'd world;
> For my enemy is dead, a man divine as myself is dead,
> I look where he lies white-faced and still in the
> > > coffin—I draw near,
> Bend down and touch lightly with my lips the white
> > > face in the coffin.
> > > > > > ("Reconciliation," *CRE,* p. 321)

Ostensibly a kiss of benediction and appeasement, this embrace at the same time upholds a narcissistic bond between the self and its dark double that implicitly challenges the prospect for detachment. While it may be true that "war and all its deeds of carnage must in time be utterly lost," the poet is by no means prepared to accept that erasure. Instead, he conjures the beautiful dumb sisters of Death and Night, whose unceasing work of bereavement, washing "again and ever again, this soil'd world," recalls the endless vigil of the Wound-Dresser tirelessly making his rounds. Laying the subject of war to rest here only results in its further internalization.

"*Power,*" comments the author of *Specimen Days* in a parenthetical aside, "so important in poetry and war" (*PW* 1:142). Though his cryptic parallel resists explication, one admirable gloss for it can be found in Stevens's description of the mind as "a violence from within that protects us from a violence without . . . the imagination pressing back against the pressure of reality."[10] On balance, however, neither aphorism accurately registers the prevailing temperament of *Drum-Taps.* While it is true that one poem near the end of the selection exhorts the troops returning from the front to "leave me your pulses of rage—bequeath them to me—fill me with currents convulsive" while another makes reference to "myself and this contentious soul of mine, / Still on our own campaigning bound, / Through untried roads with ambushes opponents lined" (*CRE,* p. 325), traces of a corresponding "violence within" are more typically muted past all recognition in these poems. The refusal of rage seems only to prolong the mourning process, to deepen the inflexible stance of a memorialist whose only defense consists in his utter defenselessness, stranded as he is between the call "to learn from crises of anguish" and the impulse to forsake any such understanding. Once set beside "the impassive hand" of the Wound-Dresser, Whitman's more militant proclamations—"I know my words are full of danger, full of death"—sound like empty bravado. A better illustration of Stevens's adage (written in 1942 as another war was getting underway) can be found in one of Whitman's contemporaries, who supplies the necessary contrast:

> Ye elms that wave on Malvern Hill
> In prime of morn and May,
> Recall ye how McClellan's men
> Here stood at bay?
> While deep in yonder forest dim
> Our rigid comrades lay;
> Some with the cartridge in their mouth—
> Others with fixed arms lifted South,
> Invoking so
> The cypress glade, ah wilds of woe![11]

Holding compassion and horror at arm's length, Melville anesthetizes both with the metaphysic of wit. Describing the "rigid comrades" of McClellan's doomed campaign as if they were the frolicsome youth of Thomas Gray's Eton College Ode serves a double purpose: it exposes to ridicule any attempt to place the war and its butchery in the literary tradition at the same time it appeases, by way of parodic displacement, the mind's craving to do just that. An absurdly inappropriate frame of reference, the language of eighteenth-century pastoralism nevertheless frames a response. And yet parody alone cannot adequately take into account the treatment of corpses mockingly stylized in attitudes no less artificial and contorted than the cadence of the lines themselves. Unlike Whitman, Melville insists on fixing his slain to the spot, but the cost of doing so is to confront figures who appear disconcertingly sentient in their rigidity, frozen as they are in clenched gestures of appeal, haplessly invoking an aloof and possibly indifferent remembrancer. If the dumbshow of "fixed arms lifted South" secures no response from impassive Nature, would this unconcern apply as well to the poet? To this implied reproach Melville answers with a vengeful vindictiveness that borders on desecration—a playing with the limbs of the dead, twisting their lifeless features into trite caricature.

Battle Pieces matches blow for blow, weighing the violence without against the violence within. As the title suggests, words and weapons share an intimacy that demonstrates how readily the poet may exchange the role of mourner for that of executioner. Melville's most memorable images consequently flash out from the page like musket fire: the recruits who "file toward Fate . . . chatting left and laughing right" are lured into battle just as inexorably as they are lured into these poems until the ambush is sprung and they find themselves "enlightened by the vollied glare." It would appear that devotion to "the THREE HUNDRED THOUSAND who in the war for the maintenance of the Union fell devotedly under the flag of their Fathers" (so reads the dedication of the volume) required slaying them all over again. That Melville overwhelms grief with rage while Whitman smothers it in compassion is no doubt in keeping with the different temperaments of these two writers, though it is instructive to note further how their vision of the war made this difference still more dramatic. Its gait spasmodic, its imagery gnarled, and its diction willfully antiquated, *Battle Pieces* is by turns everything *Drum-Taps* is not. Composed largely once the end of the conflict was in sight, it reinserts what Whitman is at pains to eliminate. Melville pieces together a narrative that moves chronologically through the war from battle to battle, alert to hidden symmetries and grimly attentive to their ironies. In this brooding, analytic stance he may no doubt be likened to Hardy interrogating his "purblind doomsters"; "an adept of neutrality," as Denis Donoghue calls him, "Melville's Great Comedian" forswears "all allegiances, partly for self-preservation, partly in devotion to the privacy of truth."[12] But were we to delete its ironic overtones, this outlook would in fact more nearly approximate Whitman's stance; in the rage pressing through the clotted syntax of *Battle Pieces* we glimpse not "an adept at neutrality" but a tortuous process of accommodation, whereby the poet shifts allegiance from the sanctity of the individual to the authority of the Union. Scarcely so naive as "those champions and enthusiasts of the state," the author of *Battle Pieces* is nonetheless forthright in his vision of a society fortified by sacrifice, "stronger for stress and strain." If slavery had laid bare the "slimed foundations" tainting the compacts of the Fathers, fratricide "purifies" in Melville's "America." By vindicating and preserving the "Iron Dome" of Union, fratricide also makes apparent the necessary subjugation of the many under the One. "In form as in content," declares Michael Paul Rogin, "*Battle Pieces* honors confinement. . . . [It] restores the state to its primacy over civil society, but it does so at the expense of the republican dream."[13]

But *Drum-Taps,* as we have seen, flees from advocacy. It holds fast to the fiction that as "schemes, politics, fail," and as the "quicksand years . . . mock and elude me" it is after all the "great and strong possess'd soul . . . the final substance that out of all is sure" (*CRE,* p. 448). Voting for the primacy of the many over the One in this fashion, though, offers little defense against the whispered enticements of "sane and sacred death," and in this respect regression stands at the opposite extreme from rage. Rather than pay homage to a state devoid of transcendent purpose, Whitman deifies death and its blissful oblivion as the final catalyst for comradeship. To be sure, in subsequent years he did find it possible to allege a providential design for the war no less emphatically than Melville. As early as *Democratic Vistas* (1870), for example, he points to "the late Secession War and its results" as evidence that "popular democracy, whatever its faults and dangers, practically justifies itself beyond the proudest claims and wildest hopes of its enthusiasts" (*PW* 2:377). Such reasoning is common enough, yet even in a random instance like this one detects a lingering diffidence in the figure of a Republic which has no need for the intervention of its enthusiasts but "justifies itself." It is only a short step from such gestures at containment to the still more disingenuous conceit, propounded five years later in an article on "Origins of Attempted Secession" (1875), that the years "1860–1865 [were not] a struggle of two distinct and separate peoples, but a conflict (often happening, very fierce) between the passions and paradoxes of one and the same identity—perhaps the only terms on which that identity could really become fused, homogeneous and lasting" (*PW* 2:427). This too would be a Republic "stronger for stress and strain."

A far more compelling treatment of these "passions and paradoxes" rending "one and the same identity" can on the other hand be found in what George Fredrickson correctly identifies as "Whitman's final word on the Civil War."[14] This is "Chanting the Square Deific," which was first printed in the "Sequel" to *Drum-Taps* along with "When Lilacs Last in the Dooryard Bloom'd" and later transposed to "Whispers of Heavenly Death." It represents something of an anomaly among the poems of this period in that it stands as Whitman's lone effort to enclose the war's significance, in this case by way of a

Hegelian masterplot of interlocking, antagonistic forces fused by a synthesizing spirit. By the poet's own account, the intent of "Chanting the Square Deific" is to give "mathematical expression" to "the idea of spiritual equity," though his comparison of "the four sides sustaining the universe" to "the north, south, east, west of the constituted universe" brings to light its relevance as political allegory (*WWC* 1:156). Appropriately, the poem begins with the irrepealable legislation of the Fathers who, "dispens[ing] from this side judgments inexorable without the least remorse," authorize "mighty laws" and stand forth as "unpersuadable, relentless, executing righteous judgments" (*CRE*, p. 443). Unto the shoulders of two descendants, Christ and Satan, fall the burdens of these stern commandments, the one ("Consolator most mild . . . with gentle hand extended") incarnating the deathless charity of social affection, the other ("aloof, dissatisfied, plotting revolt") the unending strife of war and rebellion. Finishing the square and fusing together these opposite equals, mutually dependent in their rivalry, is "Santa Spirita, breather, life." In a seeming contradiction which could be confusing were it not so familiar elsewhere in *Leaves of Grass*, Whitman's figure of Union is imagined to be both incontrovertibly real ("Essence of forms . . . permanent, positive . . . I, the most solid") and impalpable ("Ethereal, pervading all . . . namely the unseen"). As it underwrites all values by "including all life on earth, touching, including God, including Savior and Satan," so it necessarily eludes evaluation. Beyond good and evil, "beyond the light . . . beyond the flames of hell . . . beyond Paradise," Santa Spirita claims no distinctive attribute of its own apart from its power to enclose and complete the "life of the great round world, the suns and stars, and of man" (*CRE*, p. 445). So it is that Whitman holds the discordant energies of Lawgiver, Wound-Dresser, and Secessionist in suspension, here gathered in the common ground of "the general soul."

"Chanting the Square Deific" is not quite so wooden as this paraphrase would make it sound. Nevertheless, there is an unmistakably formulaic slant to the poem's development, as though Whitman had only to set up his antithetical drives and then let the work of dialectic run its course. As a consequence, the appointed synthesis achieved in the fourth and final canto cannot but strike the reader as, in the words of one critic, "something of a foregone conclusion."[15] The element of predictability, moreover, is augmented by the first three cantos, all of which drive home the theme of a monomaniacal will inflexibly locked within its destined role, as is made clear in the final words of Jehovah ("I dispense from this side judgments inexorable without the least remorse"), Christ ("And my sweet love bequeath'd here and elsewhere never dies"), and Satan ("Nor time nor change shall ever change me or my words"). While putatively "beyond" these figures of compulsive repetition, it is important to note that despite its power of integration Santa Spirita does not sponsor a final reconciliation. In order to maintain its stance of flawless receptivity Whitman's "general soul" must on the contrary exhibit no motive whatever and is therefore described as a wholly intransitive entity, "perfumed solely with my own perfume." Ironically, though, the same immutable, unchanging inertia that grips each of the three sides of the square characterizes this last one as well: it remains an empty slot of inclusion whose rigid neutrality parallels the numbed blankness of the Dresser making his hospital rounds. Like that figure, its impassive will-lessness is suggestive of a debilitating entropy which must be continually offset by the violent shock of contraries. "Santa Spirita, breather, life," far from being impaired by such dissensions, is better described as feeding upon, drawing its energy from these conflicts, and it is in this context we can more fully understand the otherwise baffling placement of this chant amid a section called "Whispers of Heavenly Death."

Although the ostensible mission of "Chanting the Square Deific" is to contain the significance of the war by evoking it through the "passions and paradoxes" of "one and the same identity," it does not in fact place its primary emphasis on the internal divisions and antagonisms threatening the vision of "One Identity." Typically, Whitman's deepest fear does not involve the fragility of the Union but its monolithic impersonality—a decaying fiction which demands fresh sacrifices for its revival. Unlike the case of Melville, there is no State for the poet to endorse since that, as we have seen elsewhere in *Drum-Taps,* is already sensed to be a corpsed abstraction, "Insensate! Insensate!" As such, we begin to perceive the point at which political apprehension and personal trauma intersect: the compulsive energy of Jehovah, Christ, and Satan in Whitman's apocalyptic covenant, forever maintained at a constant pitch of intensity so as to prevent the "general soul" from lapsing away into senescence, provides a necessary counterpart to the mourner who, joined by the sisterhood of Death and Night incessantly washing ever and ever again the soiled world, discovers himself transfixed in one unending rite of absolution. Emending Stevens, we might in this respect say that Whitman matches the degeneration within by pairing it with the degeneration without.

Yet one wants to press these equations further, if only because their implications remain so oblique in a text like "Chanting the Square Deific." Some of its obscurities come into focus near the end of *Democratic Vistas* when its author looks ahead to "the future of these States" and anticipates the need for "poets immenser far [to] make [the] great poems of death" (*PW* 2:420). This would be "a class of bards who, consistent with the Hegelian formulas, and consistent with modern science," scorn "this universal ennui, this coward fear, this shuddering at death" by doing for their own age what Lucretius had sought to do for his. The latter-day literatus is to "absorb whatever science indicates, with spiritualism, and out of them, and out of his own genius . . . compose the great poem of death" (*PW* 2:421). Needless to say, this is the project undertaken by "Chanting the Square Deific," even to the point of honoring "the Hegelian formulas" as well as emulating the precepts of "modern science" in the exactitude of its "mathematical expression." Yet an attentive reading of these concluding paragraphs reveals another kind of death less susceptible to the blessings of "spiritualism." What this portends is not the carnage of the battlefield nor the maimed in the hospitals but an ongoing loss of vitality afflicting the body politic and momentarily glimpsed by Whitman as he catalogs the costs of democratic America in "the decay of faith, the long postponement, the fossil-like lethargy, the ceaseless need of revolutions." (*PW* 2:423). Taken out of context, these phrases seem merely to echo the Jeffersonian call for a periodic upheaval in political institutions, but it quickly becomes apparent that the meaning behind "the ceaseless need of revolutions" places Whitman closer to Henry Adams and his theorems concerning *vis inertiae* than to Thomas Jefferson. What troubles him here is not "the fear of irreconcilable interiors and lack of a common skeleton knitting all close" but the tendency of democratic institutions to *seek* their own demise with an almost instinctual purposiveness. "It is useless to deny it," writes Whitman. "Democracy grows rankly up the thickest, noxious, deadliest plants and fruits of all—brings worse and worse invaders—needs newer, larger, stronger, keener compensations and compellers" (*PW* 2:422). The absence of the expected preposition is startling: democracy does not grow *among* these poisoned materials but breeds them, at once the host and the parent of the disease.

Revealed here is a political variation of the second law of thermodynamics, where the state must be rescued from its own impulse toward degeneration, must in fact be saved through "keener compensations and compellers" from its own longing for a condition of nonbeing. Because "its first instincts are fain to clip, conform, bring in stragglers, and reduce everything to a dead level," democracy—"the leveler, the unyielding principle of the average"—chronically requires some counterforce (call it "spiritualism," "Hegelian formulas," or "modern science") to restrain "the deadly original relentlessness of all her first-class laws" (*PW* 2:726, 391). Evidently, the amount of energy invested in the republic by its members is disproportionate to the amount of energy the republic can in turn generate; and it is this discrepancy which renders comparisons of the state to an unwieldly "behemoth" or unbridled "leviathan" somewhat imprecise since this notion of instability is in reality actuated by the "fossil-like lethargy" and relentless entropy of democracy's "first class laws." The machinery of Union is not beset by the danger of destruction so much as bent on it: "Our lands, embracing so much, (embracing indeed the whole, rejecting none,) held in their breast that flame also, capable of consuming themselves, consuming us all" (*PW* 2:422).

When Whitman hesitantly conjectures "perhaps, indeed . . . [democracy] is of no account in itself" (*PW* 2:380), he is not acknowledging the worthlessness of this "abstraction" so much as confronting its essential blankness. It is his own phrase for what I have termed, in characterizing his Santa Spirita, an empty slot of inclusion. As a sheer vacancy tending deathward, democracy's primal urge to "reduce everything to a dead level" suggests an ironic and haunting consummation to the dream of consensus in the guise of a uniform sameness, the unanimity of the leveler death. To be sure, *Democratic Vistas* also embraces "the principle of individuality" as "the compensating balance-wheel of the successful working machinery of Aggregate America" (*PW* 2:392), but judging from the imagery in its later pages of a machine helplessly governed by its own economy of loss, this is to restate the problem rather than resolve it. "[L]ike a physician diagnosing some deep disease," Whitman elsewhere offers his own version of the dynamo and the virgin by calling upon "a strong and sweet Female Race, a race of perfect Mothers" to arrest the "appalling depletion" of the body politic (*PW* 2:369, 372). In the end, though, Whitman's last recourse against this entropic drive was to confront it directly by making "the great poems of death," poems whose power of regeneration would be capable of both honoring the reality of loss and somehow transfiguring it. Yet in turning back to this familiar double imperative we cannot at the same time fail to note the mutually exclusive nature of this demand in the wake of his war poems. Allen Grossman rightly reminds us that "Whitman's motive was to get death out of sociability, to devise "death's outlet song,"[16] but this he does not do in *Drum-Taps*. The readiness with which the Wound-Dresser is converted into death's worshiper argues the unnerving complicity between death and sociability to such a degree that it becomes a matter of vain conjecture to say how one may be extracted from the other. His outlook, so far from curing the encroaching debility of "aggregate America," tends to replicate it, striking physician no less than patient with the same enervating affliction.

The truest and most moving expression granted to "death's outlet song of life" is on the other hand to be found in the hymn in which this phrase originally appears, "When Lilacs Last in the Dooryard Bloom'd." Unquestionably the greatest of his "great poems of death," this elegy for Lincoln marks a special advance in understanding by formulating a distinction between "the thought of death" and "the knowledge of death" in the climactic recognition scene of section fourteen, for this is precisely the distinction beyond the reach of the Wound-Dresser, who steeps himself in each occurrence of death (its "thought") in anxious disregard for its generalized "knowledge." By personifying each of these ways of knowing as "my comrades" and by placing himself "in the middle as with companions, and as holding the hands of companions," Whitman aims to recover his archetypal role as mediator or what Grossman calls "the conjunctive term between . . . general and particular, many and one—the hand in hand of union mediated only by the consciousness of continuous vitality."[17] This is not to say that the difficulties of *Drum-Taps* have thereby been surmounted, since not least of the challenges facing the elegist is here again to coax this "continuous vitality" out of "the sure-enwinding arms of cool-enfolding death" without surrendering utterly to her embrace. As I have suggested, what most alarms Whitman in the aftermath of the war is not the continued presence of "intestine strife" within the Union but the "deadly original relentlessness" of a structure which, if allowed to thrive unchecked, merely pursues its own destruction. The orphic task of "Lilacs" is to invite in order to reconstitute the "Dark Mother" of oblivion through "the tallying song of my soul, / Victorious song, death's outlet song, yet ever-altering song" (*CRE,* pp. 336–37). Although some of its more formulaic borrowings from the genre of pastoral elegy distinguish this poem from his more improvised performances, it is worth stressing from the start that Whitman's "Burial Hymn" shares an essential continuity with the other major texts in that it too undertakes to supersede the flawed constitutionalism of Union by replacing it with the poem's more capacious tallyings, a restored covenant of brotherhood brought, as Hart Crane would say, "upward from the dead."

Politically, the stances of the elegist and his subject were all but indistinguishable. Lincoln's pledge to honor the constitutional safeguards the fathers had originally placed around slavery while vowing to oppose its extension with every constitutional method at hand essentially describes Whitman's position when hostilities first broke out. Despite their divergent backgrounds as Democrat and Whig, the conservatism of both men directed their belief, at least initially, that the vital question at stake was the legitimacy of the social compact. As memories of the battlefield eventually dulled with age, Whitman in fact embraced the view that by sealing its principles with his life the slain president personified "UNIONISM in its truest and amplest sense" (*PW* 1:98). Less a death than a martyrdom, the "tragic splendor" of his assassination proved the immortality of the republic; its "incalculable value" was such that it provided the affective mortar to solidarity, "a cement to the whole People, subtler, more underlying, than anything in the written Constitution, or courts or armies— namely, the cement of a first-class tragic incident thoroughly identified with that People, at its head, and for its sake."[18] Needless to say, nothing could more severely point up the decline into mental and creative lethargy overtaking Whitman's later years than such hackneyed sentiments, whose emphasis on ties more subtle and underlying than anything in written documents seems a weak and distant echo of ambitions embraced and articulated far more energetically at the outset of his career. All the same, his indulgence in hagiography is worth mentioning in order to illustrate the kind of text "Lilacs" will not become, for while it is a commonplace of all strong elegies to lament the mourner more than the mourned, what remains striking in Whitman's account is the virtual elision of its "departing comrade," who no sooner enters the poem than he is symbolized past all recognition. A good deal of this reticence is probably owing to the circumstances of Lincoln's death, which the poem is careful to avoid, yet it is also apparent that the chief task of the traditional elegy—the apotheosis of the beloved and the restoration of the natural order—are at best peripheral subjects in Whitman's vision. This is not to imply that the assassination had little impact on the poet's imagination, only that its true extent is best measured by close attention to the poem's intricate and often overdetermined formalism rather than anything it might reveal about "the sweetest, wisest soul of all my days."

Three is the favored number for synthesis, and it is not altogether surprising that as early as the fourth line mention should be made of a "trinity sure" said to comprise lilac, western star, and the "thought of him I love." As it unfolds the poem alters this trio slightly by placing lilac, fallen star, and the hermit thrush at the center of its complex design, though these figures alone hardly exhaust the range of what explicators are prone to call Whitman's "triune symbolism." Secondary versions of this structure abound with almost confusing proliferation: Lincoln's death is for example associated by turns with "the harsh surrounding cloud" portending emasculation and bondage, with a motherly enchantress (Venus, the "western orb sailing the heaven") promising cradled tranquillity, or with the procession of the coffin westward signifying public rites of mourning; emblems for poetic expression are likewise divided among the broken sprig of lilac, the thrush's "song of the bleeding throat," and the resurrected tally of the soul—a resurrection made possible by the previous triumvirate of the poet flanked between his two "companions" of death. Further permutations of this triplicate process, ranging from the interweaving of sensory images (sight, hearing, smell) to the twining of the poem's three major symbols in the final lines, have been mapped by various commentaries. Because his primary intent throughout the opening and middle sections of the poem is to devise a field of contraries which would sanction his appearance upon the scene as reconciler or spiritual intermediary, it becomes apparent that ascertaining the precise significance of these symbols is less vital to Whitman's purpose than positioning them. In fact, so undeviating is the poet's wish to secure this middle ground—to be the mediator between death and sociability—that the more conventional burdens of the elegy are largely bypassed: Whitman's grief, for example, does not erupt into flashes of cognitive despair, nor does it bitterly contemplate the worthlessness of artistic fame; there are no recriminations against "Time, a maniac scattering dust" nor against a "thankless Muse" powerless to save her offspring. In his treatment the crisis of death does not really occasion a crisis in meaning in the sense of radically calling into question the intelligibility of the moral and social order. Scarcely an obscene and capricious force that annihilates human values, death is recognized almost from the outset to be "sane and sacred"—a force the poet is not concerned to vanquish but translate and humanize through his own terms of exchange.

Because "Lilacs" does not develop by means of a sharply delineated narrative but through the accretion of hesitantly ventured analogies and juxtapositions, its opening stanzas provide more the scaffolding for the drama that ensues than a series of actions. Indeed, the poem does not begin so much as try out a series of provisional beginnings, with each of the first four sections depicting the "I" in various attitudes of bereavement as it moves from the ceremonial poise of "I mourn'd, and yet shall mourn with ever-returning spring" in the first sentence to the outburst of panic-stricken apostrophes that overwhelm the second stanza, the formal breaking of the lilac sprig, and then to the introduction of the hermit thrush warbling its "song of the bleeding throat." Each of these vignettes may be likened to freeze-frames or still lifes which fade into only to fade out of sight and which bear a self-enclosed, discrete quality whose abrupt transitions indicate the absence of any trace carried over from one moment to the next. Evidently, there is no perspective for consciousness to inhabit which would allow it to survive the blank spaces between each of these stanzas, and in this respect the severe shifts in mood from composed recollection to outright hysteria or from wistful melancholy to laconic observation further the sense that these utterances are issuing from a splintered, centerless point of view, in one moment helplessly trapped "the black murk that hides the star" while in the next impassively witnessing the solitary thrush. Shifting abruptly as well between past and present tense as it will through much of the poem, the tenuous narrative voice seemingly distributed among these divergent attitudes makes us feel that the symbols here disclosed are anything but "elements in the undifferentiated stream of thoughts and things [which incarnate] the real process of becoming." Though critics habitually extrapolate a variety of submerged resemblances and veiled foreshadowings in these still lifes, such connections should not obscure recognition of the essentially static nature of Whitman's presentation. At this early stage and through the first half of the poem what predominates is not an "undifferentiated stream of thoughts and things"[19] but a rigid tableau of figures which not only preclude integration but refuse any sense of development or metamorphosis. The hermit thrush continues to warble its dirge, the coffin wends slowly westward, the sprig of lilac is offered—all the while the poet flits from scene to scene, juggling each segment of the story against the other. Nowhere else in *Leaves of Grass* do we encounter a text whose components are initially so stylized and so recalcitrant, as if these fixtures of mourning, left suspended in proximate but undefined relation to one another, were not the products of a creative will but so many inert forms (coffin, lilac, bird) challenging that will to stir them into sentience. "O how shall I warble myself for the dead one there I loved? And how shall I deck my song for the large sweet soul that has gone? And what shall my perfume be for the grave of him I love?": the questions point up, in their labored formality, a ponderous rhetoric insusceptible to organicism's "curious removes and indirections."

To a certain degree, the disjunctive manner of "Lilacs" may be regarded as a display of calculated propriety on Whitman's part, since in accordance with the rites of mourning he breaks his sprig of lilac, thereby breaking as well his own figure of the tally, the proper rhetoric of inclusion. Conceivably, too, the state of fragmentation recorded in the first half forms a prelude to the triumphant fusion to be achieved in the final section, where the "tally of my soul" is recuperated through "retrievements out of the night." But merely to stand fragmentation against fusion as negative to positive value is a facile exercise, particularly since the lyrics of *Drum-Taps* demonstrate how readily the ideal of fusion reaches its own *reductio ad absurdum* in the loving clasp of death. This too, no less than the disconnection we have already noted, poses a threat for the poem's protagonist which is all the more pressing given his determination to spiritualize death itself rather than simply apotheosize a fallen leader. For the explicit recipient of his song, as he explains in the seventh stanza, is not "for one alone" but "for you O sane and sacred death . . . with loaded arms I come, pouring for you, / For you and the coffins of all of you O death." No sooner does he issue this vow, however, than he confronts the first genuine moment of crisis in the poem as "the black murk" concealing the "powerful western star" momentarily lifts:

> O western orb sailing the heaven,
> Now I know what you must have meant as a month since I
>   walk'd,

As I walk'd in silence the transparent shadowy night,
As I saw you had something to tell as you bent to me
            night after night,
As you droop'd from the sky low down as if to my side,
            (while the other stars all look'd on,)
As we wander'd together the solemn night, (for
            something I know not what kept me from sleep,)
As the night advanced, and I saw on the rim of the
            west how full you were of woe,
As I stood on the rising ground in the breeze in the
            cool transparent night,
As I watch'd where you pass'd and was lost in the
            netherward black of the night,
As my soul in its trouble dissatisfied sank, as where
            you sad orb,
Concluded, dropt in the night, and was gone.

                                                                (*CRE,* p. 331)

As he reverts to the past tense, Whitman steals back to the shores of
Paumanok, where the heavens similarly descend to baptize the outsetting bard of love. ("Now I know what you must have meant" likewise
recalls the "now in a moment I know what I am for" of released
perception in "Out of the Cradle.") In the *clair-obscur* of the "transparent shadowy night" we glimpse a mild case of ecstasy in which the
lover, trembling on the verge of epiphany, appears about to step
outside himself while standing "on the rising ground in the breeze"
prepared to receive the whisperings of the now "departed comrade,"
here transfigured into the conventional role of Phosphor/Venus. Yet
the transparency of soul to soul, Whitman's hallmark for a redeemed
colloquy ("what I assume, you shall assume") heralds the wrong kind
of merging. The advances of the "western orb," rich with intimations
of a luxuriant mortality, are as yet too starkly pleasurable to be counte-
nanced, one reason why Whitman selects the notable term
"dissatisfied" to characterize the "soul in its trouble," a term which
connotes a response closer to perplexity than woe. Intimacy serves to
preclude and not promote the securing of a middle ground so that,
from a larger perspective, we find the poet stranded between two
extremes, either lost amid a mosaic of disconnected images which
fends off synthesis or enticed into an erotic communion with the dead
which threatens to consummate this synthesis prematurely. Media-

tion itself still has no stable role to perform in the poem: if elsewhere it is overdeveloped, as is evident in the phalanx of conventional symbols and motifs, here it may be too tenuous, receding suddenly with the allure of "the lustrous star" whose "silver face" peers through the night.

Thus, by the time he reaches the ninth section of the poem, all its author can know is that "the black murk" and "harsh surrounding cloud that will not free my soul" continue to hold and detain him. Ostensibly, both images specify the paralysis of grief (they also anticipate "the cloud . . . the long black trail" of death soon to cover the land); less immediately, they identify as well the perceptual bondage that has gripped Whitman from the middle of *Drum-Taps* onward. This is the condition concisely described six sections later as "the sight that was bound in my eyes unclosed," the stupefied gaze transfixed by the "netherward black" of hospital and battlefield. The need to counter that bondage is especially urgent given the poet's recognition that in order to restore visionary independence he must pass through the "hiding receiving night" where his own song is to tally and be tallied against the thrush's "carol of death." Already in section nine this "singer bashful and tender" is beckoning ("I hear your notes, I hear your call . . . I understand you"), but the listener begs off these advances too by turning instead in sections ten through twelve, to "the large unconscious scenery of my land," as if in one final attempt to enlarge the frame of reference before he is lured into the dusk of "cedars and ghostly pines so still." A landscape magically washed clean of the strayed and straying corpses of the war, these vistas include "floods of the yellow gold of the gorgeous, indolent sun . . . in the distance the flowing glaze, the breast of the river, / And the city at hand with dwellings so dense, and stacks of chimneys . . ." (*CRE,* p. 332). With these tokens of a carefree eroticism unafraid of retribution, implicitly drawn against the earlier images of emasculation and impotence, Whitman travels back to the persona of the child who goes forth and its finely etched idyllicism. Placing before him "all the scenes of life and the workshops, and the workmen homeward returning," he travels back also to antebellum America, its "varied and ample land, the South and the North in the light, Ohio's shores and flashing Missouri, / And ever the far-spreading prairies cover'd with grass and corn" (*CRE,* p. 333). Such nostalgic pastoralism is plainly inadequate to the larger task at hand, though it does possess the immediate advantage of steering the poem away from the more wooden, point-

edly stilted manner that has predominated to this point. The negligent
ease of the writing further unveils a world of assured temporal continuity where sunsets give way to "the gentle soft-born measureless
light" of dawn with its "just-felt breezes," which in turn yields to "the
fulfill'd noon" as it again welcomes "the coming eve delicious . . . enveloping man and land." As Lincoln begins to recede still
further from view, not to be mentioned again until the very end of the
text, the effect of Whitman's scene painting is not merely to "interpose
a little ease" but to win back some semblance of his own native
idiom—an idiom of panoramic vivacity and vividness which has been
not only missing from this poem until now but which has in fact been
missing from *Leaves of Grass* for nearly a decade.

From this expansive prospect we are suddenly brought back to the
"gray-brown bird" singing from the recesses of the swamp. The apparent contrast between wide and varied lands and hidden recesses
carries forward the polarity of private and public whose outline has
been evident in the numerous juxtapositions concerning mourning as
a ritual observance (the breaking of the lilac, the procession of the
coffin) and mourning as a personal, incommunicable ordeal (the mystic, solitary approach of the western star, the "shy and bashful"
thrush avoiding the settlements). Little in the poem so far has indi-
cated the likelihood of these spheres being brought together, though
in view of Whitman's desire not only to accommodate a personal loss
but to translate the meaning of loss itself for the community through
"death's outlet song of life," such an integration is crucial to his
design. As if it were repeating the tragedy all over again in still another
attempt to situate and define the relation of the many and the one,
section fourteen attempts just such an integration, only now in a
language of stately simplicity which identifies it as one of the most
powerful and authentic passages in *Leaves of Grass,* if not in American
poetry:

> Now while I sat in the day and look'd forth,
> In the close of the day with its light and the fields
>   of spring, and the farmers preparing their crops,
> In the large unconscious scenery of my land with its
>   lakes and forests,
> In the heavenly aerial beauty, (after the perturb'd
>   winds and the storms,)

Under the arching heavens of the afternoon swift
        passing, and the voices of children and women,
The many-moving sea-tides, and I saw the ships how
        they sail'd,
And the summer approaching with richness, and the
        fields all busy with labor,
And the infinite separate houses, how they all went
        on, each with its meals and minutia of daily usages,
And the streets with their throbbings throbb'd, and
        the cities pent—lo, then and there,
Falling upon them all and among them all, enveloping
        me with the rest,
Appear'd the cloud, appear'd the long black trail,
And I knew death, its thought, and the sacred
        knowledge of death.

                               (*CRE*, pp. 333–34)

In a subtle reversal of the usual platitude which holds that the trauma of loss is best assuaged by a return to the commonplaces and banalities of everyday life, Whitman pursues a different emphasis: for him the mundane routine or "minutia of daily usages" in each of those "infinite separate houses" does not dull the reality of death but furnishes a necessary context for its emergence. More than a pleasant backdrop, the placid, unlabored continuity emphasized in these vistas is vital to Whitman's design, for his essential motive is to bring death into the community without shattering the ties of that community. Thus the metaphor of the "long black trail," while it irresistibly calls up associations with a plague infecting the land, suggests at the same time a natural and perhaps even familiar phenomenon, one whose violence is considerably softened even as its more ominous shadings are respected. The role of the poet, only now beginning to take shape, here resembles that of a liminal spirit or shaman who presides over and guards the communal passage from life to death, peace to war. Explicit consideration of the significance of Lincoln's sacrifice continues, in the meantime, to be elided; the speaker exhibits no interest whatever in exploring this dimension, and still less is he moved to contemplate those principles of "UNIONISM" which that sacrifice was thought to have dignified. In fact, in this rewriting of Lincoln's demise Whitman discovers two new companions ("the sacred knowledge of death" and its "thought") who, in replacing the departed comrade, soon escort the poet in his descent down to "deep secluded recesses" of "lovely and soothing death."

With the appearance of these two companions Whitman returns to the central dilemma of the war as his verse conceives it. For that dilemma turns, as we have seen, on a deeply sensed and possibly irreconcilable incompatibility that divides "thought" from "knowledge," that divorces experience from understanding. To invoke a higher cause as justification for all those slain in battle was, as Whitman came to perceive during the fighting, to blaspheme rather than honor their memory; yet to privilege mute acknowledgment over any appeal to a rational order (whatever its source) is at the same time to invite the charge of bad faith inasmuch as this preference becomes difficult to distinguish from mere quietism—a policy of paralyzed forbearance. The result is an awed capitulation to death's mastery rather than an effort to retrieve its meaningfulness for the social world. Characteristically, Whitman here approaches this impasse between thought and knowledge—experience and understanding, acknowledgment and rationality—by personifying each of these contrary principles and, in so doing, imagines himself to be the expressive link ("And I in the middle as with companions") between them. Only then is he prepared to receive the "loud human song" of his solitary singer and its "voice of uttermost woe"—the voice he was not prepared to hear earlier when, unaccompanied, he had awaited the confidence of the western star. Whitman's crisis in understanding is not thereby resolved, though it is worth noting that by bracketing off his "Death Carol" in italics and by assigning it to another voice, he effectively insinuates a distance between himself and what amounts to another enraptured capitulation to the charms of motherly death. In itself, the song of the hermit thrush is largely unremarkable, being for the most part a reworking of material handled with more dramatic urgency in the *Sea-Drift* cycle. Its unsparing grandiloquence and stale archaisms further imply the poet's remoteness, one that is only proper given his self-declared intent to tally the mystic appeal of this "strong deliveress" rather than be "lost in the loving floating ocean" of her caresses.

The true emotional center of "Lilacs" is in any case not to be found in this "wondrous chant" but in the "long panoramas of vision" emancipated in its wake. As in "the hiding receiving night that talks not" of the previous scene, section fifteen presents the poet once again as a silent, haunted beholder, but in this case he not only tallies the "pure deliberate notes" of the thrush but supplies the indispensable and long-awaited framework for comprehending their significance:

> And I saw askant the armies,
> I saw as in noiseless dreams hundreds of battle-flags,
> Borne through the smoke of the battles and pierc'd
>   with missiles I saw them,
> And carried hither and yon through the smoke, and torn
>   and bloody,
> And at last but a few shreds left on the staffs, (and
>   all in silence,)
> And the staffs all splinter'd and broken.
>
> I saw battle-corpses, myriads of them,
> And the white skeletons of young men, I saw them,
> I saw the debris and debris of all the slain soldiers
>   of the war,
> But I saw they were not as was thought,
> They themselves were fully at rest, they suffer'd not,
> The living remain'd and suffer'd, the mother suffer'd,
> And the wife and the child and the musing comrade
>   suffer'd,
> And the armies that remain'd suffer'd.

(*CRE*, p. 336)

To mark the difference between the first six uses of the verb "saw" and its seventh and last appearance is to glimpse the tentative beginnings of a new style of commemoration. For as haunted witnessing reluctantly gives way to inward perception, the implication that emerges is that strict fidelity to the memory of the dead and acceptance of those fictions of consolation necessary to lay them at rest may not, after all, be mutually exclusive. It is indeed only when the elegist is able to supplement mere sight with insight—to negotiate some bridge between the slain and those surviving—that he can claim his proper status as one who guards the boundary between the living and the dead without neglecting or subordinating either sphere. What ideally results is neither triumphant affirmation nor continued despair but a song which joins together both elements and, in doing so, moderates their extremity. This is to be received as a

> Victorious song, death's outlet song, yet varying,
>   ever-altering song,
> As low and wailing, yet clear the notes, rising and
>   falling, flooding the night,
> Sadly sinking and fainting, as warning and warning,
>   and yet again bursting with joy,
> Covering the earth and filling the spread of heaven . . .
>   (*CRE*, p. 337)

The resurrected tally brought up from the dead makes explicit the poet's determination to honor both sides of his reality. Along with victory and jubilation, "death's outlet song" intertwines a vivid memory of the departed in the hopes of showing both strands to be interdependent. In these terms the thought of death and the knowledge of death do at last converge; the "varying ever-altering song" effectively spiritualizes loss (the essential requirement for its entrance into the social world) but not at the expense of overlooking its original occasion, its "thought." The outcome represents the better discourse of the better President, for while the democratic state such as we found diagnosed in *Democratic Vistas* required death to shore up and substantiate contested beliefs and myths unable to sustain their power of persuasion, the poet translates death into the community without subsuming the former under a higher term. In effect, his own rite of "spiritualism"—his conversion of loss into socially redeemable capital—is expressly designed to repudiate any such jargon of substantiation since the victorious joy of reunion with the community is itself predicated on and critically bound up with the continued acknowledgment of grief.

The extraordinary care shown by Whitman in defining the true function of "death's outlet song" bears eloquent witness to the real center of interest in his elegy, which has less to do with accommodating death (and still less a death) than devising a medium proper to the task of reintegrating death back into life. The result is a conjunction of nuanced judgment and unabashed compassion which invests "Lilacs" with all the tragic dignity readers have rightly appreciated almost from the time of its first appearance. But at the same time we can scarcely ignore the more disquieting features of that dignity, for in certain key respects the silence of "Lilacs" is devastating. As in the case of *Drum-Taps*, it bears repeating that Whitman's elegy discerns absolutely no purpose served in the killing of those young men who continue to haunt the mind's eye "as in noiseless dreams"; it uncovers no truth vindicated by their "white skeletons," no cause defended. Still more striking than the mere content of this implied verdict is, however, the silence which accompanies it, a silence which appears to indicate that even if the elegist can or will not speak on behalf of the Union purportedly upheld by the death of Lincoln and his soldiers, neither can he bring himself to speak against it. An inescapable consequence of his "delicacy," to recall James Wright's term, continues to issue in neither advocacy nor condemnation but a standoff between both responses which is the legacy of his involvement in the war and, beyond that, a legacy of his own conservative radicalism, here succinctly crystallized in the double imperative of *both* honoring the dead without recourse to the accepted meanings of the community *and* somehow redeeming the meaningfulness of death for that community. Stirring as the "altering, ever-varying song" which seeks to reconcile these imperatives is, its final effect only deepens the impression, in its meticulous balancing of death against sociability, that Whitman's stance most closely resembles the gods mentioned in Melville's "The Conflict of Convictions" who will utter neither "yea or nay" but stand irresolutely on their middle ground, loath to break away from the values of a community but equally reluctant to uphold them.

Judging from the scattered comments and reflections of his later years, the polarity between the thought and the knowledge of death continued to beg off resolution, growing instead ever more intransigent. The war did not deliver a death blow to Whitman's mystic Unionism, as that idealism was already severely tempered by fears and reservations evident well before its outbreak, fears and reservations which concerned not simply the fate of the Union but the rationality of the policies guiding it. What the war did do was to heighten the divide between acknowledgment and meaning to particularly distended extremes, thereby draining it of any dramatic tension. The writer whose meliorism encouraged him to believe that the nation's successful passage through disunion and bloodshed provided "by far the most signal proof yet of the stability of that experiment, Democracy, and of [its] principles, and of [its] Constitution" (*PW* 2:431) was the same who nursed as in noiseless dreams memories of the million dead strewn throughout the landscape and distilled through the air. Half realizing that his best work was behind him, Whitman loaned out the better part of his remaining years in garrulous reminiscence and endless revisions of and adjustments to *Leaves of Grass*, his *"carte de visite* to posterity." The reminiscences are mostly forgotten and forgettable; the verse and the literary "experiment" it was conceived to advance continue to reach out to us with undiminished vitality.

Notes

Introduction

1. R. W. B. Lewis, "Always Going In and Coming Out," in *Walt Whitman*, ed. Harold Bloom (New York: Chelsea, 1986), p. 125. A harsher extension of Lewis's distinction appears in Edwin Miller's contention that "as a commentator on the dream of democracy Whitman sound more like a Fourth of July orator than a perceptive critic or poet: he was a poor historian and a naive prophet of the future" (*Walt Whitman's Poetry: A Psychological Journey* [Boston: Riverside Press, 1968], p. 27). Harold Bloom appears to have spoken for many readers during the sixties in commenting that "the Whitman who will not cease affirming until we wish never to hear anything affirmed again—[this poet] is done with, and in good time" (quoted in "The Central Man: Emerson, Whitman, Wallace Stevens" [originally published in 1966], *The Ringers in the Tower: Studies in the Romantic Tradition* [Chicago: University of Chicago Press, 1971], p. 226). Santayana's dissenting opinion on Whitman and his "Poetry of Barbarism" has been widely reprinted. Also notable are his remarks on the poet in "Genteel Tradition in American Philosophy."

2. "Observations on Walt Whitman," in *A Century of Whitman Criticism*, ed. Miller (Bloomington: Indiana University Press, 1968), p. 163. Brief though it is, Eliot's review is one of the first to comment on Whitman's essential conservatism: "Tennyson liked monarchs, Whitman liked presidents. Both were conservative, rather than reactionary or revolutionary; that is to say, they believed explicitly in progress, and believed implicitly that progress consists in things remaining essentially as they are." These remarks, appearing in 1926, come around the same time as Eliot's conversion to the Anglican church.

3. Among those I have found most helpful are Donald Pease, "Blake, Crane, Whitman, and Modernism: A Poetics of Pure Possibility," *PMLA* 96 (1981): 64–85; Mitchell Breitwieser, "Who Speaks in Whitman's Poems?" in *The American Renaissance: New Dimensions*, ed. Harry R. Garvin (Lewis-

burg, Pa: Associated University Press, 1983), pp. 121–43; Lewis Hyde, *The Gift: Imagination and the Erotic Life of Property* (New York: Random House, 1983), pp. 160–215; Allen Grossman, "The Poetics of Union in Lincoln and Whitman: An Inquiry Toward the Relationship of Art and Policy," *The American Renaissance Reconsidered,* ed. Pease and Walter Benn Michaels (Baltimore: Johns Hopkins University Press, 1985), pp. 183–208.

4. "Blake, Crane, Whitman, and Modernism," p. 76.

5. See Gay Wilson Allen, *The Solitary Singer: A Critical Biography* (1955; reprint, New York: New York University Press, 1967), p. 131. Whitman originally happened upon Keats's famous definition in the *North British Review.*

6. William Wordsworth, *The Prelude,* bk. 1, lines 341–44.

7. "The Poetics of Union in Lincoln and Whitman," p. 194. Grossman's essay deserves special mention, not only for its provocative reflections on the "poetics of Union" in *Leaves of Grass* but because many of the issues it explores parallel those taken up at length in the present study. Although I came across his inquiry when my own was well under way, it has been instrumental in helping me to clarify my own thoughts as well as to sharpen my sense of the complexity of the concerns addressed by Whitman. My treatment diverges from Grossman's primarily on the fate of Whitman's "policy," for where he sees the pathos of Whitman's song to be such that its ethic of "free sense" effectively places it outside any "natural standpoint" or "social institution" which could receive it, my own sense—as will be developed in the introduction as well as throughout the ensuing chapters—is that this pathos more particularly inheres not in his alienation from accepted institutions but in his standing neither altogether in nor outside this sphere.

8. *The Solitary Singer,* p. 199. Daniel Aaron's assessment of this document is still more severe: he calls it "a preposterous solution for his country's redemption" (*The Unwritten War: American Writers and the Civil War* [New York: Oxford University Press, 1973], p. 57). So far as I can tell, no one has taken note of this essay's pointedly cautious, conservative stand.

9. George Fredrickson, *The Inner Civil War: Northern Intellectuals and the Crisis of the Union* (New York: Harper and Row, 1965), pp. 7–8. For a recent development of Fredrickson's position see M. Wynn Thomas, "Whitman and the American Democratic Identity Before and During the Civil War," *Journal of American Studies* 15 (1981): 73–93.

10. *The Inner Civil War,* p. 21.

11. *The Selected Essays of William Carlos Williams* (New York: New Directions, 1969), p. 180.

12. In other words, the problem with the Fugitive Slave Law is that it is superfluous, not unconstitutional. Whitman's reasoning, contorted as it may be, is a far cry from Emerson's embittered response to the passage of this law. For reasons I explore in the second chapter of this study, Whitman was much more likely to be swayed by what Jefferson called "the magic supposed to be in

the word *constitution*" than was Emerson. For Jefferson's phrase see *Notes on the State of Virginia*, ed. William Peden (Chapel Hill: University of North Carolina, 1955), p. 124.

13. Newton Arvin, *Whitman* (New York: Macmillan, 1938), p. 30–31. Arvin's point comes primarily in reference to Whitman's politics, particularly on the subject of slavery.

14. *Lucifer in Harness: American Meter, Metaphor, and Diction* (Princeton, N.J.: Princeton University Press, 1973), p. 52.

15. The phrase appears in a letter from the poet on 7 January 1860 to *Harper's* magazine, where Whitman was hoping to place one of his poems. The full context is worth restoring:

> The theory of "A Chant of National Feuillage" is to bring in, (devoting a line, or two or three lines, to each,) a comprehensive collection of touches, locales, incidents, idiomatic scenes, from every section, South, West, North, East, Kanada, Texas, Maine, Virginia, the Mississippi Valley, &c.&c.&c.—all intensely fused to the urgency of compact America, "America always"—all in a vein of graphic, short, clear, hasting along—as having a huge bouquet to collect, and quickly taking and binding in every characteristic subject that offers itself—making a compact, the-whole-surrounding, *National Poem*, after its sort, after my own style.
>
> Is there any other poem of the sort extant—or indeed hitherto attempted? (*Corr* 1:46)

16. *The Pursuit of Signs: Semiotics, Literature, Deconstruction* (Ithaca, N.Y.: Cornell University Press, 1981), p. 135.

17. Malcolm Cowley launched the campaign for a return to the early Whitman with his republication of the inaugural volume (*The 1855 Edition of Leaves of Grass* [New York: Viking, 1959]). He makes a case for the superiority of the first edition in his introduction, pp. xxxii–xxxvii. Quentin Anderson has argued for the merits of the second edition (originally issued in 1856) in *The Imperial Self* (New York: Knopf, 1971), pp. 125–65; Roy Harvey Pearce has done the same for the third edition (originally issued in 1860) in "Whitman Justified: The Poet in 1860," *Minnesota Review* 1 (1961); 261–94. See also his introduction to *Leaves of Grass by Walt Whitman: Facsimile Edition of the 1860 Text* (Ithaca, N.Y.: Cornell University Press, 1961).

Part One

1. *Autobiography and Literary Essays,* ed. John M. Robson and Jack Stillinger (Toronto: University of Toronto Press, 1981), pp. 348–49.

2. See *Anatomy of Criticism: Four Essays* (Princeton, N.J.: Princeton Uni-

versity Press, 1957), p. 33 and T. S. Eliot, *On Poetry And Poets* (New York: Harbinger, 1952), p. 96.

3. *A Rhetoric of Motives* (1950; reprint, Berkeley: University of California Press, 1969), pp. 221–45.

4. *The 1855 Edition of "Leaves of Grass,"* ed. Malcolm Cowley (New York: Viking Press, 1959), p. 44.

5. *Rivers and Mountains* (New York: Holt Rinehart, 1966), p. 26. Ashbery's poem is entitled "A Blessing in Disguise."

Chapter One

1. In "Dante's Address to the Reader," *Romance Philology* 7 (1953–54): 268–78, Erich Auerbach remarks that "classical apostrophe . . . is not identical with the address to the reader; this address constitutes a special and individual development" (271). The distinction rests on the fact that while imperatives abound in address, they remain comparatively inessential for written apostrophe. Whether this implies a greater degree of access or control is questionable; Whitman's "you, whoever you are" may be no less of a mystery than Yeats's "Presences." Auerbach notes that the ancient rhetoricians "never described or listed the address as a special figure of speech," and I shall follow the common practice of viewing address as a subgenre of apostrophic discourse.

2. On this decline see C. Carroll Hollis, *Language and Style in "Leaves of Grass"* (Baton Rouge: Louisiana State University Press, 1983), pp. 88–124.

3. *The Prose Works of William Wordsworth,* ed. W. J. B. Owen and J. W. Smyser, 2 vols. (Oxford: Oxford University Press, 1974), 1:120.

4. Arthur Golden uses these terms in his introduction to *Walt Whitman's Blue Book* (New York: New York Public Library, 1968), though such designations are in fact widespread in Whitman criticism. See, for example, Howard J. Waskow, *Whitman: Explanations in Form* (Chicago: University of Chicago Press, 1966), pp. 49–69.

5. *Literary Friends and Acquaintances* (Bloomington: Indiana University Press, 1968), p. 68.

6. *Connoisseurs of Chaos* (1965; reprint, New York: Columbia University Press, 1983), p. 12.

7. *A Grammar of Motives* (1945; reprint, Berkeley: University of California Press, 1966), p. 352.

8. *Selected Critical Writings of George Santayana,* ed. Norman Henfrey, 2 vols. (Cambridge: Cambridge University Press, 1968), 2:98.

9. *Poetry and the Age* (New York: Alfred A. Knopf, 1953), pp. 102, 107, 108. I am aware that Jarrell's rhetoric of appreciation was in fact a common practice for him, one reason why Robert Lowell termed his criticism "eulogistic." What interests me here, however, is less a critique of Jarrell's

position than the reasons it has proven so amenable to the study of Whitman. For more recent variations on the same theme, see, for example, *Walt Whitman: The Making of the Poet* (New York: Basic Books, 1983) by Paul Zweig, who notes that "most of Whitman's writing has effectively resisted the critical intelligence lavished on other poets of Whitman's stature. . . . It seems to suggest nothing could or should be said about it" (p. 168).

10. *Poetry and the Age,* p. 119.

11. I borrow the term from Burke's discussion of the grammar of constitutionality in *A Grammar of Motives,* pp. 323–91.

12. See John Lynen, *The Design of the Present: Essays on Time and Structure in American Literature* (New Haven, Conn.: Yale University Press, 1969), p. 191.

13. *The Mirror and the Lamp* (New York: Oxford University Press, 1954), p. 25. Abrams also goes on to remark that "the audience had no modal existence in Romantic poetry."

14. "The Poetics of Union in Whitman and Lincoln: An Inquiry toward the Relationship of Art and Poetry," in *The American Renaissance Reconsidered,* ed. Walter Benn Michaels and Donald Pease (Baltimore: Johns Hopkins University Press, 1985), p. 205.

15. *Thomas Paine: Selected Writings,* ed. Harry Hayden Clark (New York: Hill and Wang, 1961), p. 197. Similar sentiments abound in Whitman, in prose as well as poetry. "The theory of the American Confederation," he observes in one his notes on antislavery, "as outlined in the Declaration of Independence and embodied in the Constitution; and the harmonious workings of the several states, is the most perfect theory in the world, because it is the best in the world in practice. —He fails utterly of understanding its key, however, who supposes we have delegated to any portion of the government, either federal, state, or municipal or the courts any of the most important of our rights. —We have given to these just so much power" (*WWW,* p. 81).

16. *Thomas Paine,* p. 203.

17. Ibid., p. 83. For a suggestive meditation on these and other quandaries with respect to constitution-making, see Hannah Arendt, *On Revolution* (New York: Viking Press, 1963), pp. 139–78.

18. See Erich Auerbach, *Scenes from the Drama of European Realism,* trans. Ralph Manheim (Gloucester, Mass.: Peter Smith, 1973), p. 26.

19. See *The Imperial Self* (New York: Knopf, 1971), pp. 125–65.

20. Before venturing an analysis of this poem, I should note that many of its tensions may no doubt be ascribed to the poet's wary and often explosive relation to his own homosexuality, this text being, after all, included in a sequence devoted to the theme of "adhesiveness." Yet so far as the treatment of the reader in this instance remains consonant with other texts, it remains illustrative of the kind of quandaries I am attempting to isolate here.

21. Thoreau's letter has been reprinted in *A Century of Whitman Criticism,* ed. Edwin H. Miller (Bloomington: Indiana University Press, 1968), p. 14.

22. *Hart Crane and Yvor Winters; Their Literary Correspondence,* ed. Thomas Parkinson (Berkeley: University of California Press, 1978), p. 70.

23. "Who Speaks in Whitman's Poems?" in *The American Renaissance: New Dimensions,* ed. Harry R. Garvin (Lewisburg, Pa.: Associated University Press, 1983), p. 131.

24. *Self-Portrait in a Convex Mirror* (Harmondsworth: Penguin Books, 1975), p. 82.

25. *The Political Unconscious: Narrative as a Socially Symbolic Act* (Ithaca, N.Y.: Cornell University Press, 1981), p. 106–7.

26. Ibid., p. 106.

27. See William Finkel, "Walt Whitman's Manuscript Notes on Oratory," *American Literature* 22 (1950): 27–53. For further discussion of Whitman's journal entry, see Hollis, *Language and Style in "Leaves of Grass,"* p. 147.

28. *Illuminations,* ed. Arendt, trans. Harry Zohn (New York: Schocken Books, 1969), pp. 180, 179.

29. *Biographia Literaria,* ed. J. Shawcross, 2 vols. (Oxford: Clarendon Press, 1907), 2:65–66.

30. James's review has been reprinted in *A Century of Whitman Criticism,* pp. 7–11.

31. "The Novels of George Eliot," *Atlantic Monthly* (1866); quoted in Wayne Booth, *The Rhetoric of Fiction* (Chicago: University of Chicago Press, 1961), p. 49.

32. John Ashbery, "Fragment," *The Double Dream of Spring* (New York: Ecco Press, 1976), p. 79.

Chapter Two

1. See, for example, Hyatt Waggoner, *American Poets and Poetry* (New York: Harcourt, 1968), p. 151–54 for a useful summary of Whitman's extensive borrowings. When addressing the significance of Emerson's influence, most commentators dwell upon Whitman's later recantations of his mentor, as in Roger Asselineau's *The Evolution of Walt Whitman: The Creation of A Personality* (Cambridge, Mass.: Belknap Press, 1960), pp. 52–62 or Justin Kaplan's *Walt Whitman: A Life* (New York: Simon and Schuster, 1980), pp. 209–12. In *Emerson, Whitman, and the American Muse* (Chapel Hill: University of North Carolina Press, 1982), Jerome Loving situates both figures against the backdrop of their historical circumstances.

2. Sacvan Bercovitch, *The American Jeremiad* (Madison: University of Wisconsin Press, 1978), p. 23.

3. *Walden and Civil Disobedience,* ed. Owen Thomas (New York: Norton, 1966), p. 70.

4. *Longinus on Sublimity,* trans. D. A. Russell (Oxford: Clarendon Press, 1969), p. 7.

5. *The Senses of Walden: An Expanded Edition* (San Francisco: North Point Press, 1980), p. 160.

6. *The Correspondence of Thomas Carlyle and Ralph Waldo Emerson,* 2 vols. (Cambridge, Mass.: Riverside Press, 1884), 2:218–19.

7. *The Palm At The End Of The Mind,* ed. Holly Stevens (New York: Vintage Books, 1972), p. 257. In tracing out a similar dynamic of sacrifice and retribution, Julie Ellison speaks perceptively of Emerson's attraction to strategies tending to augment "the critic's power over the text he interprets and the scholar's power to shape myth and history retroactively" (*Emerson's Romantic Style* [Princeton, N.J.: Princeton University Press, 1984], p. 5).

8. *Journals and Miscellaneous Notebooks of Ralph Waldo Emerson,* ed. William Gilman and Alfred Ferguson, 16 vols. (Cambridge, Mass.: Belknap Press, 1960–), 9:331, 350.

9. See *Studies in Classic American Literature* (New York: Viking Press, 1969), pp. 163–77.

10. These phrases are drawn from a characteristic account of the Jeremiad form offered in Sacvan Bercovitch's *The American Jeremiad* p. 136.

11. See ibid., chaps. 2 and 5.

12. *The Gift: Imagination and the Erotic Life of Property* (New York: Vintage Books, 1983), p. 179.

13. Ibid., p. 197.

14. *Pragmatism* (Cambridge, Mass.: Belknap Press, 1975), p. 131.

15. R. W. B. Lewis, *Trials of the Word* (New Haven, Conn.: Yale University Press, 1965), p. 11. In his path-breaking account of *The Continuity of American Poetry* (Princeton, N.J.: Princeton University Press, 1961), Roy Harvey Pearce also remarks that because Whitman's world "contains the poet's readers as well as the poet, his is an insight which, if his readers are bold enough, will move them to transform themselves as he has transformed himself. . . . Yielding to the poem, in short, they will release in themselves the creative energies which will make them nothing less than heroic" (p. 71). I do not wish to overthrow or deny such a view but suggest that Pearce's notion of "containment" has a double-edged use.

16. See *Visions of Excess: Selected Writings, 1927–1939,* ed. Allan Stoekl (Minneapolis: University of Minnesota Press, 1985), p. 121. Valuable discussion of the *potlatch* may also be found in Marcel Mauss, *The Gift: Forms and Functions of Exchange in Archaic Societies,* trans. I. Cunnison (New York: Norton, 1967) and Hyde, *The Gift,* pp. 28–32.

17. *Personae* (New York: New Directions, 1971), p. 89.

18. "Closing Statement: Linguistics and Poetics," in *Style in Language,* ed. Thomas Sebeok (Cambridge, Mass.: Harvard University Press, 1960), p. 357. A further discussion of "To You," one that also draws upon Jakobson's article, may be found in C. Carroll Hollis, *Language and Style in "Leaves of Grass"* (Baton Rouge: Louisiana State University Press, 1983), pp. 98–101.

19. *The Social Contract*, ed. Maurice Cranston (Harmondsworth, Middlesex: Penguin Books, 1968), p. 64. For further discussion of Rousseau's remark see Cranston's introduction to his Edition, pp. 34–36, 42–43.

20. Quoted in Ivan Marki, *The Trial of the Poet: An Interpretation of the First Edition of "Leaves of Grass,"* (New York: Columbia University Press, 1975), pp. 67–69.

21. See Santayana, "The Genteel Tradition," in *Selected Critical Writings of George Santayana,* ed. Norman Henfrey, 2 vols. (Cambridge: Cambridge University Press), 2:97–100; Lawrence, *Studies in Classic American Literature*, p. 167; and Neruda, "We Live in a Whitmanesque Age (A Speech to P.E.N.)," reprinted in *Walt Whitman: The Measure of His Song,* ed. Jim Perlman, Ed Folsom, and Dan Campion (Minneapolis: Holy Cow! Press, 1981), p. 140.

22. *Death and Sensuality: A Study of Eroticism and the Taboo* (New York: Walker and Company, 1962).

23. *Adultery in the Novel: Contract and Transgression* (Baltimore: Johns Hopkins University Press, 1979), p. 7.

24. *A Rhetoric of Motives* (Berkeley: University of California Press, 1969), p. 22.

Chapter Three

1. See *On Revolution* (New York: Viking Press, 1963), pp. 139–42.

2. Quoted in Clifton J. Furness, "Walt Whitman's Politics," *The American Mercury* 16 (1929) :460.

3. See *The Writings and Speeches of Daniel Webster,* ed. James W. McIntyre, 18 vols. (Boston: Little, Brown, 1903), 4:198–201. For an informative discussion of Webster's legal background and its bearing on his Unionism, see Robert Ferguson, *Law and Letters in American Culture* (Cambridge, Mass.: Harvard University Press, 1984), pp. 208–10.

4. Even so restrained a reading as that offered in Richard Chase's *Walt Whitman Reconsidered* (New York: Sloane Associates, 1955) speaks without fear of qualification about "the descent of the as yet unformed and unstable ego into the id, its confrontation there of the dark, human tragedy, its emergence into a new, more stable form" (p. 54). More sophisticated variations on the same theme are to be found in Edwin Miller, *Walt Whitman's Poetry: A Psychological Journey* (Boston: Riverside Press, 1968), pp. 72–84, and Stephen A. Black, *Whitman's Journeys into Chaos: A Psychoanalytic Study of the Poetic Process* (Princeton, N.J.: Princeton University Press, 1975), pp. 125–37.

5. *The 1855 Edition of "Leaves of Grass,"* ed. Malcolm Cowley (New York: Viking Press, 1959), p. 111.

6. The fragment may be found among the lines rejected from *Leaves of*

Grass as cited in Oscar Triggs's *The Complete Writings of Walt Whitman*, ed. Richard Maurice Bucke, Thomas B. Harned, and Horace Traubel (New York: G. P. Putnam's Sons, 1902), 3:263, item 29. The other reference to "Black Lucifer," not contained in the Triggs edition, is quoted in *Notes and Fragments,* ed. Bucke, (1899; reprint Folcroft, Pa.: Folcroft Library Editions, 1972), p. 19, item 135.

7. Immanuel Kant, *The Critique of Judgement,* trans. James Creed Meredith, 2 vols. (London: Oxford University Press, 1952), 1:56.

8. Ibid., pp. 56, 139.

Part Two

1. Whitman's lament may be found in Thomas Brasher's edition of the *Early Prose and Poetry of Walt Whitman* (New York: New York University Press, 1963), pp. 21–22. See also other recantations in this vein, such as "Our Future Lot," "Fame's Vanity," "Time to Come," and, of course, "The Punishment of Pride."

2. Emerson's famous letter has been widely reprinted. Though receptive at first, Emerson's admiration for Whitman soon cooled, and only two months after his congratulatory letter he was writing to correspondents of "our wild Whitman, with real inspiration, but choked by Titanic abdomen." As I hope to show in this chapter, Emerson's characterization is remarkably prescient. See *The Letters of Ralph Waldo Emerson,* ed. Ralph Rusk, 6 vols. (New York: Columbia University Press, 1939), 4:552.

3. Esther Shepard first advanced George Sand's possible influence on Whitman in *Walt Whitman's Pose* (New York: Harcourt Brace, 1936), while Maurice Bucke is responsible for the mystical seizure hypothesis, which he first proposed in "Walt Whitman and the Cosmic Sense," and which may be found in *In Re Walt Whitman* (Philadelphia: David McKay, 1893). For more recent accounts of the young Whitman see Joseph Jay Rubin's lively *The Historic Whitman* (University Park: University of Pennsylvania Press, 1973) and Floyd Stovall, *The Foreground of "Leaves of Grass"* (Charlottesville: University of Virginia Press, 1974).

4. Roger Asselineau, *The Evolution of Walt Whitman* (Cambridge, Mass.: Harvard University Press, 1960), p. 2.

5. *Studies in Classic American Literature* (New York: Viking Press, 1969), p. 163.

6. As James A. Miller, Jr., remarks helpfully of this juncture in the poem, "the poet himself appears to admit that his symbol has become so burdened with meaning that it ceases to function effectively" (*A Critical Guide to "Leaves of Grass"* [Chicago: University of Chicago Press, 1957], p. 74).

7. Attempts to map out a sequence for "Song of Myself" are legion. Among the most prominent are: Malcolm Cowley, "Introduction," *The 1855*

Edition of "Leaves of Grass" (New York: Viking Press, 1959), pp. vii–xxvii; Miller, *A Critical Guide to "Leaves of Grass,"* pp. 6–36; Ivan Marki, *The Trial of the Poet: An Interpretation of the First Edition of "Leaves of Grass"* (New York: Columbia University Press, 1976), pp. 150–206; Thomas Crawley, *The Structure of "Leaves of Grass"* (Austin: University of Texas Press, 1970). For a cogent summary of the difficulties entailed by such projects see John Lynen, *The Design of the Present: Essays on Time and Structure in American Literature* (New Haven, Conn.: Yale University Press, 1969), pp. 290–91.

Chapter Four

1. See C. Carroll Hollis, "Whitman and William Swinton: A Cooperative Friendship," *American Literature* 30 (1959): 425–49. Hollis also reviews the notebooks on language in "Whitman and the American Idiom," *Quarterly Journal of Speech* 43 (1957): 408–20, while Michael Dressman discusses the dictionary project in "Walt Whitman's Plans for a Perfect Dictionary," in *Studies in the American Renaissance, 1979,* ed. Joel Myerson (Boston: Twayne, 1979), pp. 457–73. For an interesting attempt to apply some of Whitman's linguistic speculations to "Song of Myself," see James Perrin Warren, "The 'Real Grammar': Deverbal Style in 'Song of Myself,'" *American Literature* 56 (1984): 1–16.

2. The observation appears in *New York Dissected: A Sheaf of Recently Discovered Newspaper Articles by the Author of "Leaves of Grass,"* ed. Emory Holloway and Ralph Adimari (New York: Rufus Rockwell Wilson, Inc., 1936), p. 56.

3. *The Literary Remains of Samuel Taylor Coleridge,* ed. Henry Nelson Coleridge, 4 vols. (London: 1836), 2:67–8. The best overview of the organic movement, one to which I am indebted, remains M. H. Abrams, *The Mirror and the Lamp* (New York: Oxford University Press, 1954), pp. 156–226.

4. *Selected Writings of Walter Pater,* ed. Harold Bloom, (New York: Signet, 1974), p. 152.

5. *The 1855 Edition of "Leaves of Grass,"* ed. Malcolm Cowley (New York: Viking Press, 1959), pp. 20–21.

6. *American Hieroglyphics: The Symbol of Egyptian Hieroglyphics in the American Renaissance* (New Haven, Conn.: Yale University Press, 1980), p. 92.

7. See *The Gathering of the Forces,* ed. Cleveland Rogers and John Black, 2 vols. (New York: Putnam, 1920), 1:213.

8. Quoted in Michael Kammen, *A Machine That Would Go Of Itself* (New York: Knopf, 1986), p. xxiii. A useful survey of Constitutional disputes and ambiguities in the antebellum years can be found in Don E. Fehrenbacher, *Slavery, Law, and Politics* (New York: Oxford University Press, 1981), chap. 1.

9. *Symbolism and American Literature* (Chicago: University of Chicago Press, 1953), pp. 146, 150. The immediate subject of Feidelson's critique is Emerson, though his apprehensions echo similar misgivings with regard to Whitman's poetry that extend back to Santayana's attack on its "barbarism."

10. My use of this distinction is indebted to Mark Conroy's informative discussion in *Modernism and Authority: Strategies of Legitimation in Flaubert and Conrad* (Baltimore: Johns Hopkins University Press, 1985). See esp. p. 31.

11. See *American Hieroglyphics,* pp. 94–114. While I agree with Irwin's contention that Whitman's language aims "to evoke immediate conviction," I diverge from his suggestion that this entails for the poet a quest to transcend language. Thus, as will emerge from my reading of "Song of Myself," while Irwin takes statements such as "I carry the plenum of proof and everything else in my face" as an ideal policy, my inclination is to read these as expressions of desperation or avoidance.

12. Reasoning along similar lines and in terms to which I am indebted, Donald Pease labels this phenomenon "the scene of cultural persuasion"—a manifestly ironic designation for Pease since he is referring to that procedure in which the very terms deployed to articulate a given issue will predetermine the course of its "resolution." Under such conditions, rhetorical configurations work to "*pre*occupy all the positions—and all the oppositions as well." See "*Moby-Dick* and the Cold War," *The American Renaissance Reconsidered,* ed. Walter Benn Michaels and Donald Pease (Baltimore: Johns Hopkins University Press, 1985), pp. 113–55.

13. *A Rhetoric of Motives* (1950; reprint, Berkeley: University of California Press, 1969), p. 13. Burke's speculations here, now a commonplace in narrative theory, expand on earlier reflections on the same theme in *A Grammar of Motives* (1945; reprint, Berkeley: University of California Press, 1966), pp. 430–40.

14. See *The Design of the Present: Essays on Time and Structure in American Literature* (New Haven, Conn.: Yale University Press, 1969), pp. 196–225.

15. These citations can be found, respectively, in Lawrence Lipking, *The Life of the Poet: Beginning and Ending Poetic Careers* (Chicago: University of Chicago Press, 1982), p. 114; Albert Gelpi, *The Tenth Muse: The Psyche of the American Poet* (Cambridge, Mass.: Harvard University Press, 1975), p. 163; and Lawrence Buell, *Literary Transcendentalism: Style and Vision in the American Renaissance* (Ithaca: Cornell University Press, 1973), p. 326.

16. *Walt Whitman Reconsidered* (New York: Sloane Associates, 1955), pp. 58–98.

17. "The Anxiety of Performance," *New Literary History* 13 (1981): 171.

18. Commenting on section twenty-five Harold Bloom finds that "at this, almost the mid-point of his greatest poem, Whitman is sliding knowingly toward crisis," though I would claim that this crisis has in fact already begun,

with the next three sections being but an elaboration of the challenge here presented. (See *Agon: Towards a Theory of Revisionism* [New York: Oxford University Press, 1982], p. 187.) For an informative discussion of the poet's "cagey maneuvering" and how the final lines of the section "mark an unmistakable redeployment and retraction" of its earlier bravado, see Gelpi, *The Tenth Muse,* pp. 194–95.

19. As a point in contrast we can cite the example of Henry James, another writer much given to brooding upon "these fascinations of the fabulist's art, these lurking forces of expansion, the necessities of upspringing in the seed," although the novelist is considerably more explicit than Whitman in going on to question "if one could do so subtle, if not so monstrous a thing as to write the history of the growth of one's imagination." He is more explicit since his own prefaces, in their incessant quest to root out the "germ" of the story, candidly recount the deviations of "some unforeseen principle of growth" that willfully swells "the short subject" into "comparative monsters." From such unnatural gestations there is spawned an orphaned host of "poor fatherless and motherless" fictions, "unrecognized and unacknowledged birth[s]" that portend the "triumph of intentions never entertained and that throw "mocking shadows" over "the early bloom of one's good faith." The citations appear in *The Art of the Novel,* ed. R. P. Blackmur (New York: Scribner's, 1932), pp. 98, 296–97.

20. The figure of demonic, unauthorized beginnings is of course a common topic of anxiety in British poetry as well and has been usefully summarized in the following overview by Paul Fry: "Left to their own devices, the odes of Gray and Collins, as much as those of Jonson, Milton, and Dryden, must continuously allay the fear that self-conception may yield a monstrous birth, 'called with thought' from dark and uncontrollable sources" (*The Poet's Calling in the English Ode* [New Haven, Conn.: Yale University Press, 1980], p. 131).

21. *Three Case Histories,* ed. Philip Rieff (New York: Collier Books, 1963), p. 184.

22. Fisher Ames, "American Literature," in *The American Literary Revolution, 1787–1837,* ed. Robert E. Spiller (Garden City, N.Y.: Doubleday, 1967), p. 86. Ames's essay was first published in 1809.

23. *Whitman's Journeys into Chaos: A Psychological Interpretation of "Leaves of Grass"* (Princeton, N.J.: Princeton University Press, 1975), p. 109.

24. To this extent, Stephen Black's suggestion that "by abruptly transforming the metaphor of 'blind loving wrestling touch' into a less threatening landscape, [the poet] wards off the threat of actual sexual relations and reverts to masturbation" sounds unduly captious since it falls short of acknowledging how deeply recursive (rather than merely evasive) this moment is. His comments can be found in *Whitman's Journeys into Chaos,* pp. 108–9.

25. Though often derided as anachronistic or revanchist, the notion that

the proof of literature *as* literature resides in its indifference to proof has scarcely disappeared. So Hayden White, in a thoughtful essay, argues that "it is their nondisconfirmability that testifies to the essentially *literary* nature of the historical classics" ("The Historical Text as Literary Artifact," *The Tropics of Discourse* [Baltimore: The John Hopkins University Press, 1981]). Richard Rorty offers another version of the same point in the course of explaining that "it is a feature of what I call 'literature' that one can achieve success by introducing a quite new genre of poem or novel or critical essay . . . *without argument*. . . . By 'literature,' then, I shall mean the areas of culture which, quite self-consciously, forgo agreement on an encompassing critical vocabulary, and thus forgo argumentation" (*The Consequences of Pragmatism* [Minneapolis: University of Minnesota Press, 1982], p. 142).

Chapter Five

1. See Whitman's letter to Emerson in 1856, reprinted in *CRE*, p. 739.

2. See Garry Wills, *Inventing America: Jefferson's Declaration of Independence* (New York: Vintage Books, 1978), p. xiv. My treatment of Lincoln's perception of a "moral hiatus" between Declaration and Constitution is also indebted to Dwight Anderson, *Abraham Lincoln: The Quest for Immortality* (New York: Knopf, 1982).

3. Fisher Ames, "American Literature," in *The American Literary Revolution: 1787–1837,* ed. Robert Spiller (Garden City, N.Y.: Anchor Books, 1967), p. 86; Harriet Martineau, *Society in America,* 3 vols. (London: Saunders and Otley, 1837), 3:206.

4. R. W. B. Lewis, *The American Adam: Innocence, Tragedy, and Tradition in the Nineteenth Century* (Chicago: University of Chicago Press, 1955), p. 45. On the relation between the American Renaissance and literary nationalism William Hedges justly notes that "we are seldom made to feel that there is any *vital* connection between the great writers of American literature and the literature of the years that are supposed to have prepared the way for it" ("The Myth of the Republic and the Theory of American Literature," *Prospects* 4 [1979]: 102).

5. I paraphrase the opening sentence of Margaret Fuller's "American Literature; Its Position in the Present Time, and Prospects for the Future," reprinted in *The American Transcendentalists: Their Prose and Poetry,* ed. Perry Miller (Garden City, N.Y.: Anchor, 1957), pp. 189–94. Whitman was much taken by Fuller's essay, first issued in 1846 among her *Papers on Literature and Art.* See his references to her "high-pitched taunt" (*PW* 2:539, 666–67), as well as William Carlos Williams's ironic adaptation of it in *Paterson* (New York: New Directions, 1969), p. 140.

6. D. H. Lawrence, *Studies in Classic American Literature* (New York: Viking Press, 1969), p. viii.

7. *The Native Muse: Theories of American Literature,* ed. Richard Ruland (New York: Dutton, 1972), pp. 313, 310, 312. For a comprehensive account of this period, the reader is referred to Benjamin Spencer, *The Quest for Nationality: An American Literary Campaign* (Syracuse, N.Y.: Syracuse University Press, 1957). Robert Weisbuch also provides a lively and informative overview in *Atlantic Double-Cross: American Literature and British Influence in the Age of Emerson* (Chicago: University of Chicago Press, 1986).

8. *The American Literary Revolution,* p. 309.

9. *The Native Muse,* pp. 86, 90.

10. *Ibid,* p. 143.

11. *The Will to Power,* ed. Walter Kaufmann, trans. Kaufmann and R. J. Hollingdale (New York: Viking Press, 1968), p. 3.

12. *The Native Muse,* p. 147.

13. See Perry Miller, *The Raven and the Whale: The War of Wits and Words in the Era of Melville and Poe* (New York: Harcourt, 1956), p. 207.

14. *The American Literary Revolution,* p. 74.

15. *The Journals and Miscellaneous Notebooks of Ralph Waldo Emerson,* ed. William Gilman and Alfred Ferguson, 16 vols. (Cambridge, Mass.: Belknap Press, 1960–), 7:521. Fisher Ames's opinions regarding "a right perception of genius" may be found in *The American Literary Revolution,* p. 75.

16. Or, as Frank Lentrichhia more bluntly states, "There can be no Emersonian action." See his discussion "On the Ideologies of Poetic Modernism, 1890–1913: The Example of William James," in *Reconstructing American Literary History,* ed. Sacvan Bercovitch (Cambridge, Mass.: Harvard University Press, 1986), p. 241.

17. See n. 2, Part 2.

18. Responding along similar lines, Donald Pease describes "an interlocutive process" whereby the poet's presence is not "identified with a psychological identity that existed before these songs. . . . Instead . . . when Whitman wrote 'I sing myself' he literally meant that his singing brought a self into being" ("Blake, Crane, and Whitman: A Poetics of Pure Possibility," PMLA 96 [1981]: 77).

19. For a succinct description of this form see Northrop Frye, *Anatomy of Criticism* (Princeton, N.J.: Princeton University Press, 1957), p. 294. "Pars epica" I borrow from Kurt Schulter's study of *Die Englische Ode* (Bonn: H. Bouvier u. Co. Verlag, 1964), p. 31.

20. Richard M. Adams, *Strains of Discord: Studies in Literary Openness* (Ithaca: Cornell University Press, 1959), p. 181.

21. Barrett Wendell, *A Literary History of American Literature* (New York: Macmillan, 1900), p. 468.

22. Ivan Marki, *The Trial of the Poet: An Interpretation of the First Edition of "Leaves of Grass"* (New York: Columbia University Press, 1975), p. 137.

23. *A World Elsewhere: The Place of Style in American Literature* (New York: Oxford University Press, 1966), p. 21.

24. Ibid.

25. Commentators frequently cite the influence of Isaiah ("the son of man is as the grass") as standing behind Whitman's meditation on "the beautiful uncut hair of the grave." Yet as this familiar conceit modulates into the "faint red roofs of the mouth," the proximate source may be found in the Psalmist's curse "let them be as the grass on the housetops that withereth before it groweth up," a curse which again plays upon the proleptic convergence of start and finish that I have been discussing.

26. *Love and Death in the American Novel* (New York: Criterion Books, 1960), p. xix.

27. See *The Fate of Reading* (Chicago: University of Chicago Press, 1975), p. 152.

28. *Natural Supernaturalism: Tradition and Revolution in Romantic Literature* (New York: Norton, 1971), pp. 37–56. We have of course already seen Whitman's variation on this "apocalyptic marriage" at the end of the twenty-fourth section of "Song of Myself."

29. In 1871, Whitman would have his way with the muse of the Old World Epic, charmingly beseeching her "To cross out please those immensely overpaid accounts, / That matter of Achilles's wrath . . ." But that would come later.

30. *The Prelude*, ed. E. de Selincourt, 2d ed. revised by Helen Gardner (London: Oxford University Press, 1959), bk. 2, line 221, *passim*; bk. 13, lines 199–205. A useful discussion of Wordsworth's treatment of this issue and its bearing on subsequent nineteenth-century literature may be found in David Simpson, *Fetishism and Imagination: Dickens, Melville, Conrad* (Baltimore: Johns Hopkins University Press, 1982).

31. *Wordworth's Poetry, 1787–1814* (New Haven, Conn.: Yale University Press, 1964).

32. *The American Literary Revolution*, p. 296.

33. See Basil de Selincourt, *Walt Whitman: A Critical Study* (1914; reprint, New York: Russell and Russell, 1965), pp. 124–55, 149–51; Lynen, *The Design of the Present: Essays on Time and Structure in American Literature* (New Haven, Conn.: Yale University Press, 1969), pp. 290–95; and Ziff, *Literary Democracy: The Declaration of Cultural Independence* (New York: Viking, 1981), pp. 233–34.

34. *The 1855 Edition of "Leaves of Grass,"* ed. Malcolm Cowley (New York: Viking Press, 1959), p. 11.

35. I therefore cannot agree with Quentin Anderson's contention that the catalogs, "at their brilliant best, are successful efforts to melt things together, to make the sum of things ring with one note . . . he dowers his world with

only so much quiddity as he can dissolve, or cants each created thing on the slope of process down which it will slide to oblivion." Anderson's "poet of decreation," whoever it may be, is certainly not Whitman. See *The Imperial Self* (New York: Knopf, 1971), pp. 95, 94.

36. *Studies in Classic American Literature*, p. 218.

37. *Symbolism and American Literature* (Chicago: University of Chicago Press, 1953), p. 25.

38. David Cavitch points up this aspect of Whitman's originality in remarking that "the figure of the child in Whitman's poetry conveys neither the challenging innocence of Blake's radical infants nor the natural piety of Wordsworth's 'best philosopher'. Whitman's child is not Rousseau's animal with perfectly balanced instincts. . . . Whitman is less sentimental than most writers who participated in the aggrandizement of childhood in the nineteenth century" (*My Soul and I: Whitman's Inner Mystery* [Boston: Beacon Press, 1985], p. 36).

39. "I. A. Richards and the Dream of Communication," *The Fate of Reading*, p. 38.

40. William James, *Pragmatism* (Cambridge, Mass.: Harvard University Press, 1975), pp. 76–77.

Chapter Six

1. *American Renaissance: Art and Expression in the Age of Emerson and Whitman* (New York: Oxford University Press, 1941), p. 547.

2. *Fearful Symmetry: A Study of William Blake* (Princeton, N.J.: Princeton University Press, 1947), p. 316.

3. *The Complete Works of Edgar Allan Poe*, ed. James Harrison, 17 vols. (New York: Thomas Crowell, 1902), 16:200.

4. *The Works of Joel Barlow*, 2 vols. (Gainesville, Fla.: Scholar's Facsimiles and Reprints, 1970), 2:542.

5. *Walden and Civil Disobedience*, ed. Owen Thomas (New York: Norton, 1967), p. 11. On variants, political, religious and otherwise, of this millenialism, see also Sacvan Bercovitch, *The American Jeremiad* (Madison: University of Wisconsin Press, 1978), pp. 141–52.

6. *Letters of Wallace Stevens*, ed. Holly Stevens (New York: Knopf, 1966), p. 871.

7. T. S. Eliot, "Notes towards the Definition of Culture," in *Christianity and Culture* (New York: Harcourt Brace Jovanovich, 1968), p. 100.

Part Three

1. Daniel Aaron, *The Unwritten War: American Writers and the Civil War* (New York: Oxford University Press, 1973), p. 59.

2. *I Sit and Look Out,* ed. Emory Holloway and Vernolian Schwarz (New York: Columbia University Press, 1932), p. 98.

Chapter Seven

1. On the dating of both *Children of Adam* and *Calamus,* see Fredson Bowers, *Whitman's Manuscripts: "Leaves of Grass" (1860)* (Chicago: University of Chicago Press, 1955), pp. lxiii–lxxiv.

2. Justin Kaplan, *Walt Whitman: A Life* (New York: Simon and Schuster, 1980), pp. 238–39.

3. The best general treatment dealing with Whitman's attitudes on this subject can be found in Daniel Aaron, *The Unwritten War: American Writers and the Civil War* (New York: Oxford University Press, 1973), pp. 59–62. These attitudes were not uncharacteristic of a good many Northerners at the time; Whitman's stance on miscegenation, for example, is typical. In an editorial for the *Brooklyn Daily Times* in May of 1858 he asks: "Who believes that the Whites and Blacks can ever amalgamate in America? Or who wishes it to happen? Nature has set an impassable seal against it. Besides, is not America for the Whites? And is it not better so? As long as the Blacks remain here how are they to become anything like an independent and heroic race? There is no chance for it" (quoted in *I Sit and Look Out,* ed. Emory Holloway and Vernolian Schwarz [New York: Columbia University Press, 1932], p. 90).

4. *Walt Whitman: The Making of a Poet* (New York: Basic Books, 1983), pp. 190, 187.

5. *The Imperial Self* (New York: Knopf, 1971), p. 104.

6. For additional comments on Whitman's evasion of metaphor in these lines, see David Cavitch's discussion in *My Soul and I: Whitman's Inner Mystery* (Boston: Beacon Press, 1985), pp. 37–39.

7. My treatment of "The Tyger" draws upon Harold Bloom's ironic reading, as presented in *The Visionary Company: A Reading of English Romantic Poetry* (Garden City, N.Y.: Doubleday and Company, 1961), pp. 33–38.

8. Ivan Marki, *The Trial of the Poet: An Interpretation of the First Edition of "Leaves of Grass"* (New York: Columbia University Press, 1975), p. 73.

9. *My Soul and I,* p. 127.

10. For background, see Gay Wilson Allen, *The Solitary Singer: A Critical Biography of Walt Whitman* (1955; reprint, New York: New York University Press, 1967), p. 220. Allen conjectures that internal evidence dates this speech not earlier than 1858 and that it may have been delivered on at least one occasion about this time.

11. Quoted in Clifton J. Furness, "Walt Whitman's Politics," *American Mercury* 16 (1929): 461.

12. Ibid.

13. See *Leaves of Grass: Facsimile Edition of the 1860 Text,* ed. Roy Harvey Pearce (Ithaca, N.Y.: Cornell University Press, 1961), pp. 354–55.

14. "Creative Writers and Day-dreaming," *The Standard Edition of the Complete Psychological Works of Sigmund Freud*, ed. and trans. James Strachey, 24 vols. (London: Hogarth Press, 1953–74), 9:141–54.

15. *The Liberal Imagination: Essays on Literature and Society* (New York: Anchor, 1950), p. 40.

16. James E. Miller, Jr., *A Critical Guide to "Leaves of Grass"* (Chicago: University of Chicago Press, 1957), p. 70.

17. Sherwood Anderson, *Winesburg, Ohio* (New York: Modern Library, 1919), p. 11. Other readings in this vein can be found in Edwin Miller, *Walt Whitman's Poetry: A Psychological Journey* (Boston: Riverside Press, 1968), pp. 146–50 and Stephen Black, *Whitman's Journeys into Chaos: A Psychoanalytic Study of the Poetic Process* (Princeton, N.J.: Princeton University Press, 1975), pp. 171–82, 185–97.

18. *The Romantic Sublime: Studies in the Structure and Psychology of Transcendence* (Baltimore: Johns Hopkins University Press, 1976), pp. 59, 58.

19. Samuel Taylor Coleridge, *Biographia Literaria*, ed. J. Shawcross, 2 vols. (London: Oxford University Press, 1954), 1:202.

20. *Between Men: English Literature and Male Homosocial Desire* (New York: Columbia University Press, 1985), p. 205.

21. Alan Trachtenberg, "This Compost," in *Medicine and Literature*, ed. Enid R. Peschel (New York: Neale Watson, 1980), p. 368.

Chapter Eight

1. "Modern Poetry," *The Complete Poems and Selected Letters and Prose of Hart Crane*, ed. Brom Weber (New York: Doubleday, 1966), p. 263. Crane adds that Whitman's "bequest is still to be realized in all its implications." The essay was written in 1930.

2. See "Cape Hatteras," *The Bridge, The Complete Poems*, pp. 94, 93.

3. In the New York *Saturday Press* (Dec. 24, 1859) under the title of "A Child's Reminiscence." Two poems from the 1855 edition, "A Boston Ballad" and "Europe, the 72nd and 73rd Years of These States," had been published as early as 1850, though these angry tracts are not typical of the more finished poems in that volume.

4. The remarks of Saintsbury and Swinburne are collected in *A Century of Whitman Criticism*, ed. Edwin Miller (Bloomington: Indiana University Press, 1968), pp. 50–53; 81–89.

5. Paul Fry, *The Poet's Calling in the English Ode* (New Haven, Conn.: Yale University Press, 1980), p. 138.

6. *Walt Whitman and Wallace Stevens* (Ithaca, N.Y.: Cornell University Press, 1976), p. 113.

7. See the headnote in *CRE* pp. 246–47.

8. See Edwin Fussell, *Lucifer in Harness: American Meter, Metaphor, and Diction* (Princeton, N.J.: Princeton University Press, 1973), pp. 130–34.

9. *The Complete Works of Edgar Allen Poe,* ed. James Harrison, 17 vols. (New York: Thomas Crowell, 1902), 14:195, 207.

10. Ibid., p. 193.

11. T. S. Eliot, "From Poe to Valery," *The Recognition of Edgar Allan Poe,* ed. Eric W. Carlson (Ann Arbor: University of Michigan Press, 1966), p. 207.

12. *The Complete Works of Edgar Allan Poe,* 14:207.

13. So called by Donald Pease in "Blake, Crane, Whitman and Modernism: A Poetics of Pure Possibility," *PMLA* 96 (1981): 77, 78.

14. *The Birth of Tragedy and The Case of Wagner,* trans. Walter Kaufmann (New York: Vintage Books, 1967), p. 37.

15. Ibid., pp. 133, 103. For a more extensive discussion of both texts, see John Irwin, *American Hieroglyphics: The Symbol of Egyptian Hieroglyphics in the American Renaissance* (New Haven, Conn.: Yale University Press, 1980), pp. 97–111.

16. *The Birth of Tragedy,* pp. 17, 59.

17. Stephen Whicher, "Whitman's Awakening to Death," *The Presence of Walt Whitman,* ed. R. W. B. Lewis (New York: Columbia University Press, 1962), p. 13. Harold Bloom's influential commentary also deserves citation: "[Whitman] says 'I Ebb'd' but he means that 'this electric self' ebb'd, for it is the pride out of which he is able to write poems, the self of 'Song of Myself' that is ebbing. He is dying as a poet, as he rightly fears" (*A Map of Misreading* [New York: Oxford University Press, 1975], p. 181). My own reading of the poem stresses, in turn, that the concealed aim of the poem is to do away with this "electric self," not mourn its departure.

18. *Agon: Towards a Theory of Revisionism* (New York: Oxford University Press, 1982), p. 29.

19. *The Evolution of Walt Whitman: The Creation of a Personality* (Cambridge, Mass.: Harvard University Press, 1960), p. 119.

Chapter Nine

1. James M. Cox, "Walt Whitman, Mark Twain, and the Civil War," *Sewanee Review* 69 (1961): 187.

2. Ibid. Whitman's letter can be found in *Faint Clews and Indirections,* ed. Clarence Ghodes and Rollo G. Silver (Durham, N.C.: Duke University Press, 1949), p. 135.

3. *A Critical Guide to "Leaves of Grass"* (Chicago: University of Chicago Press, 1957), pp. 219–25. See also M. Wynn Thomas, "Whitman and the American Democratic Identity," *Journal of American Studies* 15 (1981): 73–93.

4. *Studies in Classic American Literature* (New York: Viking Press, 1969), p. 170.

5. On analogies drawn at the time between the Revolutionary and Civil

Wars see George Fredrickson, *The Inner Civil War: Northern Intellectuals and the Crisis of the Union* (New York: Harper and Row, 1965), pp. 60–64. The Melville quote appears in a poem from *Battle Pieces* entitled "Fort Donelson."

6. See James Wright, "Whitman's Delicacy," in *The Presence of Walt Whitman,* ed. R. W. B. Lewis (New York: Columbia University Press, 1962); Daniel Aaron, *The Unwritten War: American Writers and the Civil War* (New York: Oxford University Press, 1973), p. 67. Santayana's comments on Whitman's involvement in the war in "The Poetry of Barbarism" anticipate Aaron's more critical remarks.

7. James's early review has been reprinted in *A Century of Whitman Criticism,* ed. Edwin Miller (Bloomington: Indiana University Press, 1968); his later comments appear in *Notes of A Son and Brother,* which is collected in *Henry James: Autobiography,* ed. F. W. Dupee (New York: Criterion Books, 1956), p. 424.

8. Howells's phrase appears in a review of *Drum-Taps* that has been collected in *A Century of Whitman Criticism,* p. 9. Harold Bloom's reflections on Whitman's "pragmatic saintliness" during this period are also worth mentioning. See *Walt Whitman: A Collection of Critical Views,* ed. Harold Bloom (New York: Chelsea House, 1985), p. 4.

9. *Walt Whitman: The Making of a Poet* (New York: Basic Books, 1983), p. 330.

10. Wallace Stevens, *The Necessary Angel: Essays on Reality and Imagination* (New York: Vintage Books, 1951), p. 36.

11. "Malvern Hill," *Selected Poems of Herman Melville,* ed. Robert Penn Warren (New York: Random House, 1967), p. 123.

12. *Connoisseurs of Chaos* (1965; reprint, New York: Columbia University Press, 1983), pp. 97, 87.

13. *Subversive Genealogy: The Politics and Art of Herman Melville* (New York: Knopf, 1983), pp. 278, 264.

14. *The Inner Civil War,* p. 96.

15. C. Carroll Hollis, *Language and Style in "Leaves of Grass"* (Baton Rouge: Louisiana State University Press, 1983), p. 153.

16. The Poetics of Union in Lincoln and Whitman: An Inquiry toward the Relationship of Art and Policy," *The American Renaissance Reconsidered,* ed. Walter Benn Michaels and Donald E. Pease (Baltimore: Johns Hopkins University Press, 1985), p. 191.

17. Ibid., p. 201.

18. *Walt Whitman's Memoranda During the War,* ed. Roy P. Basler (Bloomington: Indiana University Press, 1962), p. 12.

19. See Charles Feidelson, Jr., *Symbolism and American Literature* (Chicago: University of Chicago Press, 1953), p. 22.

Index